# Communications and Culture

*Communications* has been defined as the conveying or exchanging of information and ideas. This wide definition is taken as the starting-point for this series of books, which are not bound by conventional academic divisions. The series aims to document or analyse a broad range of cultural forms and ideas.

It encompasses works from areas as esoteric as linguistics and as exoteric as television. The language of communication may be the written word or the moving picture, the static icon or the living gesture. These means of communicating can at their best blossom into and form an essential part of the other mysterious concept, *culture*.

There is no sharp or intended split in the series between communication and culture. On one definition, culture refers to the organisation of experience shared by members of a community, a process which includes the standards and values for judging or perceiving, for predicting and acting. In this sense, creative communication can make for a better and livelier culture.

The series reaches towards the widest possible audience. Some of the works concern themselves with activities as general as play and games; others offer a narrower focus, such as the ways of understanding the visual image. It is hoped that some moves in the transformation of the artful and the scientific can be achieved, and that both can begin to be understood by a wider and more comprehending community. Some of these books are written by practitioners – broadcasters, journalists and artists; others come from critics, scholars, scientists and historians.

The series has an ancient and laudable, though perhaps untenable, aim – an aim as old as the Greeks and as new as holography: it aspires to help heal the split between cultures, between the practitioners and the thinkers, between science and art, between the academy and life.

PAUL WALTON

# COMMUNICATIONS AND CULTURE

**SERIES EDITORS**   ROSALIND BRUNT, SIMON FRITH, STUART HALL, ANGELA MCROBBIE
**FOUNDING EDITOR**   PAUL WALTON

## Series Standing Order

If you would like to receive future titles in this series as they
are published, you can make use of our standing order
facility. To place a standing order please contact your
bookseller or, in case of difficulty, write to us at the address
below with your name and address and the name of the
series. Please state with which title you wish to begin your
standing order. (If you live outside the UK we may not have
the rights for your area, in which case we will forward your
order to the publisher concerned.)

Standing Order Service, Macmillan Distribution Ltd,
Houndmills, Basingstoke, Hampshire, RG21 2XS, England.

# Postmodernism and Society

*Edited by*

**ROY BOYNE AND
ALI RATTANSI**

**MACMILLAN**

First published 1990
Reprinted 1991

Published by
MACMILLAN EDUCATION LTD
Houndmills, Basingstoke, Hampshire RG21 2XS
and London
Companies and representatives
throughout the world

Typeset by Footnote Graphics, Warminster, Wilts

Printed in Hong Kong

British Library Cataloguing in Publication Data
Postmodernism and society.—(Communications and culture).
1. Western culture. Modernism & postmodernism
I. Boyne, Roy    II. Rattansi, Ali    III. Series
306
ISBN 0–333–47510–0 (hardcover)
ISBN 0–333–47511–9 (paperback)

# Contents

# List of Illustrations

# Acknowledgements

We would like to express thanks to the members of the Theory Group of the British Sociological Association. Nicky Turnbull, James Donald, Mike Gane and Sallie Westwood offered valuable advice and support for which we are very grateful.

ROY BOYNE
ALI RATTANSI

# Chapter 1

# The Theory and Politics of Postmodernism: By Way of an Introduction

Roy Boyne and Ali Rattansi

Many sociologists, cultural commentators, literary theorists and philosophers have been intrigued by the idea of postmodernity for some time now, and this interest is reflected in the considerable outpouring of writing on the topic which has appeared over the last year or two. There seems, however, to be scant agreement on how the crucial terms in these discussions are to be understood. 'Modernity' and 'postmodernity', 'modernism' and 'postmodernism' appear and reappear in philosophical, literary and other texts in what is at first sight a bewildering array of guises. Combined, especially in Britain, with a scepticism towards fashionable – especially French – debates as well as resistance to what are seen as trendy neologisms, particularly in the realm of culture and aesthetics, there is a danger that much of the debate about postmodernism will remain on the academic and cultural margins, the property of an *avant-garde* but held generally in deep suspicion and even derision by the rest.

This collection is offered in the belief that the debate about postmodernism addresses issues that are actually of crucial significance to the humanities and the social sciences and, more generally, raise profound political questions for the late twentieth century and beyond.

But a fuller engagement with the debates needs some preliminary clarification of the key terms and interventions around which the discussions are constructed. We attempt to provide this in what follows, which is intended more as an over-arching essay that frames the papers in the volume, rather than the sort of conventional editorial introduction which focuses primarily on the essays in a collection. Our strategy is borne of the strong sense that an accessible overview of the key terms and issues would help many to get an initial purchase on what appears at first sight to be an impenetrable and specialised debate. Moreover, we hope that our essay will make simplistic, dismissive judgements on the theoretical and political significance of these developments more difficult to sustain.

We must inquire first into whatever it is that postmodernity is taken to have replaced. We must ask, therefore, what is the nature of modernity.

## The Two Sides of Modernity

In a widely read and indeed justly celebrated discussion, Berman attempts to encapsulate the experience of modernity by describing it as a maelstrom that 'promises adventure, joy and growth, transformation of ourselves and the world', but also threatens to destroy cherished traditions and securities; it unites by cutting across class, region and ideology and yet disintegrates through incessant change, contradiction and ambiguity. It is generated, he says, by

> great discoveries in the physical sciences, changing our images of the universe and our place in it; the industrialization of production, which transforms scientific knowledge into technology, creates new human environments and destroys old ones, speeds up the whole tempo of life, generates new forms of corporate power and class struggle; immense demographic upheavals, severing millions of people from their ancestral habitats, hurtling them half-way across the world into new lives; rapid and often cataclysmic urban growth; systems of mass communication, dynamic in their development, enveloping and

binding together the most diverse people and societies; increasingly powerful national states, bureaucratically structured and operated, constantly striving to expand their powers; mass social movements of people, and peoples, challenging their political and economic rulers, striving to gain some control over their lives; finally, bearing and driving all these people and institutions along an ever-expanding, drastically fluctuating capitalist world market. (Berman, 1983, p. 16).

Berman's powerful prose captures the global social and political consequences of the forces unleashed on the world by urbanisation, the industrial revolution and the French revolution which are generally taken to have produced the distinctly 'modern' experience. Yet Berman makes little of the term postmodernism, assimilating it as an uninteresting phase of 'modernism', and his description of modernity also absorbs features that many regard as distinctly *post*modern.

Importantly, Berman also underplays the significance of an Enlightenment *Weltanschauung*, a belief in the omnipotence and liberating potential immanent in the application of reason and science to both the natural environment and to social relations, a totalising confidence in the ability of human reason to penetrate to the essential truth of physical and social conditions, thus making them amenable to rational control. In the debates about postmodernism, the Enlightenment and its legacy have become a polarising axis, defended by those, such as Habermas, intent upon completing what they see as an unfinished, emancipatory project, and attacked by Lyotard and others as the ultimate source of the totalitarian and ecological nightmares that have bedevilled the twentieth century. Of course, the Enlightenment functions here as a symbol, both sides ignoring the influence of the scientific revolution and philosophical contributions of seventeenth-century England as well as the more pessimistic, so-called 'dark' side of Enlightenment thinking.

With the emergence of the industrial working classes and socialist movements in the nineteenth century, modernity in a sense bifurcated, generating an internal critique and opposition pressing for the fulfilment of egalitarian promises belied by 'bourgeois' society. After 1917 this polarity developed on a global scale, generating, we would argue, a distinctive version and set of

experiences of modernity that need to be distinguished from
what broadly we would want to refer to as 'capitalist modernity'.
However crude and preliminary the distinction between capitalist
and non-capitalist versions of modernity, it is important to register
the necessity of some such discrimination as a starting point and in
so doing to enter a strong reservation against the bluntness of
'modernity' *tout court*. In its flattening effects the concept of
modernity shares far too much with the notions of 'industrialism'
and 'modernisation' that hegemonised American sociology in the
1950s and 1960s and which discerned everywhere a neutral tech-
nicist logic, destroying especially in the Third World what were
taken to be traditional 'obstacles' to 'progress', the latter taking
the forms of urbanisation, 'national integration', embryonic
private enterprise industrialisation, the emergence of 'modern'
élites, etc., and also supposedly subjecting the state socialist world
to an industrial logic of 'convergence' with the West that was said
to be enforcing an economic and political pluralisation (Taylor,
1976 pp. 3–41; Giddens, 1985, pp. 137–47).

Sociology, of course, is itself a child of modernity, emerging in
the Enlightenment as a set of systematic meditations in the
writings of Condorcet, Montesquieu, Ferguson, Smith and others
on the structure and evolution of societies. And as with modernity
more generally, the emergence of socialist discourses and especially
Marxism has introduced a chronic internal polarity within the
social sciences. However, it would certainly be wrong to imagine
that non-Marxist sociology has merely elaborated a series of
apologetics for the capitalist industrial modernity of which it has
formed a constitutive element. The writings of the most influential
figures, Weber especially, but those of Durkheim too, have an
acute ambivalence and a critical edge in relation to the pathos,
contradictions and unfulfilled promise of modernity, which it is
impossible to ignore.

Nevertheless, classical sociology paid little attention to the
existential demands of the single human individual whose fate it
was to live through the maelstrom of modernity. With one or two
significant exceptions, often of a theological cast, such as the
philosophy of Kierkegaard, this side of modernity was mostly
explored within art and literature. In 1843, we find Kierkegaard

(1958, p. 89) reflecting upon what Matthew Arnold (1978) regarded as the 'repose' and 'confidence' of modern society as follows:

> I could perhaps reproduce the tragedy of my childhood, the terrifying mysterious explanation of religion which an anxious foreboding played into my hands, which my imagination worked upon, and the scandal which religion aroused in me, all in a novel called 'the mysterious family.' *It would begin on an entirely idyllic patriarchal note so that no one would suspect anything until suddenly the word sounded which translated everything into terror.* (Italics added).

The two sides of modernity, progressive union of scientific objectivity and politico-economic rationality somehow mirrored in disturbed visions of unalleviated existential despair, are poignantly expressed in the art of Goya. His royal portraits capture the confidence of the ruler, while representations of manual labour, in pictures like *The Forge* and *The Knife Grinder*, suggest the awesome power at their command; against this putative union of bourgeois command and proletarian productivity, however, Goya invites us to see the 'dark' side of modernity, its loss of values, faith and purpose reflected in a lithographic output depicting war, madness and absurdity. No matter which of the countless interpretations of this exemplary artist's work that we take, whether, for instance, we listen to Louis MacNiece's *Autumn Journal* (1939, p. 27), in which we are told that Goya's royal portaiture is to be seen as ultimately ineffectual parodies of self-importance, or whether we follow Baudelaire who wrote:

> Goya
> Nightmare crammed with unfathomable things,
> witches roasting foetuses in a pan,
> crones at a mirror served by naked girls
> who straighten stockings to entice the fiend;

what is clear is that such work seeks to penetrate beneath surfaces, to reveal truths, whether they be of the darkness lurking on the other side of reality or of a luminescent future blocked only by the absurdities of the present.

## Modernism

What, then, of modernism? Berman, in his account, sees modernism very broadly as the set of 'visions and ideas that aim to make men and women the subjects as well as the objects of modernisation, to give them the power to change the world that is changing them' (1983 p. 16), thus including figures in literature, art and music from both the nineteenth and twentieth centuries. But, as will become apparent, it is important to restrict the term *modernism* to refer to the set of artistic, musical, literary, more generally aesthetic movements that emerged in Europe in the 1880s, flourished before and after the First World War and became institutionalised in the academies and art galleries of post-Second World War Europe and America. A brief and selective list of eminent figures usually regarded as distinctly modernist begins to give an indication of the nature of the modernist project: Matisse, Picasso and Kandinsky in painting, Stravinsky, Debussy and Schoenberg in music, Henry James, Joyce and Kafka in literature, poets such as Eliot, Pound, Rilke and Mallarmé, and dramatists such as Strindberg and Pirandello. Of course, at this point the heterogeneity of modernism also becomes apparent, both across artistic languages and aesthetic projects. Can there be anything that unites Schoenberg's atonality in music, for example, with cubism or surrealism in art? Alternatively, what unites post-impressionism, cubism, surrealism and abstract expressionism in art?

Despite this heterogeneity, itself partly a product of a modernist tendency to launch 'movements' (Bradbury and MacFarlane, 1976, pp. 192–3), it is possible to excavate a set of key aesthetic strategies which can be seen broadly to underlie the modernist project and which distinguish it from the aesthetic realisms and naturalisms which preceded it. In a perceptive account, Lunn, for instance, identifies four main distinguishing *motifs* in modernism (Lunn, 1985, pp. 34–7). First, an aesthetic self-reflexiveness, reflected in the tendency of modern artists, writers and composers to make their media of creation and artistic procedures objects of attention in their own work. Joyce's exploration of the problem of novel writing in *Ulysses*, Matisse's use of colour and perspective to emphasise the significance of colour as art, Picasso's play on the two-dimensionality of the painting surface in cubism (see

Crowther's essay in our volume), Brecht's strategies to reveal the mechanisms of theatricality in his plays are all prime examples. In each there is a deliberate distancing from the naturalist aesthetic of mere reflection of an objectively given outer reality, and an exploration of the 'reality' of artistic representation and construction. Secondly, juxtaposition or 'montage', which implies a weakening of straightforward narrative and the creation of unities out of the simultaneous presence of different perspectives. The rhythmic and tonal simultaneity of Bartok's music, the use of dissonance in Debussy and Schoenberg, the visual montage of an Eisenstein film are all part of attempts to disrupt the simpler harmonies and narrative structure of an earlier period. Past, present and future appear more as aspects of a 'continuous present'. Paradox, ambiguity and uncertainty figure as the third major theme. Typical here are the creation of multiple narrative voices rather than a single infallible narrator, allowing either the audience to attempt a resolution of the contradictions thus opened up, as in some of Brecht's work, or leaving the reader, in the manner of Kafka, with an enigmatic experience, or providing very provisional syntheses in the style of cubist painters. Finally, Lunn underlines the significance of the demise of the 'integrated individual subject'. In contrast to the coherent personalities of the realist novel, for example, the modernist novel presents individuals as riven by psychic conflicts, while in expressionist and cubist art the human form is either distorted or geometrically recomposed.

This preoccupation of modernism with highlighting the means of representation, the disruption of narrative, contradiction and fragmentation in subjectivity and identity, and so on, should not, however, be allowed to obscure the significance of an underlying, and sometimes contradictory, tendency within most modernist projects to cling to the belief that in principle the deep structure of reality is knowable, that it is intellectually and culturally penetrable, as it were, but requires aesthetic, philosophical and psychic strategies more complex, inventive and self-reflexive than the ones typically deployed in realist and naturalist forms. Surrealism, in fact, exemplifies this, mingling a surrender to the unconscious and the celebration of fragmentation and incongruous juxtaposition with varying degrees of commitment to the rational control of the unconscious as well as to social revolution through various forms of affiliation wih Marxist theory and the French Communist Party (Schneede, 1973, pp. 21–47; Short, 1976, p. 308).

Modernity, then, on all of its sides, may also be defined in terms of an aspiration to reveal the essential truth of the world. That truth will not reside on the surface of things, but will be hidden by appearances, masked behind the phenomenal forms of the present or secreted away in the distance of the future. Defining modernity in the terms of *uncovering*, of ripping away the layers of disguise, of disclosing and realising the promise or threat of the future *by moving on and through where we are now*, enables us to reconcile the various sides of modernity.

The importance, nevertheless, of treating *modernism* in a relatively distinct manner derives from the fact that despite its inevitable links with modernity, modernism always also constituted, in a sense, a *critique* of modernity, for it clearly refused to endorse any simplistic beliefs in the progressive capacity of science and technology to resolve all problems, nor did it hold with positivism and the idea of the integrated individual subject that provided the aesthetic, philosophical and psychological underpinning for the celebratory grand narratives of both capitalist and socialist versions of modernity.

On the other hand, it is partly because of this critical distancing and the form it took that there are lines of continuity between modernism and what has come to be called postmodernism, for the latter also constitutes a critique of the pretensions of modernity and in some senses may be said to extend and deepen the critique already begun by modernism. At this point, however, it is worth remarking that what has come to be identified as the 'modernist' movement in *architecture* – the field in which the impact of postmodernism has become most widely known – actually constituted a celebration of the possibilities of modernity and in this sense should be understood as distinct from modernisms in painting, music, literature and poetry. The transition in *Bauhaus* from an earlier expressionist influence to a commitment to function and industrial design in architecture (Whitford, 1984) is indeed illustrative of the contrast between modernisms in other fields and the so-called modernist current in architecture which, in the form of the 'International Style', became hegemonic in post-war mass urban building programmes.

**The Reality of Postmodernism**

The term 'postmodernism', Hassan says, 'has shifted from awkward neologism to derelict cliché without ever attaining to the dignity of concept' (1985, p. 119). First apparently used in Spanish by Frederico de Onis in the 1930s, it is in the literary commentaries of Irving Howe, Harry Levin, Leslie Fiedler and Ihab Hassan himself that the term gained currency in the 1950s and 1960s, then acquiring both prominence and notoriety in the 1970s and 1980s, especially through the architectural criticism of Charles Jencks and the philosophical intervention of Jean-François Lyotard's *The Postmodern Condition*.

Many doubt whether the term can ever be dignified by conceptual coherence. But there is encouragement in the paradox of a set of cultural projects united by a self-proclaimed commitment to heterogeneity, fragmentation and difference. And there are other commonalities too, at least in part deriving from the reaction against modernism. On the other hand, as we have remarked earlier, the distinctiveness of postmodernism in relation to modernism is inevitably blurred, for it is, like modernism, in part a critique of what it takes as the defining features of modernity. And as with modernity/modernism, we shall insist on a relative distinction between 'postmodernism', as a term that characterises a series of broadly aesthetic projects, and 'postmodernity', as a social, political and cultural configuration of which 'postmodernism' is supposedly a constitutive element.

The following may serve as a schematisation of the defining features of postmodernism in the arts, but with the qualifications already entered and more, for in a rapidly changing terrain it can only be provisional, and indeed we would argue that the term itself can only be transitional and is likely to be replaced by a series of other terms, as the cultural projects labelled postmodernist begin to diverge, especially in the face of the kind of cooptation that repeatedly recuperated new movements within modernism (a point explored by Crowther here). In any case, no single typification can expect to exhaust the sheer variety of projects that claim or are saddled with the label, although we would like to draw attention to the similarity between our account and those of our contributors (Callinicos, Wolff and Caygill for example).

There is, in the first place, an attempt to dissolve the boundaries between 'high' and 'mass' culture, to find new languages which synthesise and reconstitute new forms out of and beyond the old divisions. Here one can see the significance of the reaction against the élitism of high modernism and also its institutionalisation and domestication especially in New York's Museum of Modern Art and the Tate Gallery in London, the blunting of its earlier critical edge through incorporation into the lucrative art market and its elevation into the new orthodoxy. In this sense, the postmodernists constitute the sort of avant-garde that the Dadaists and Surrealists represented against the alleged recuperation of various forms of post-impressionism, but there is now a distinctive concern to appropriate many of the popular cultural forms of the post-war period. Warhol's Pop Art, with its recycling of popular images, and the combination of features from 'jazz' and 'classical' music in Cage and Glass furnish some well-known instances. There is, too, a concern to merge 'art' and 'life', again reminiscent of an earlier *avant-garde*, which is evident in 'happenings' and other art forms. An eclectic mixing of codes and styles, as in architecture which uses *motifs* from Egyptian, classical and modernist styles – James Stirling's *Neue Staatsgalerie* in Stuttgart is often cited (Jencks, 1986, pp. 18–19) – and in the work of artists such as Colin Self, whose exhibition at the Hayward Gallery displayed work in a wide range of styles including 'Women's Institute Evening Class style' (Taylor, 1987, p. 45). The electicism meshes with an ironic playfulness which refers to previous styles and famous works, as in Peter Blake's 'The Meeting' or 'Have a Nice Day, Mr. Hockney' (Jencks, 1986, pp. 4–5). Fantasy and reality are interwoven seamlessly, as in Rushdie's novels, and Kureishi's film *My Beautiful Launderette* (Henriques, 1989, pp. 18–20). Indeed, the exploration of ethnic minority and feminist perspectives is a significant element of postmodernism, as is the impact of post-structuralism and Lacanian psychoanalytic theory, with many of these influences coalescing in individual projects such as Kelly's *Post-Partum Document* (discussed by Paul Crowther in this collection).

The term postmodernism, then, has some purchase on a set of aesthetic and cultural projects. But it is often extended to include poststructuralist work in literary theory, philosophy and history (Derrida, Foucault, Lyotard), Rorty's form of pragmatist philosophy, post-positivist philosophy of science (Kuhn, Feyerabend), the textual movement in cultural anthropology (Clifford, Marcus), and so on. However, this is arguably an over-extension of the term. For one thing, not all the figures who appear on this sort of list would accept the label. Moreover, if the postmodernisms we have identified gain at least part of their commonality by their reaction against forms of modernism in the arts, then it has to be said that it is hard to identify 'modernist' moments in philosophy, anthropology, etc. which are direct counterparts to modernism in the arts and to which the so-called postmodernisms are a reaction. Indeed, as we have pointed out, modernisms in part emerged as a critique of the empiricism and positivism embedded in the projects to which the so-called postmodernists in philosophy and the social sciences are also reacting, and in this sense, on the one hand, there are some commonalities between earlier modernisms and the so-called postmodernists in literary theory, linguistics, philosophy and social analysis. On the other hand, it is difficult to assimilate particular postmodernist strategies in fields like art and music to what are alleged to be postmodernist trends in linguistics, philosophy and social theory.

Thus it can be highly misleading to lump together Cage, Derrida and Lyotard, or Foucault, Rushdie and Rorty as postmodernists and expect to derive significant commonalities which enable collective appropriation or provide a collective critical target. Lyotard's own appropriation of the label has contributed considerably to the confusion that surrounds the term (we discuss Lyotard's intervention below).

Nevertheless, we would suggest that, given the overextension that has already taken place, and the terms of debate that have already been set, it is at the present time not helpful simply to refuse to characterise the work of Derrida or Foucault or Rorty as 'postmodernist' and thus to exclude them from further discussions around the question of postmodernism. Thus, in our introduction and in the volume as a whole, we think it legitimate to use the term broadly to include discussions of, especially, poststructuralism in literary theory, philosophy and historical and social analysis of the kind inspired by Foucault and Derrida, but that this should be done with a recognition of the fundamental difficulties of such an assimilation and the probability that with futher developments the divergences will become more pronounced and the term postmodernism will lose even further its classificatory power.

This having been said, it remains to point out that what has made the extension of the term credible has been its purchase on a

relatively widespread mood in literary theory, philosophy and the
social sciences concerning the inability of these disciplines to
deliver totalising theories and doctrines, or enduring 'answers' to
fundamental dilemmas and puzzles posed by objects of inquiry,
and a growing feeling, on the contrary, that chronic provisionality,
plurality of perspectives and incommensurable appearances of the
objects of inquiry in competing discourses make the search for
ultimate answers or even answers that can command widespread
consensus a futile exercise. And this coincides with a relatively
widespread interest in how various discourses within these disciplines rhetorically work to create illusions of theoretical coherence and empirical credibility, with institutional and intellectual
preconditions and effects of these discourses as forms of power
relations, and the deconstruction of the pretensions of these discourses and their replacement by strategies of inquiry and debate
(the genealogical method in Foucault, deconstruction in Derrida)
which are undertaken without the epistemological baggage of
earlier periods. And in turn, some of these themes have actually
been appropriated by artists, novelists, etc. who have come to be
regarded as 'postmodernists', thus creating further grounds (albeit
provisional and temporary) for allowing 'postmodernism' to be
deployed in the way it has been in this collection.

To put our argument differently, what allows an extension of the
term postmodernism to both the fine arts and trends within the
disciplines of literary theory, philosophy and the social sciences is
that they share a common condition which we would characterise
as a crisis of 'representation' or, more accurately, a series of crises
of representation, in which older modes of defining, appropriating
and recomposing the objects of artistic, philosophical, literary and
social scientific languages are no longer credible and in which one
common aspect is the dissolution of the very boundary between
the language and its object, this in turn being related to the
acceptance of the inevitability of a plurality of perspectives and
the dissolution of various older polarities (popular/élite forms,
subject/object) and boundaries (for instance between disciplines
such as philosophy, sociology, history and psychoanalysis). It is
arguable that the idea of 'crises of representation' can be extended
to cover the crises of social class-dominated political movements
and discourses and some of the problems of political representation now apparent in both liberal democratic polities and state

socialist systems, thus allowing a characterisation of the 'post-modern condition' as one of a coincidence between crises of representation in the fine arts, philosophy, the social sciences and 'modern' political institutions.

Of course, the concept of representation is being used here in various senses – epistemological, artistic and in relation to the political articulation of social 'interests' – which cannot be assimilated to one another. Nevertheless, once this caveat is borne in mind, the idea of the postmodern condition as constituted by a series of crises of representation provides a potentially fruitful characterisation of many fundamental aspects of the 'new times'.

However, this is not an account we can elaborate upon here. Instead, we intend to examine other conceptions of the post-modern condition and most especially that advanced by Jean-François Lyotard, who remains today perhaps the most influential theorist of postmodernity. Some key conceptions associated with him were anticipated in earlier American contributions that are worth revisiting.

## Post-Industrialism and the End of Ideology Thesis

If modernism was always a compound of futurism, nihilism, conservatism and revolution, a contradictory celebration and condemnation of technology, and a thoroughly fearful invitation of social change, it is because whatever difference lies beyond the perceptions of the present, one can only conceive of it with apprehension. One way of defining postmodernity, then, might be in terms of the end of apprehension, the final arrival at the future and the end of revelations. A vision of this kind lay behind the *end of ideology* thesis advanced by Bell, Lipset and others in the 1950s and early 1960s, and also behind various conceptions of post-industrial society (Bell, 1988; Lipset, 1981).

The core of the 'end of ideology' thesis was not exactly that historical progress had brought us to the point where the truth of the world was plainly written on its finally revealed deeper surfaces, but it was not, in fact, too far from this. For the 'end of ideology' theorists, the power of general ideologies, such as Marxism, was definitely on the wane. By the mid-sixties, 'prot-estantism and catholicism, fascism, capitalism, communism, and social democracy [had] all lost their power to inspire Western people to work hard, to live morally, or to change the world'. (Lipset, 1981, p. 531). The basic 'end of ideology' thesis was, then, that the days of alliance between politics and revelation were over. This was taken to mean that we have reached the age of consensus, that one vision of the ideal against which the modernist spirit measures human achievement is no longer contested, and is finally in sight.

The 'end of ideology' theorists' celebration of America as *the* Good Society, and the political and ideological eruptions of the 1960s amongst students, anti-war activists, black minorities, third world nationalists and feminists led to the rapid decline of the thesis. With the benefit of hindsight, however, it can be seen that the thesis was in some senses prefigurative, anticipating, especially in its critique of Marxism, the thesis of the end of metanarratives proclaimed by the theorists of postmodernity.

In 1974 Daniel Bell published *The Coming of Post-Industrial Society*. He claimed (1974, pp. 14ff) that the basic structure of the emerging post-industrial society would be that of a service economy dominated by a technical–professional class whose technical knowledge would not only make them the key decision makers, but would also place them in control of the surveillance (information and data banks) and fine tuning mechanisms (econometrics, for example) of society. Bell not only thought that the irrational outcomes of uncontrolled market processes were going to be replaced by the calculated outcomes of the technical application of rational choice theories to the computer-modelled and system-analysed problems of administering a mass society, he also now dreamed of politics, beyond crude material interests, which would return to genuine debate over the nature of the good society. As he put it,

> the major source of structural change in society ... is the change in the character of knowledge: the exponential growth and branching of science ... At first man sought to conquer the natural order; and in this he has almost succeeded. In the last hundred years he has sought to substitute a technical order for the natural order; and in this he is well on his way. (1974, pp. 44–5).

At first glance, it looks as if the post-industrial society thesis meshes perfectly with the 'end of ideology' thesis: the notion that a technical élite might control the application of a universally valid rational analytic method to all aspects of social policy would appear to support the idea that total ideologies had become defunct, made powerless by the finally acknowledged arrival of codified theoretical knowledge. The situation is, however, not quite as clear as this. Bell does not, for example, support the idea of a convergence between the USA and the USSR. The reason for this is that, in Bell's view, the notion of the post-industrial society applies only to the social strucure, and he distinguishes and – somewhat intermittently – disconnects the social structure from the polity, on the one hand, and from the culture on the other. Two things may be said here. First, in addition to the many critiques of Bell's post-industrialism concept (see Miller, 1975; Kumar, 1978), there is a clear contradiction between Bell's prognosis for Western politics as participatory democracy crowned by impassioned debate among the technical élite on the nature of the good life, and his statement that societal convergence is not to be expected, since a similar social structure can exist in conjunction with a dissimilar political regime. If, however, democratic and authoritarian (and presumably any others that one might mention) regimes are both on the post-industrial agenda, does that not seem to be a scenario for reinvigorated ideological competition of the total kind that Bell had earlier dismissed? Second, and the reason for the ultimate compatibility of the 'end of ideology' thesis and the post-industrial society thesis, Bell's notion of post-industrial culture, which is seen to be increasingly 'anti-institutional and antinomian' (1974, p. 114) as opposed to the orientation within the social structure which is marked by rationality and meritocracy, constitutes an opening for multiple kinds of cultural formation. In their very diversity, such plural cultural forms may come to constitute a kind of prophylactic against *all* forms of total political ideology. It must be said, however, that while such arguments and conclusions are quite widespread today, as can be seen, for example, in Abercrombie et al's critique of the dominant ideology thesis (1980), much radical thought, particularly among Marxists and feminists, still holds that the widespread hegemony of capitalist and/or patriarchal values still functions as total ideology which stands in need of opposition, demystification and dismantling.

It is perhaps no coincidence that the opposition in Bell's work between culture and structure mirrors the two sides of modernity that we have discussed. The question that we now have to address is how many of the well-recognised theoretical inconsistencies and empirical misdiagnoses that we find in the work of Bell are to be found in the central social scientific text of postmodernism – Jean-François Lyotard's, *The Postmodern Condition*.

## The Postmodern Condition

In 1977, the President of the Conseil des Universités of the Government of Quebec asked one of France's premier philosophers – Jean-François Lyotard – to construct a report on the current state of knowledge in the advanced societies. In response to this request, Lyotard published *La Condition postmoderne* in 1979.

This book continues some of the themes which are to be found in the writings of both the end of ideology theorists and the post-industrialist society theorists. It accepts that Western societies can be understood as post-industrial, and that the revolution in microelectronics has had, and will continue to have, a profound effect on the culture and social structure of the Western world. It continues the attack upon Marxist grand theory, but this time Marxism is not the principal target. Rather, it is subsumed under the category of the metanarrative. For what Lyotard argues is that all of the grand discourses of Western society, which is to say all of the legitimating narratives which purport to provide valid and definitive principles, in any sphere, applicable across all societies, can now be seen to be defunct. He provides (1984, p. xxii) the following examples of metanarratives: 'the dialectics of Spirit, the hermeneutics of meaning, the emancipation of the rational or working subject, [] the creation of wealth'. Lyotard, then, extends the critique of ideology beyond the attacks upon Marxism that we have discussed, into the realms of liberal political economy and even into science.

How does Lyotard move from the given fact of technological progress to a definition of postmodern society as characterised by 'incredulity toward metanarratives'? In the first place, there is a kind of submerged Weberianism in his account. He argues that refusal of metanarrative discourses (a refusal, by the way, which he only demonstrates by selective references to theoretical work across a number of scientific disciplines) is a consequence of progress in science. Because of this progress, science and technology stand in no need of legitimation: their achievements function perfectly well on the practical plane. As a result of this, Lyotard argues, somewhat elliptically, narrative begins to lose its functions, its symbolic and legitimating role finally smashed by the onward march of rationalisation.

There is however, no despondent conclusion. Lyotard does not see an iron cage of bureaucracy built upon the printed circuit boards of the computer society. Rather, he sees the postmodern attitude as one of incredulity toward all statements which make out that things have to be done in one particular way, and that way only. The metanarrative of the bureaucratic imperative falls discredited in postmodern society, just as the metanarratives of Marxism, progress, liberal consensus, and unified science do. Thus, although Lyotard would fiercely contest Daniel Bell's belief in the universal applicability of some form of metanarrative of consensus, he nevertheless shares the latter's hope for a form of politics which might best be described as the art of judgement formation in the absence of fixed rules (for fixed rules, applicable across all cases, are metanarrativistic; what is more, what need is there for *real* political debate if there are fixed formulae to be applied?). As Lyotard (1984, p. xxv) puts it: 'Postmodern knowledge is not simply a tool of the authorities; it refines our sensitivity to differences and reinforces our ability to tolerate the incommensurable. Its principle is not the expert's homology, but the inventor's paralogy'.

What sort of understanding can we bring to our societies if indeed these changes are taking place, and if the consequences of these changes are as Lyotard describes them? Traditional sociology may not be of much help. Lyotard argues that sociology is still largely based on one of two competing models: either functionalist systems theory (based on a kind of organismic metanarrative) or evolutionary conflict theory (ultimately based on the Christian–Hegelian metanarrative of the final redemption of the human spirit). Neither of these models, with their innumerable variants, can perform the task of grounding a true analysis of human societies. As Stephen Crook argues in his chapter in this volume, the general failures of social theory may be explained in terms of its obsession with 'ends', with visions of finished worlds and finalities; his hope is that a set of 'post-foundationalist' social theoretic projects will in some way improve on the earlier record. For Lyotard, what is required is a focus on the 'what happens', a focus on the pragmatics of social worlds. This leads him to suggest that a more adequate sociological method will be based on the notion of communicative performance within language games, a suggestion which echoes, in the field of linguistics, in Lecercle's paper in this volume.

Wittgenstein's notion of language games seems to offer a theoretical heuristic appropriate to postmodernity because it stresses the simultaneously parochial and rule-bound nature of social activities. In Wittgenstein's replacement of the logical atomism of the *Tractatus* with the agonist approach of the *Philosophical Investigations*, we can see a version of the repudiation of the metanarrative. But Lyotard is well aware that the postmodern suspicion of general concepts does not mean that ideas like justice and truth can now be regarded as obsolete, a point which it is important to recognise in view of the powerful critique of Baudrillard's postmodern scepticism which Christopher Norris erects in this volume. It is at this point that Lyotard injects a mysterious dynamism into the language game concept by making use of the Kantian notion of the sublime which is shifted away from the aesthetic concern with transcendence, characteristic of modern art, and toward a sociological and psychological impulse to find new moves within the language games of social life. Thus, in discussing postmodern science as 'the search for instabilities', Lyotard suggests that social development in the postmodern epoch cannot now be seen as the fulfilment of some grand historical narrative, but that it will be a pragmatic matter of inventing new rules whose validity will reside in their effectivity rather than in their compatibility with some legitimating discourse.

For Lyotard, then, postmodernity is seen as a post-metaphysical, postindustrial, pluralist, pragmatic and restless set of partially differentiated social orders. His view is consonant with the work of both Michel Foucault and Jacques Derrida, with the former's notion of ubiquitous but ultimately uncentred power relations, and with the latter's critique of the conceptual monism that underlies the Western philosophical tradition.

It must be pointed out, however, that this vision is open to the kinds of critique that were levelled at the theorists of post-industrial society. In particular, we would argue that the theorists of postmodernity have considerably overestimated the significance of the theoretical debates and technological developments that have marked the last ten years in the Western world. Structural social inequality, economic-logic defying associations of inflation and underemployment, the paradoxes of representative democracy, the continuing drive for profit, efficiency, cultural hegemony and increased market share by the mega-corporations, to name just some of the abiding features of contemporary Western capitalist society, seem to be little affected by the changing patterns of knowledge, production and consumption identified within *avant-garde* theoretical debate. This is not to doubt that we are living through what the journal *Marxism Today* (October 1988) has infectiously called 'new times', a combination of a new global interdependency, an emergent post-Fordism in production and consumption, a decline in the dominance of manufacturing and traditional class politics, and so on, but to question whether terms like post-industrialism or postmodernity are able to characterise with sufficient complexity and clarity the shape of the new times.

Like modernity, then, postmodernity is a highly problematic term. Although the present period is culturally, politically and economically distinctive, the terms capitalist and socialist, for example, have by no means lost their purchase on significant social divisions, pressures and possibilities. 'Modernity' and 'postmodernity', although useful shorthand markers for the emergence initially of urban industrialism and then for a period marked by 'new times' and various global crises, most especially of socialism, and by the profound effects of post-colonialism, nevertheless lack the theoretical and analytical discrimination necessary to grapple with the complexities of the social, political and economic formations that exist as part of a heterogeneous but interdependent global configuration.

There are, nevertheless, other aspects to these issues that we need to look at more deeply. As we have remarked earlier and as the contributions to this volume show, the postmodernism debate is located particularly in regard to questions of social context, political form, aesthetic practice and philosophical legitimation. One area where all of these discourses come together is urban design. The construction of the spaces in which we live and work

forms the object of a key set of discourses and practices and
has provided a significant focal point for the debates around
postmodernism.

## Architecture and the City

Los Angeles has often been referred to as a postmodern city. It
lacks a centre, having a downtown area which, in Reyner
Banham's words (1971, p. 208), 'began to disintegrate long
ago – out of sheer irrelevance as far as one can see'. It is a city
of movement, something which is perfectly symbolised by a
parallelogrammatic freeway system which efficiently disperses the
Angelenos, who are quite at home in the ordered language game
of urban freeway driving, to the various parts of a plural urban
order. It is a city of pragmatic adaptation to the innumerable
differentiated urban micro-orders which constitute it, and which
collectively make up an unplanned mega-space (in spite of the
millions of words in the volumes of planning regulations), which
threatens the metanarrativistic principles upon which the theory
and practice of Western urban planning and design have been
based for millennia. It is, finally, a city which cannot be reduced to
a single principle: not the motor car, not the freeways nor the
railway system that preceded them, not its lack of history (for
mythical and 'real' histories it has in plenty), not Hollywood and
the dream factory, not the giant corporation, not the high technology company, not the beach, not the smog nor the sun. Wrapped
around all these principles, language games have developed and
still – paralogically – develop; each game with its own rules,
experts, argot, myths, and finally unsuccessful countervailing
claims to represent the essence of urban life. As Kenneth Frampton
has noted (1987, p. 12): 'when all the dust has finally settled in the
great debate that surrounds the rise and fall of a suspect Post-
Modernism, we may possibly look to Los Angeles, to begin again,
with an "other" modernity'. Read in this way, Los Angeles provides
an illustration of the point and purpose of postmodern theorising as
providing the deprivileged conceptual tools for appre-
hending (post)modern life, and this notion of 'deprivileging' is
crucial, for, as Elizabeth Wilson makes plain in her contribution to
this book, which looks at the question of fashion, the ambiguities

of the postmodern condition are its most valuable features, and underlie its potential to deconstruct privileged moments of all kinds.

This brings us to a major paradox within postmodern theorising concerning so-called postmodern architecture. Charles Jencks, proselytiser extraordinary for postmodern architecture, defines postmodernism in architecture as follows (1986, pp. 14–5):

> *double-coding: the combination of modern techniques with something else (usually traditional building) in order for architecture to communicate with the public and a concerned minority, usually other architects* . . . Modern architecture had failed to remain credible partly because it didn't communicate effectively with its ultimate users . . . and partly because it didn't make effective links with the city and history. Thus the solution I perceived and defined as Post-modern: an architecture that was professionally based and popular as well as one that was· based on new techniques and old patterns. Double coding to simplify means both elite/popular and new/old. (Author's italics)

Double-coding, then, brings together two key elements of the postmodernist project, the stylistic eclecticism and the critique of modernist élitism. And Jencks is correct to refer to the discrediting of modern architecture in the face of the failure of many (not all) award-winning housing developments to provide a tolerable social environment for the people who would exist there. But his 'solution' to this failure, his recipe for better communication between architecture and society, the city and history is symbolic and institutional. The exemplars of postmodern architectural achievement are museums, façades, banks, and a couple of housing schemes where local residents have been able to make a contribution to the design process. Now, without denying the success of some of these buildings (Stirling's *Neue Staatsgalerie* being notable here), the addition of neo-classical adornment to the modernist scale and temper seems to be a barely adequate response to the well documented sociological dysfunctions of modern architecture, amongst which one might mention litter, graffiti, vandalism, excremental pollution, burglary, theft, robbery, mugging, sexual assault, family breakdown, and a whole panoply of psychiatric disorders (Coleman, 1986). When one bears in mind that, as Deyan Sudjic (1986, p. 35) put it, in a view which is also found in Paul Crowther's chapter in this volume, 'architects have always looked back in order to move forward', it is difficult not to agree with him that the affair of postmodern architecture appears to have been greatly oversold, and to have underestimated the importance of historical traditions and continuities in locating any forms of artwork.

This is where the paradox of postmodern architecture is located. There is no doubt that the grip of modernist design, with its institutional and functional symbolics and its concomitant paternalism and élitism, is *potentially* weakened by the development of the 'postmodern' city. This is the case whether one takes Los Angeles, at one extreme, or Beirut, at the other. But the nature of the 'postmodern' city may be such as to make it impossible for architectural practice to communicate at the level of the city as a whole. If postmodern life is about pragmatic responses to plural dynamics within unities whose totality is only notional, then a truly postmodern architecture would be reduced in both scale and pretension. The self-proclaimed postmodern monuments do not accord very well with such a logic, which suggests that the view of much postmodern architecture as really late-modern architecture is probably correct. Perhaps Rem Koolhaas is right (1987, p. 450) when he says: 'Through the parallel actions of reconstruction and deconstruction, the city becomes an archipelago of "architectural" islands in a postarchitectural landscape of erasure; where the city is replaced by a highly charged nothingness'.

Edward Soja (1989, p. 190) may also be right when he suggests that 'It all comes together in Los Angeles'; but his vision of Los Angeles as 'a constellation of Foucaultian heterotopias "capable of juxtaposing in a single real place several spaces, several sites that are in themselves incompatible"' (p. 240) is not the only model which we have for thinking through the asymmetrical trajectory of the 'postmodern' built environment. Indeed, the anti-metanarrativistic quasi-logic of postmodernity would give us as a rule that there is always a plurality of forms, always an excess which cannot be captured by the subordinations of a mechanistic conceptualism. Thus we have, for example, Tokyo, a site of a Buddhist culture which recognises, in the concept of *mujo*, the immanence of change, uncertainty, and the mutability of forms and forces within the human condition. Hiroshi Hara, architect of the Yamamoto International Building on reclaimed land in Tokyo

Bay, speaks of 'the fusion or overlapping of humans, machines and nature' and tells us that Tokyo 'is a city where there are no real distinctions between living and working areas – they're all mixed up' (1986, p. 25).

Confronted with an analytical spectrum for the postmodern city which runs from Los Angeleno 'Autopia' through a conspicuously self-dramatising Berlin and on to sites of simultaneous production, consumption and cultural otherness in Japan, leading finally to the violently disjointed language wars of Beirut (Squiers, 1987), our 'postmodernist' conclusion is that one would search in vain for an urban sociological metanarrative, or any metanarrative, that would collect without remainder the phenomena under analysis.

One lesson of all this might be that total social analyses of the sort advanced by economists, architects, sociologists, art historians, and the rest will tend to fail the test of full epistemological legitimation. They are unlikely to summon up a definitive ordering principle upon which their claim to be total could rest. Perhaps this means that the utterances of both expert and layperson alike should be apprehended not merely in terms of their truth, but rather more in terms of their performativity, in terms of what they do. This distinction, which is effectively that between achievement and excuse, leads us to conclude that the final import of postmodern thinking, with its panopoly of concepts developed out of different fields and applied in different ways, might be political.

## The Politics of Postmodernism

In areas as disparate as the nature of scientific knowledge, the structure of the contemporary city, industrial sociology, political theory, modern fiction (McHale, 1987), consumer behaviour (Haug, 1986; Featherstone, 1983), sexuality and the body (Kroker and Kroker, 1988; Boyne, 1988), architecture, contemporary aesthetic production (Kraus, 1985), one common theme can be found across all the writings concerned with delineating the new postmodern perspective. This common theme is that postmodernism is, in the broadest sense, 'political'. Through its entire range, postmodernist discourse presents questions about how social relations should be organised and lived, about the social possibilities of our age, and about the social visions it is desirable to underwrite in the postmodern epoch. But what are the politics of postmodernism? Is there a postmodern politics appropriate to a supposedly new postmodern era?

Initially, we might attend to terms – for example, *progressive* and *conservative* – which many postmodern theorists would already exclude from discussion on account of their origins in grand narratives which, out of the alleged arrogance of a supposedly superior vantage point, claim to identify the political virtues and vices of all aesthetic and social projects. There has, of course, been considerable disagreement over definitions of progress and reaction. Modernists have been roughly divided between 'left' and 'right', between those who regard capitalism as unable to deliver the triple Enlightenment promise of natural abundance, economic equality and social freedom, and those who see capitalism as the only guarantee of wealth and liberty against what they see as the inevitable nightmare of totalitarianism to which the left-modernist pursuit of equality succumbs. Modernists have also quarrelled because successive aesthetic tendencies have been set up as arbiters of authentic artistic expression, just as various philosophical currents within the general problematic of modernism have claimed epistemological privilege. In the face of the contentiousness and variety of modernist political debate, it may seem tempting to accede to the postmodernist rejection of the terms of modernist political discourse, and to conclude that to try and specify the political moments of postmodernism in terms of progress or reaction would be futile. We do not find this position convincing.

The postmodern critique of the Enlightenment project and of its embodiment in various forms, such as art or architecture or politics, is itself undertaken from particular standpoints, from preferred stances which are open to 'political' inspection and interrogation. Lyotard, as a prime example, after all paints a very broad picture, and is unable to escape positing some kind of functional equivalent to a metanarrative in the course of his search for a postmodern social theory. In fact, several postmodernist themes immediately suggest themselves as obvious targets for political analysis: for example, the privileging of 'pluralism', the ironic appropriation of historical episodes, the celebration of the death of the author and the fragmentation of identity, and the recovery of the discourses of 'the other'.

**The Two Sides of Postmodernism**

Our starting point for what might be regarded as a traditionally
formed political analysis of postmodernism is the fact that many
socialists and feminist writers have actually rejected the social
theory and cultural practice of postmodernism, seeing it as antithetical to emancipatory strategies toward socialism and the
abolition of women's subordination. Bauman, for example, char-
acterising postmodernist social theory as a response to the crisis of
the intellectual left's loss of its traditional historical agent, the proletariat, sees postmodernism primarily as a last-ditch philosophy of
resignation and futility which can be at best only provide a partial
foundation for the rethinking and the new self-identity that the left
urgently needs. Although – given his recent approbation of the
trend against universalist thinking, and his deployment of Baudrillard's notion of *seduction* as a main analytical tool of contemporary social analysis (1988, pp. 221–2, 226) – his position now is
not quite as clear as he implied when he wrote, 'There is no
conceivable way a realistic Left programme can be patched
together out of postmodernist theory' (1986, p. 86). Overall,
Bauman takes the view that postmodern theorising is at serious
risk of imploding into intellectual irrelevance. Callinicos, writing
in the present volume from a revolutionary Marxist perspective
which, unlike Bauman's, appears to see little need for serious
rethinking on the Marxist left, presents a more uncompromising
condemnation of postmodernism as a *cul de sac* which reflects the
intellectual left's 'sense of an ending', seeing this, however, not as
a dangerous gesture of despair, but rather as a blissful surrender to
the temptations of affluence and consumption made available by
capitalism to intellectuals and other members of the 'new middle
class'. 'Who,' Callinicos asks, 'could be better qualified to provide
a rationale for lying back and enjoying late capitalism than
Lyotard, himself an ex-militant of the semi-Trotskyist *Socialisme
ou Barbarie* group? That this is what Lyotard effectively does
seems to me beyond question'.

The need for feminists to take their distance from the characteristic themes of postmodernist theorising is argued by Lovibond in
the present collection. She exposes the notorious anti-feminism of
Nietzsche, who is a major reference point for the postmoderns, as
well as underlining the problem of constructing any effective

feminist analysis if the postmodernist proscriptions against any type of metanarrative are taken seriously. As she asks, 'If there can be no systematic political approach to questions of wealth, power and labour, how can there be any effective challenge to a social order which distributes its benefits and burdens in a systematically unequal way between the sexes?' The epistemology and political theory of postmodernism, Lovibond argues, simply disallow the possibility of analysing the structural causes of sexual inequality and therefore cannot be called upon to underwrite the feminist project, indeed they undermine its very foundation.

Such readings of the politics of postmodernism are, however, open to question on a variety of grounds. One problem is that postmodernism, despite the relative internal coherence we have earlier demonstrated, nevertheless also contains a range of positions across a diversity of intellectual and cultural fields; especially, a critique of the social theory of Lyotard or Baudrillard, or of Rorty's epistemology, cannot necessarily be held to undermine the critical effects and radical potential of postmodernist strategies in painting, the cinema or architecture. Thus, even the sharpest feminist or Marxist critique of one stream of postmodernist thought does not, for example, vitiate Rosalind Kraus's brilliant demonstration (1985, pp. 151–70) of the unconscious subterfuges associated with the presentation of Rodin's sculpture, which functioned to preserve the aura of orginality and genius surrounding his work, and which expose the extent to which the art establishment legitimates itself by reference to such ultimately dubious notions.

There is actually a political variety and indeterminancy to the postmodernist project which it is all too easy to smother with blanket judgements of condemnation (see Edgar, 1987 and Hall, 1986 for views closer to ours). This can lead to a failure to appreciate the significance of the more constructive dialogue that some socialists and feminists have already opened up with postmodernism. Moreover, as we shall also show, there are important developments around the questions of anti-racism and the analysis of the West's 'others' which have emerged out of postmodernist concerns and which it would, in fact, be reactionary to ignore or dismiss as irrelevant.

One precondition for developing a more complex understanding of the politics of postmodernism is a refusal of the assumption that the political meaning of artistic products, to focus on these for the time being, will simply be revealed to an attentive and theoretically informed gaze which, however, is oblivious to the manner in which the meaning and relevance of artistic works is influenced by the political context of production and reception. An instructive contrary analysis is provided by Huyssen in an essay on 'The cultural politics of Pop' (1986a). He points out that while in America the Pop Art of Warhol, Lichtenstein and others preceded student, new-Left and counter-cultural radicalisation, and thus soon came to be seen as a mere celebration of the commodification of mass culture by capitalist manufacturing and advertising industry, and moreover found itself within a relatively short period incorporated by museums and collectors as the 'newest form of high art', in West Germany, on the other hand, the emergence of Pop coincided with the rise of the anti-authoritarian New Left. In the West German case, serial productions of Coke bottles or comic strips were not seen as 'affirmative reproductions of mass produced reality', but rather as a critique of the establishment, and of conventional art criticism and its distinction between 'high' and 'low' art. This significance was largely lost with the collapse of the student movement, and the 'politics' of Pop subsequently followed the American pattern, as its incorporation by the Museum and the Academy restored to Pop the 'aura' it had formerly sought to shatter with its recycled commonplace images of commercialised mass culture. The point here does not concern the negation of the radical moment, but the different political contexts of Pop's reception in West Germany and America.

The elementary lesson for the interpretation of postmodern art (and surely art in general) is that the meaning of individual products is not essentially and exhaustively given by its techniques of pastiche and irony, nor by conceptual glosses on themes such as 'depthlessness' and so on. Interpretation is also a function of how a particular work is inserted into the ensemble of relations between artistic intentions, forms of institutionalisation, styles of interpretation, and modes of appropriation by political movements and projects. This insight is partly evident in Hebdige's (1983) discussion of British Pop Art, a movement which not only signified the transition from the austere traditionalism of the fifties to the 'Swinging Sixties', but also disrupted high art's disdain for the 'popular'.

Now, we have seen that critics of postmodernism are often very concerned about the political implications of postmodern writings and art works. But, in fact, this engagement is very often based upon a rough theoretical appreciation, rather than a fine-grained analysis which is attuned to qualitative differences between varying contexts. Thus there is a tendency, on the left, to run together a reductive political economy or sociology of postmodernism with particular readings of its characteristic products, and this can squeeze out crucial contextual features which, if attended to, would tend to weaken any universalistic judgements upon postmodernist work. Jameson's discussion of Warhol, in his influential *New Left Review* essay (1984), for example, completely misses Huyssen's point about the differing political contexts of reception for Pop art, despite his interest in the critical potential of Pop.

More importantly, perhaps, Habermas's polemic against the French postmoderns also reveals a tendency to impute political meanings without paying due attention to the relative political indeterminacy of texts, and without attending to the significance of political networks and allegiances in determining, in part, their political meaning. In his widely read essay, 'Modernity – an incomplete project' (1985), Habermas, in addition to presenting a critique of those he calls the 'old conservatives' (Leo Strauss et al) and the 'neoconservatives' (Daniel Bell et al), challenges the antimodernism of Foucault and Derrida, whom he labels 'young conservatives'. However, Habermas is mistaken in assuming that the work of Foucault or Derrida can be so simply categorised as in reactionary opposition to the emancipatory project whose epistemological foundations he has for so long sought to ground by his philosophical and social reflections on communicative action. In reality, both in France and elsewhere, the texts of Foucault and Derrida have been called upon for support by both left and right, and it is not at all clear that their writings are unambiguously and all of a piece either 'conservative' or 'progressive'. Textual politics depend in part upon the modes of appropriation adopted by other actors, by activists, writers, artists, and so on. Derrida, for example, was asked to write an introductory piece for an exhibition entitled *Art Against Apartheid*, which opened in Paris in November 1983; but from a contrary standpoint, the furore over the discovery of the pro-fascist war-time writings of Paul de Man, standard-bearer for a quasi-Derridean approach to literary criticism in America, has provided the occasion for some to affirm that deconstruction was always a deeply regressive theoretical practice.

If this singularly striking opposition is not enough, we can mention that both Poulantzas (1978) and Giddens (1981; 1982) have drawn upon Foucault to develop left analyses of the state and power, and Ryan (1982) has argued for an articulation of Derrida and Marx, while Fraser (1984) has drawn attention to the divergent political appropriations of Derrida's work in France, and some of the political ambiguities of both writers have been exposed in Peter Dews's *Logics of Disintegration* (1988). Norris has even postulated a convergence between Derrida's recent texts and Habermas's project, holding that both seek 'new grounds for the exercise of enlightened critique through an idea of communicative competence with allows for specific *distortions* in present day discourse, but which holds out the possibility of grasping and transcending these irrational blocks' (1987, p. 169). It is the absence of even a ghost of such a vision which underlies the comprehensive critique of Baudrillard which Norris has written for this volume.

Habermas's critique of postmodernism, then, is insensitive to the varying political contexts of its reception. His critique does not engage with the conflicting reception of poststructuralism by feminists (Weedon, 1987; Boyne 1990), nor does it begin to address the complexities of Paul de Man's work, which, war-time writings apart, may easily be seen as an extended plea for demystification and honesty, but which has been received in American literary criticism, with one or two exceptions (Sprinker, 1987), in a politically abstentionist mode; nor, lastly, does he consider the writings of Edward Said and others, upon which we comment below, which display a political engagement which can hardly be dismissed as 'conservative'. No doubt Habermas's rejection of postmodernism needs to be understood, as Callinicos remarks in his essay here, in the German context, given the conjunction of a certain irrationalism with Nazism. But, for all that, his lack of attention to the ambiguities of political reception that we have mentioned vitiates his critique to a considerable extent.

It is time to express our point more broadly. There is, as Foster (1985, p. xii) has argued, a postmodernism of 'resistance' as well as a postmodernism of 'reaction'. Elements of each intertwine in highly complex ways in the political intentions, conceptual structures, styles and effects of postmodernist products and practices. To reduce the whole variegated 'movement' to a single political essence is in effect to fail to perceive the real crisis of modernist projects, especially of the left, which provide a crucial context for postmodernism. It is also to block off, unnecessarily and prematurely, a dialogue that has already begun to enrich and reinvigorate many elements of social theory and cultural practice. We will illustrate this further in the fields of architecture and feminism.

One of the problematic features of postmodernism is undoubtedly its style of appropriation of history, particularly in artistic and architectural projects. Jameson, for example, reserves some of his strongest criticisms for 'the complacent eclecticism of postmodern architecture, which randomly and without principle but with gusto cannibalises all the architectural styles of the past and combines them in overstimulating ensembles' (1984, p. 66). He is also critical of the nostalgia mode of such films as *American Graffiti* and *Chinatown*. What Jencks admires as 'double coding', Jameson dismisses as 'pastiche'. There is, of course, much to be said for the left's impatience with historical references which in fact do little to illuminate specific histories, but which, rather, as in the case of some postmodern architecture, destroy the historical integrity of particular architectural forms in a search for plurality, locality, ornament, and so on. Nevertheless, whatever its shortcomings, postmodern architectural departures must be seen in the light of the colossal failure of modernism especially in the guise of the 'international style' in architecture. There is now also widespread rejection of its élitism (analysed by Caygill in this volume) as well as its stark functionalism and soullessness. Thus, whatever objections it may be necessary to enter against postmodern architecture, and marginal as yet though it might be, it can hardly be doubted that so far as architecture is concerned, a break with some of the defining tenets of modernism has long been necessary. The opening of such a rupture is visible in the commendable populism which has characterised some postmodern architectural projects, and here we could locate the desire to reflect the wishes and interests of ordinary users of buildings as part of the postmodern challenge to the modernist division between élite and mass culture.

As one would expect, given the massive vested interests that are

involved, the going is tough. As Caygill shows here, the populist
element of postmodern architecture is attenuated by the reaffir-
mation of a strong professional ideology which reproduces the
élitism of the modernist project, and thereby undercuts the theory
and practice of Jencks, Venturi and their followers. It is further
unfortunate that, although perhaps in a more subtle mode, this
élitism also appears in the other antimodernist tendency within
architecture, the so-called 'community architecture movement',
championed among others by the Prince of Wales. But, whatever
the failings of postmodern architects, in both their theory and their
practice, it cannot be definitively stated that the development of a
successful architecture of resistance would require a complete
abandonment of postmodern strategies; for many people, both the
populism and the playfulness, humour and ornamentation of
postmodern architecture promise a welcome replacement for
brutal power statements in steel and glass. There is also a potential
for the articulation of a populist postmodern architecture, emptied
of its residual élitism, with the discourse of feminism and with that
of non-Western others. Perhaps such developments are not so far
off, since the hidden racism of modernist architectural education
and the possibilities for a different set of feminist and anti-racist
practices are beginning to be revealed in accounts and projects
which are bound to multiply in the future (Haque, 1988).

The dismissal of postmodernism as conservative is additionally
and particularly difficult to sustain in the face of the intellectual
support that feminism has managed to derive from some central
elements of the postmodernist project. We can first guage the
significance of this by considering the often neglected reality of
male domination in constructing and sustaining modernism.
Women's diverse experiences of modernity, as Janet Wolff (1985)
has shown, have generally been ignored within the major literary
and sociological accounts of modernity. One major reason for this
is that the primary object of discussion has been the *public sphere*,
from which most women were increasingly excluded from the
eighteenth century onward. This exclusion meant that the dominant literary and sociological analyses were mostly produced by
men, who had the freedom to enjoy the public spaces of the city as
well as the power to dominate academic and cultural institutions.
Drawing upon recent feminist art history, Wolff points out, in her
essay in this collection, that the marginalisation and exclusion of

women from aesthetic modernism in the late nineteenth and twentieth centuries arises in part out of the practices of the major modernist institutions like the Tate Gallery in London and the Museum of Modern Art in New York, but also out of the discourse of the major commentators on modern art. These strategies of marginalisation and exclusion have made it necessary for feminist art historians both to explain and criticise this historical neglect and to labour to recover women's contributions to modernism. The consequent critique of male domination as one of the central defining features of modernism has led to an understanding of the various ways in which the unadmitted gender of modernist discourse has been sustained. Amongst the various mechanisms and processes, we might mention Pollock's (1982) demonstration that the concept of creativity in art has been theorised as fundamentally and prejudicially male, and Huyssen's argument (1986b) that the specification of women as part of, and identical with, 'the masses' has functioned to legitimate the devaluation of both categories.

It is not our argument that modernism is essentially and irredeemably male, or that all authentic feminisms must take up an active postmodernist stance, although, for example, Janet Wolff's chapter in this book presents a very strong case for the use of postmodern deconstructive strategies by feminist artists. We do argue, however, that any political evaluation of postmodernism has first to acknowledge the significance of sexual hierarchy in modernism, and then to inspect the spaces opened up within postmodernism for a questioning of male domination and the insertion of feminist agendas. The key (postmodernist/post-structuralist) operation here is that of deconstruction, understood in this context as interrogating, evaluating, overturning and disrupting. In postmodernist art, these strategies can be and have been applied to the male gaze, to forms of representations which 'naturalise' entirely questionable forms of subordination, to presentations of apparently simple but actually corrupt examples of gender characteristics and human attributes, and to the various metadiscourses upon the human condition whose pronunciations conceal partiality and prejudice. Janet Wolff and others (Owens, 1984) cite Cindy Sherman's haunting photographs of herself, dressed to resemble a Hollywood B-movie heroine, which in their suggestion of hidden danger work to question male desire and its stereotyped representations. A series of Barbara Kruger's black and white photographs are overwritten with what Wolff calls 'accusatory texts' aimed to disorient the male spectator and to elicit the shock of recognition and understanding from women: *'Your gaze hits the side of my face'* or *'We won't play nature to your culture'*. Such work challenges the power of the male gaze, and disrupts the common modes, with their discriminatory functions, of the representation of women. Another good example is Mary Kelly's much-discussed *Post-Partum Document*, a combination of image, objects and text which disputes the Lacanian theorisation of the mother–child relationship through a deployment of an autobiographical method that does not succumb to the home-maker ideal of an integrated woman subject unifying the whole work.

These intersections of postmodernist artistic practice, post-structuralism and feminism constitute a further challenge to any general identification of postmodernism and conservatism, and we find the same story if we attend to the application of post-structuralist theories in feminist literary and social analysis. Feminist literary theorists have challenged earlier essentialist excavations of the authentic 'woman's voice' or 'lesbian voice' or 'black woman's voice' in women's writing, replacing this with a concern for the various contradictory and socio-historically specific ways in which texts produce meanings and construct subject positions for the reader (Weedon, 1987). The engagement of feminist social and political theorists with poststructuralism has highlighted the problematic nature of universalist theories of gender-identity formation of the type developed by Rosaldo, Chodorow, Hartsock and others, and have begun to redefine the agenda for feminist analyses, emphasising the historical variability of gender identities and the mechanisms involved in their forma-tion (Fraser and Nicholson, 1988). However, this is not a Lyotardian collapse into local narratives devoid of wider relevance. Fraser and Nicholson, for instance, restrict their scaling down of the feminist theoretical project only to the abandonment of the search for *'the* causes of sexism' which would hold good for all societies in all historical periods, while arguing for a postmodernist feminism which retains what they call an essential genre of political theory – 'the identification and critique of macrostructures of inequality and injustice which cut across the boundaries separating relatively discrete practices and institutions' (1988, pp. 377–8). This is a

stance which brings them close to the position outlined by Sabina
Lovibond, in her critique of Lyotard, Rorty, et al. in this volume,
and it can be clearly seen that such a position does not amount to a
reckless relativism. It is worth remembering that an abandonment
of the search for the unchanging (and therefore unchangeable?)
causes of sexism does not mean abandoning the search for its
causes here and now, and is no more unreasonable a step than the
abandonment of the search for *the* theory of the state urged within
Marxism by Poulantzas (1978) and Jessop (1982).

Nothing in our argument implies that poststructuralist or postmodernist feminisms represent the only way forward, or that the
articulation between postmodernism and feminism is unprob-
lematic. For instance, legitimate critical reservations have been
entered about the inaccessibility of many postmodern feminist
artworks, requiring as they often do an initiation into post-
structuralist and Lacanian theories of the subject. Furthermore,
the radical potential of feminist cultural practices which draw upon
humanist conceptions of the subject may be quite considerable,
especially given their greater accessibility; and while there are
powerful grounds for doubting the viability of a universal theory of
male domination, the case is not overwhelming and is open to
contestation in the light of further developments in psychoanalysis,
anthropology, history and sociology. Indeed, one of the conditions
of postmodernist sensibility must be the refusal to prescribe some
discourses as essentially and unchallengeably True, and to pro-
scribe others as irredeemably False. This does not mean that
critical judgement as to the present relation of theorisations to the
available evidence must be abandoned – despite all the difficulties
this entails in the light of the inevitable theoretical 'contamination'
of evidence, and given the ever-present under-determination of
theories by evidence but which, and this is the point, makes *all*
theories vulnerable to challenge and displacement.

'Woman' has aptly been described as modernism's 'other'
(Huyssen, 1986b), but there have been and continue to be
different 'others'. The advent of modernity in the shape of
capitalist industrialism in the West coincided with, and indeed
in some considerable measure relied upon, an imperialist and
colonialist expansion that 'discovered', explored, exploited and
subjugated large sections of the non-Western world. The economic and political domination that formed the key elements of

imperialism and colonialism in the eighteenth and nineteenth centuries was always accompanied by the formation of discourses in which the 'otherness' of the peoples of Asia and Africa was apprehended and culturally colonised, and in which the cultural and moral superiority of the Western imperial power was always affirmed without reservation. This discursively produced cultural superiority established the 'right' of a commercially expansive Britain or France or Germany to exercise political and cultural domination over the 'Orient', Africa and elsewhere.

Remarkably, only a minority of Western intellectuals have ever seriously attempted to explore the significance of imperialism and colonialism in the 'rise' of the West and in the formation of its self-understanding and its attitudes toward the rest of the world. Amongst that small number today, however, is a growing proportion – often of 'hybrid' origin in so far as many of these individual intellectuals (Edward Said, Gayatri Chakravorty Spivak, Homi Bhabha, Abjul JanMohamed) combine Third World origins with Western education and positions in Western universities and cultural establishments – who have begun to challenge, with poststructuralist inspiration, the varieties of colonial and imperialist discourse that have been so crucial in the intellectual formation of modernity.

Despite Michel Foucault's own silence on questions of imperial domination (Spivak, 1988, pp. 289–91), his work has been pivotal here because of the purchase of his concepts on the apparatuses and processes involved in the formation of discourses implicated in the exercise of imperial power. Said's magisterial *Orientalism* (1978), a brilliant exposition of the discourses through which the West has constructed and governed the 'Arabs' and 'Islam', has been a key Foucauldian contribution, challenging the freezing of the 'Oriental' into a timeless 'other', all of whose supposedly uniform characteristics serve only to highlight the Occident's difference and superiority in matters cultural, moral and technological. Foucault is not the only significant influence. Derrida, too, has been important, for example in Spivak's meditations on female and subaltern 'others' in the Indian context, 'recovered' against the grain of colonial discourses as well as the universalising metanarratives of indigenous Marxisms (Spivak, 1987). Bhabha's work (1983, 1984) combines poststructuralist, especially Foucauldian, concepts with psychoanalytic themes from Freud,

Lacan and Fanon to produce effective deconstructions of colonial discourse which move beyond the unified image of the 'other', implied in Said's *Orientalism* and elsewhere, to focus on the ambivalences and contradictions of colonial stereotypification. The anti-imperialism of poststructuralist deconstructions of Orientalism and colonial discourse, extended by Said into powerful exposés of the contemporary power–knowledge complex which institutionalises the collusion between Western academics and American state agencies and interests involved in dealing with the Middle East, provide a serious challenge to any essentialising conception of the inevitable conservatism of poststructuralism. The radical, emancipatory impulse of these researches has been defined by Said (1984, p.25) as residing in three underlying features, all of them with clear poststructuralist inflections:

[first] none of the works ... claims to be working on behalf of one audience ... or for one supervening, over-coming truth ... allied to Western (or for that matter Eastern) reason, objectivity, science. On the contrary, we note here a plurality of terrains, multiple experiences and different constituencies. Second, these activities and praxes are consciously secular, marginal and oppositional with reference to the mainstream, generally authoritarian systems from which they emanate, and against which they now agitate. Thirdly, they are political and practical in as much as they intend ... the end of dominating, coercive systems of knowledge.

## The Political Possibilities and Limits of Postmodernism

Yet, at the very point of affirming the liberatory impulse of poststructuralism (which we take to be one of postmodernism's major intellectual strands), one can begin to glimpse some of its limitations.

The first difficulty which must be noted concerns the epistemological ambivalence, seized upon by several of Said's critics and characteristic of much poststructuralist analysis, in relation to the 'object' of analysis, in Said's case, the 'Orient'. Sometimes Said seems to assume the existence of a 'real' Orient which is allegedly misrepresented in Western discourses, while at other times he

explicitly refuses to offer a 'more valid' account of the Orient and
wonders whether 'there can be a true representation of anything'
(Said, 1978, p. 272). Foucault, a key source of inspiration for
Said's work, has been criticised for a similar ambivalence, refusing
in his remarks on genealogical method and elsewhere to be drawn
on questions of truth and validity beyond a demonstration of their
connection with the exercise of forms of power (Cousins and
Hussain, 1984, pp. 263–5; Jay, 1984, pp. 528–9; see also Said,
1983, p. 243). It is hard to avoid concluding that the critical force
of work such as the deconstruction of Orientalism or the genealogical analysis of the disciplinary society is weakened by the
poststructuralist/postmodernist reluctance to provide contextual
clarification and sustained justification of their underlying values.
Postmodernist and poststructuralist intellectual endeavours, like
those of others, depend after all upon the (albeit provisional)
possibility of evaluation of claims to empirical validity as well as
the construction of coherent and persuasive argument, and
it is disingenuous to engage in such practices, or to produce
devastating critiques of the projects of other researchers, while
disclaiming any possibility of elaborating and justifying the principles from which the practices and critiques are undertaken.

The epistemological agnosticism of the poststructuralists, while
allowing the development of iconoclastic research projects like
those of Foucault and Said, can at the same time be politically
disabling. Although oppositional activity, such as the Prison
Information Group (GIP) in which Foucault was involved, may be
encouraged, especially if it is allied to a fundamental mistrust of all
attempts to theorise totalities or to posit systematic connections
between institutional orders, wider strategic thinking about linking
up forms of struggle into broader programmes for the reform of
bureaucratic and authoritarian institutions does not get much
support from poststructuralist theory. Foucauldian politics seems
actually to reject any notion of social reform which would be based
on reflexive action to achieve a preferred set of alternative
institutional arrangements, and his relatively unclarified alternative is founded on a strategy of, on the one side, constant
problematisation and dissent, and on the other, a near-blind
submission to the co-optational seductions of established social
institutions, commended because the resulting changes in those
institutions may well change the game (Gandal, 1986; Boyne, 1990).

Given the undoubted significance of the work undertaken by
Foucault, Said and others, but in view of the kinds of theoretical
and political limitations identified above, a future task could be
expressed as one of joining the Lyotardian/Derridean themes of
difference and anti-transcendentalism together with Foucauldian
themes of power–knowledge, surveillance, discipline, and so on,
but without losing the Gramscian engagement with hegemonic
domination (perhaps given a Baudrillardian twist through the
notion of seduction [Bauman, 1988]), power blocs and alliances
(Hall, 1988). There is little doubt that one must guard against any
tendency to collapse support for the new social movements
(feminism, gay rights, anti-racism, anti-nuclear protest, the
'Greens') into the kind of indiscriminate pluralism which will lead
not to sharpened awareness of difference but to uncritical sponge-
headedness. Nevertheless, if the 'left' is to be reconstituted as a
political force with an institutional focus, what is needed is an
articulation of these themes mentioned above into an anti-
authoritarian political theory which will thereby have at least a
reasonable chance of being adequate to the last years of the
century and beyond.

If postmodernist thinking has been weak on the question of
global strategies and cross institutional alliances, it has been strong
in an area unduly neglected by much political thought – the nature
of subjectivity. Postmodernism's pluralism intersects with its acute
insight into the fragmentation of subjectivity and individual identity,
a consequence of the decentring and splitting of the individual in
poststructuralist social and psychoanalytical theory, a way of
conceiving identity that is considerably reinformed by developments in feminism (Weedon, 1987), political theory (Laclau and
Mouffe, 1985), and social psychology (Henriques et al. 1984).

It connects also with the growing realisation of the West's
declining cultural place in a post-colonial world and with the
emergence and revival of ethnic identities, presenting the same
kind of threat to the Western metaphysical notion of the unitary
post-Enlightenment subject as does the subversion of traditional
gender identities and sexualities consequent upon the rise of
feminism and movements for gay rights.

While it is true that there is a negative and destructive side to the
postmodernist delight in unmasking imaginary unities, whether
enshrined in monocultural conceptions of social totalities or

embedded in the notion of the sovereign individual as origin of meaning and supreme author of his or her actions, the postmodernist emphasis on fragmentation, difference and plurality, and on the liberation of individuality from the fixity of identity, has great relevance. Not only is it more adequate to the kaleidoscopic experience of modern life, it is also more appropriate to a politics sensitive to the crucial feminist insight that the personal is political, especially in the highly charged context of diverse struggles in different fields of power and conflict. Once again, however, one must guard against the hypostasis of postmodern tendencies in this direction; for any coherent and effective politics may also require forms of provisional closure which allow the establishment of identities – 'black', 'feminist', 'socialist', etc. – which can provide the basis for commitment to particular political projects (Hall, 1987).

There are important points of connection between the postmodernist decentring of the subject, its rejection of 'grand narratives', its espousal of 'local narratives', language games, and genealogies, its dread of totalising discourses leading to totalitarianism, and its political pluralism. In spite, however, of this coherence that we find in postmodern thinking, and even bearing in mind that we have illustrated the untenability of any wholesale rejection of postmodernism as reactionary, we have seen that there are real problems of epistemological ambivalence, political ambiguity and occasionally unconstrained pluralism within postmodernism. Have we not reached an *impasse*? How can attempts to develop alternative forms of politics overcome challenges to the very possibility of the metanarrative underpinning which may well be necessary for any serious political initiative? How also will it be possible for the left genuinely to reconstruct its politics in the wake of the new social movements without falling between a pluralism of indifference (Foster, 1985) and an aimless confusion of ungroundable social contractarianism and value-for-money utilitarianism?

The first point to notice here is that even the most trenchant postmodernist critics of 'grand narratives' are actually unable to formulate their critiques and analyses without recourse to theorisations which, by their own criteria, look suspiciously close to the very metanarratives they want to rule out of court, a point that is discussed by Crook and Norris in this volume. Lyotard's concepts of postmodernism and postindustrial society, and Baudrillard's

notions of the masses and social implosion, for instance, themselves presuppose a general social condition, a grand narrative of
transition from modernity and industrial society. Indeed the
problem that Kellner (1988) has identified in Lyotard's case is
actually a general one, and it is that the refusal to specify the
metanarrative elements underlying concepts like postmodernity
leaves us with ideas which are underdeveloped, underjustified,
and perhaps unnecessarily prone to the kinds of critique which
were earlier successful in demolishing the postindustrial society
and 'end of ideology' theses. Foucault's work is faced with the
same set of issues. His genealogical excavations of history uncover
a series of power–knowledge complexes and regimes of truth,
against which his comments on modern society seem to rest on a
diagnosis of it as an *integrated* set of disciplinary mechanisms. Not
only is Balbus (1987, p. 122) right to point out that, 'To hold, as
Foucault does, disciplinary ideologies responsible for the very
constitution of the modern-individual-as-object-and-subject is
necessarily to attribute to them a totalising power that only a
totalising theory can name', there is also a certain duplicity
involved in refusing to engage in totalising practice in one sense
while effectively engaging in it in another. The inability of Lyotard
and Foucault to formulate cogent social analysis without implicit
recourse to metanarratives (which can always be defined as
provisional and open to amendment if they are openly acknowledged rather than problematically denied or rhetorically disputed)
can be drawn upon to support the view that what is currently
required is not the abandonment of the whole enterprise of grand
narratives, but the replacement of obviously flawed ones with
versions that can command both theoretical and political credibility.

   This enterprise, however, cannot proceed without absorbing
some crucial lessons from postmodernism. No contemporary
social theory can be deemed adequate if it relies on guarantees
concerning the central role of the 'working class' (Hall, 1983;
Laclau and Mouffe, 1985), however defined, nor if it relies,
without a great deal of reformulation, upon traditional conceptions of the 'Socialist Commonwealth'. And, to introduce further
elements, no social theory or political practice deserves credibility
if it fails to grasp the importance of non-class sites of domination,
or if it refuses to address itself to the phenomenon of the Gulag
and the very real possibility of the degeneration of movements into

coercive monsters that tragically and totally subvert their demo-
cratising intentions. There is, too, the significance of acknowledging the contradictoriness and provisionality of subjectivities and
personal identities and the crucial role of contradictory discourses
in the formation of subjectivities, identities and social relations,
thus inserting Foucauldian and other forms of discourse theory
as key elements in any rethinking in social, psychological and
historical analysis (Stedman Jones, 1983; Potter and Weatherall,
1987; Henriques, et al., 1984; Woodiwiss, 1990).

There are encouraging signs that such serious re-thinking and
reformulation are under way and that they may contribute to an
alternative politics. Without any pretensions to a comprehensive
survey, the following may be referred to as some indications of
new projects which signal radical departures: encounters between
Marxism and postmodernism in which dialogue rather than dog-
matic foreclosure create genuine theoretical and political spaces
(Hall, 1987, 1988); a rethinking of the fundamental justification
for socialism (Levine, 1984); serious attempts to reflect on the
political conditions of pluralist socialist democracy (Hirst, 1986;
Rustin, 1985; Held, 1987; Keane, 1988); feminist and anti-racist
contributions which engage with, rather than deflect, questions
thrown up by Marxism and postmodernism (Gilroy, 1987; Fraser
and Nicholson, 1988; Benhabib and Cornell, 1987; Chapman and
Rutherford, 1988; Barrett, 1988); discussions of art, aesthetics and
culture which register a clear awareness of a postmodernism of
resistance, while being acutely mindful of the aesthetic limitations
and political drawbacks of postmodernist practices in the arts
(Huyssen, 1986; Foster, 1988).

This volume is offered as a constructive contribution to this
dialogue already under way, recognising that although modernity
as Habermas says is an unfinished project, our task is not merely to
complete what is yet unfulfilled, but also to reassess some of its
central presumptions.

## Bibliography

ABERCROMBIE, NICHOLAS; HILL, STEPHEN, and TURNER,
BRYAN (1980), *The Dominant Ideology Thesis*, London, Allen and
Unwin.

42        *The Theory and Politics of Postmodernism*

ARNOLD, MATTHEW (1978), *Matthew Arnold: Selected Poems and Prose*, edited by Miriam Allott, London, Dent.

BALBUS, ISAAC (1987), 'Disciplining Women: Michel Foucault and the Power of Feminist Discourse', in Seyla Benhabib and Drucilla Cornell (eds), *Feminism as Critique*, Cambridge, Polity Press.

BANHAM, REYNER (1971), *Los Angeles*, Harmondsworth, Penguin.

BARRETT, MICHELLE (1988), 'Introduction to the 1988 Edition', in her *Women's Oppression Today*, 2nd edn, London, Verso.

BAUDELAIRE, CHARLES (1982), *Les fleurs de mal*, translated by Richard Howard, Brighton, Harvester.

BAUMAN, ZYGMUNT (1986), 'The Left as the Counter-Culture of Modernity', *Telos*, No. 70.

BAUMAN, ZYGMUNT (1988), 'Is there a postmodern sociology?', *Theory, Culture and Society*, Vol. 5, No. 2/3.

BELL, DANIEL (1974), *The Coming of Post-Industrial Society*, London, Heinemann.

BELL, DANIEL (1988), *The End of Ideology*, second edition with a new afterword, Cambridge, Mass., Harvard UP.

BENHABIB, SEYLA and CORNELL, DRUCILLA (eds) (1987) *Feminism as Critique*, Cambridge, Polity Press.

BERMAN, MARSHALL (1983), *All That is Solid Melts into Air*, London, Verso.

BHABHA, HOMI (1983), 'The Other Question', *Screen*, Vol. 24, No. 4.

BHABHA, HOMI (1984), 'Signs Taken for Wonders: Questions of Ambivalence and Authority under a Tree Outside Delhi, May 1817', in Francis Barker, Peter Hulme, Margaret Iversen and Diana Loxley (eds) *Europe and Its Others*, Vol. 1, Colchester, University of Essex.

BOYNE, ROY (1988), 'The art of the body in the discourse of postmodernity', *Theory, Culture and Society*, Vol. 5, No. 2/3.

BOYNE, ROY (1990), *Foucault and Derrida: the Other Side of Reason*, London, Unwin-Hyman.

BRADBURY, MALCOLM and MACFARLANE, JAMES (eds) (1976), *Modernism*, Harmondsworth, Penguin.

CHAPMAN, ROWENA and RUTHERFORD, JONATHAN (eds) (1988), *Unwrapping Masculinity*, London, Lawrence and Wishart.

COLEMAN, ALICE (1986), 'Whither Post-Modern housing?', *Architectural Review*, No. 10/11, 1986.

COUSINS, MARK and HUSSAIN, ATHAR (1984): *Michel Foucault*, London, Macmillan.

DERRIDA, JACQUES (1986), 'Racism's last word' in Henry Louis Gates Jr. (ed.), *'Race', Writing and Difference*, Chicago, University of Chicago Press.

DEWS, PETER (1987), *Logics of Disintegration*, London, Verso.

EDGAR, DAVID (1987), 'The New Nostalgia', *Marxism Today*, March 1987.

FEATHERSTONE, MIKE (1983), 'Consumer culture: an introduction', *Theory, Culture and Society*, Vol. 1, No. 3, 1983.

FOSTER, HAL (ed.) (1985), *Postmodern Culture*, London: Pluto Press.

FOSTER, HAL (1985), *Recodings*, Seattle, Bay Press.

FRAMPTON, KENNETH (1987), 'The Usonian legacy', *Architectural Review*, No. 1090.

FRASER, NANCY (1984) 'The French Derrideans: Politicising Deconstruction or Deconstructing the Political?', *New German Critique*, no. 33.

FRASER, NANCY and NICHOLSON, LINDA (1988), 'Social Criticism Without Philosophy: an Encounter between Feminism and Postmodernism', *Theory, Culture and Society*, Vol. 5, Nos. 2–3.

GANDAL, KEITH (1986), 'Michel Foucault: Intellectual work and politics', *Telos*, No. 67.

GIDDENS, ANTHONY (1981), *A Contemporary Critique of Historical Materialism*, London, Macmillan.

GIDDENS, ANTHONY (1982), 'From Marx to Neitzsche? Neo-Conservatism, Foucault and Problems in Contemporary Political Theory', in his *Profiles and Critiques in Social Theory*, London, Macmillan.

GIDDENS, ANTHONY (1985), *The Nation-State and Violence*, Cambridge, Polity Press.

GILROY, PAUL (1987), *There Ain't No Black in the Union Jack*, London, Hutchinson.

HABERMAS, JÜRGEN (1985), 'Modernity – an Incomplete Project', in Hal Foster (ed.) *Postmodern Culture*, London, Pluto Press.

HALL, STUART (1987), 'Minimal Selves', in Homi Bhabha (ed.) *Identity*, London, ICA.

HALL, STUART (1986), 'On Postmodernism and Articulation: an Interview with Stuart Hall' (ed. Lawrence Grossberg), *Journal of Communications Inquiry*, Vol. 10, No. 2.

HALL, STUART, (1988), 'The Toad in the Garden: Thatcherism among the Theorists', in Cary Nelson and Lawrence Grossberg (eds), *Marxism and the Interpretation of Culture*, London, Macmillan.

HAQUE, SHAHEEN (1988), 'The Experience of a Black Woman Architect', in Kwesi Owusu (ed.), *Storms of the Heart*, London, Camden Press.

HASSAN, IHAB (1985), 'The Culture of Postmodernism', *Theory, Culture and Society*, Vol. 2, No. 3.

HARA, HIROSHI (1986), 'Working', *Design Quarterly*, No. 134.

HAUG, WOLFGANG FRITZ (1986), *Critique of Commodity Aesthetics*, Cambridge, Polity Press.

HEBDIGE, DICK (1983), 'In Poor Taste: Notes on Pop', *Block*, 8.

HELD, DAVID (1987), *Models of Democracy*, Cambridge, Polity Press.

HENRIQUES, JULIAN (1989), 'Realism and the New Language', in Kobena Mercer (ed.), *Black Film, British Cinema*, London, British Film Institute.

HENRIQUES, JULIAN; HOLLOWAY, WENDY; URWIN, CATHY; COUZE, VENN; and WALKERDINE, VALERIE (1984), *Changing the Subject*, London, Methuen.

HIRST, PAUL (1986), *Law, Socialism and Democracy*, London, Allen & Unwin.

HUYSSEN, ANDREAS (1986a), 'The Cultural Politics of Pop', in his *After the Great Divide: Modernism, Mass Culture and Postmodernism*, London, Macmillan.

HUYSSEN, ANDREAS (1986b), 'Mass Culture as Woman: Modernism's Other', in his *After the Great Divide*.

JAMESON, FREDERIC (1984), 'Postmodernism, or the Cultural Logic of Capital', *New Left Review*, No. 146.

JAY, MARTIN (1984) *Marxism and Totality*, Cambridge, Polity Press.

JENCKS, CHARLES (1986), *What is Post-Modernism?*, London, Academy Editions.

JESSOP, BOB (1982), *The Capitalist State*, Oxford, Martin Robertson.

KEANE, JOHN (1988), *Democracy and Civil Society*, London, Verso.

KELLNER, DOUGLAS (1988), 'Postmodernism as Social Theory: Some Challenges and Problems', *Theory, Culture and Society*, Vol. 5, Nos. 2–3.

KIERKEGAARD, SØREN (1958), *The Journals of Kierkegaard 1834–1854*, edited and translated by Alexander Dru, London, Fontana.

KOOLHAAS, REM (1987), 'Berlin', *Zone* No. 1/2.

KRAUS, ROSALIND (1985), *The Originality of the Avant-Garde and Other Modernist Myths*, Cambridge, Mass., MIT Press.

KROKER, ARTHUR and KROKER, MARILOUISE (1988), *Body Invaders*, London, Macmillan.

KUMAR, KRISHAN (1978), *Prophecy and Progress*, Harmondsworth, Penguin.

LACLAU, ERNESTO and MOUFFE, CHANTAL (1985), *Hegemony and Socialist Strategy*, London, Verso.

LEVINE, ANDREW (1984), *Arguing for Socialism*, London, Routledge & Kegan Paul.

LIPSET, SEYMOUR MARTIN (1981), *Political Man*, Second Edition, Baltimore, Johns Hopkins UP.

LUNN, EUGENE (1985), *Marxism and Modernism*, London, Verso.

LYOTARD, JEAN-FRANÇOIS (1984), *The Postmodern Condition*, Manchester, Manchester University Press.

MACNIECE, LOUIS (1939), *Autumn Journal*, London, Faber & Faber.

McHALE, BRIAN (1987), *Postmodernist Fiction*, London, Methuen.

MILLER, S. MICHAEL (1975), 'Notes on neo-capitalism', *Theory and Society*, Vol. 2.

NORRIS, CHRISTOPHER (1987), *Derrida*, London, Fontana.

OWENS, CRAIG (1985), 'The Discourse of Others: Feminism and Postmodernism,' in Hal Foster (ed)., *Postmodern Culture*, London, Pluto Press.

POLLOCK, GRISELDA (1982), 'Vision, Voice and Power: Feminist Art History and Marxism', *Block*, 6.

POTTER, JONATHAN and WEATHERALL, MARGARET (1987) *Discourse Analysis and Social Psychology*, London, Sage.

POULANTZAS, NICOS (1978), *State, Power, Socialism*, London, New Left Books.

RUSTIN, MICHAEL (1985), *For a Pluralist Socialism*, London, Verso.

## Roy Boyne and Ali Rattansi

RYAN, MICHAEL, (1982), *Marxism and Deconstruction*, Baltimore, Johns Hopkins University Press.

SAID, EDWARD (1978), *Orientalism*, London, Routledge & Kegan Paul.

SAID, EDWARD (1983), *The World, the Text and the Critic*, Cambridge, Mass., Harvard University Press.

SAID, EDWARD (1984), 'Orientalism Reconsidered', in Francis Barker et al. (eds), above.

SCHNEEDE, VIVE (1973), *Surrealism*, New York, Harry N. Abrams.

SHORT, ROBERT (1976), 'Dada and Surrealism', in Bradbury and MacFarlane, above.

SOJA, EDWARD W. (1989), *Postmodern Geographies*, London, Verso.

SPIVAK, GAYATRI CHAKRAVORTY (1987), *In Other Worlds*, London, Methuen.

SPIVAK GAYATRI CHAKRAVORTY (1988), 'Can the Subaltern Speak?' in Cary Nelson and Lawrence Grossberg (eds), above.

SPRINKER, MICHAEL (1987), *Imaginary Relations*, London, Verso.

SQUIERS, CAROL (1987), 'A short history of Beirut in the 20th Century', *Zone*, No. 1/2.

SUDJIC, DEYAN (1986), *New Architecture: Foster, Rogers, Stirling*, London, Royal Academy of Arts.

TAYLOR, BRANDON (1987), *Modernism, Post-Modernism and Realism*, Winchester, Winchester School of Art Press.

TAYLOR, JOHN (1976), *From Modernization to Modes of Production*, London, Macmillan.

WEEDON, CHRIS (1987), *Feminist Practice and Poststructuralist Theory*, London, Methuen.

WHITFORD, FRANK (1984), *Bauhaus*, London, Thames and Hudson.

WOLFF, JANET (1985), 'The Invisible *Flaneuse:* Women and the Literature of Modernity', *Theory, Culture and Society*, Vol. 2, No. 3.

WOODIWISS, TONY (1990), *Social Theory after Postmodernism*, London, Pluto Press.

# ter 2

# The End of Radical Social Theory? Radicalism, Modernism and Postmodernism

Stephen Crook

## 1. Introduction

French social theory has long been fashionable, if not dominant, on the academic left in anglophone countries. In the mid 1970s, for example, Althusserian Marxism and Lacanian psychoanalysis came close to defining the range of options open to radical social theory in Britain. Since the demise of these orthodoxies, attention has come to focus on the work of a diverse group of writers which includes Baudrillard, Deleuze, Foucault, Lyotard and their epigones. These writers would all (more or less) reject Marxist models of radical theory and practice, but would all (more or less) claim credentials as radical theorists. Indeed, each makes a strong claim that a wholly new kind of radical theory is now required, a claim which draws on a diffused but potent belief that massive historical shifts and dislocations are underway in culture and society. Whitebook's reaction to these 'postmodernist' themes captures the *fin de siècle* atmosphere. 'While the announcement that Minerva's owl is about to depart may be premature, one is increasingly struck by the sense of living in the closing of an epoch' (Whitebook, 1982, p. 53).

The suggestion that historical thresholds are about to be crossed, that epochal change is in the wind, can affect social theory in at least two ways. Most obviously, it can prompt suggestions that the object which social theory is 'about' is changing radically. It may be that 'industrial society' is turning into 'post-industrial society', for example. While such suggestions lead to vigorous debate on the extent to which specific themes from the theory of industrial society retain their salience, they need not involve any deeper critique of the idea of social theory as such.[1] One of the distinguishing features of the French postmodernisms noted above is precisely that they do mount such a critique. Those 'classical' projects of the nineteenth and early twentieth centuries which came to define the nature and tasks of modern social theory, the projects of Comte, Marx, Durkheim and the rest, are held to be anachronistic in a strong sense. It is not simply that their substantive claims have been rendered 'out of date' by social change, the problem lies in the very idea of a totalising social theory which can legislate for a privileged form of social practice. Postmodernist critics of 'modernist' social theory locate this idea within a discrediting line of continuity back from contemporary to classical social theory and (crucially) back from classical social theory to metaphysics.

The postmodernist claim, then, is that the modernist project in social theory, in all its Marxist and sociological variants, is both historically and conceptually exhausted. The substance of this claim will not be challenged here. Indeed, the next section will outline some of the characteristics which render the project of 'modernist radicalism' inherently suspect. The problem which the paper takes up is that of specifying an alternative to modernist radicalism. Two sections are given to the argument that French postmodernisms cannot furnish such an alternative. In the first it is claimed that postmodernist theory resolves into a monistic metaphysics which is no more acceptable than the modernism it contests. The second of the sections argues that postmodernism's radical pretensions are fatally flawed by the nihilistic implications of its monism. The final section of the paper attempts to sketch some of the main dimensions and resources of a radicalism which might evade the circles of metaphysics and nihilism which trap the debate between modernism and postmodernism. This alternative gives up many of the traditional pretensions of 'theory', and might be understood as a proposal to abandon the idea of 'radical social theory' in favour of that of 'radical social enquiry'.

## 2. Modernist Radicalism

The pattern of modernist radicalism is set in the claims of nineteenth-century social science to have achieved a decisive break with speculative, merely philosophical or metaphysical, accounts of the social world. Kilminster offers a sympathetic account of Marx's claims in this area which underlines the point.

> The practical–theoretical social science inaugurated by Marx constituted an early stage of the historical transcendence of philosophy. That is, first, its supersession as the competent discipline to analyse the complex societies in course of formation in Marx's time: the social sciences took on this task. Moreover, secondly, the category of *practice* provided for the trans-cendence of philosophy ... as wisdom and as traditional episte-mology (Kilminster, 1982, p. 159).

Durkheim's 'sociology', as well as Marx's 'historical materialism', insists that the discovery of social structures and processes as an autonomous reality, subject to its own patterns of causality, will release the study of society from the grasp of metaphysics and mere opinion, and revolutionise social practice.

Modernist radicalism defines itself in terms of the unique trans-formative power of its integration of a radicalised social theory with a radicalised social practice. This power derives from a conjunction of theoretical and historical thresholds: the discovery of the principles of a scientific understanding of society coincides with the massive transformations which give birth to specifically modern societies. Historical materialism and sociology are 'modernist' projects in that they claim privileged access to the formative principles of modernity. On the basis of that access, each can make the radical claim to be the instrument through which alone the as yet unrealised potential of modernity can be brought to fruition.

These claims shape Marx's well-known critiques of other

projects of social theory which purport to be the key to modernity. His principal objection to Hegelianism and to political economy is that each, in its way, denies the autonomy of social structures and processes. His critique of Hegel's idealism is from the outset a methodological one: 'The true way is turned upside down. The most simple thing becomes the most complicated and the most complicated becomes the most simple. What should be a starting point becomes a mystical result and what should be a rational result becomes a mystical starting point' (Marx, 1975, pp. 99–100). If Hegel seeks to derive social relations from an abstract concept of historical totality, political economy is given to the 'unimaginative conceits of the eighteenth-century Robinsonades' (Marx, 1973, p. 83) which begin from an equally abstract concept of the isolated individual. The dense formulae on 'The Method of Political Economy' in the 1857 'Introduction' (Marx, 1973, pp. 100–11) share with the earlier critique of Hegel a concern with the proper relations between whole and part, beginning and result, concrete and abstract. The methodological confusions of Hegelianism and political economy prevent them from recognising the autonomy of social structures and processes. In turn, this failure of recognition prevents them from comprehending the actuality and potentiality of modernity, so that they can have nothing of value to say about the requirements of social practice. Only an historical materialism which follows Marx's methodological precepts can grasp the movement of social reality, comprehend modernity and link theoretical knowledge to practical action.

At this very general level, the convergences between the programmes of Marx and Durkheim are quite marked. Durkheim, too, seeks a 'unity of theory and practice' through which the potential of modernity can be realised. The central claim of *The Rules of The Sociological Method* is that society is a reality *sui generis*, whose laws are accessible only to a sociological science. Unregulated, human consciousness conceives society in relation to its images of what is desirable. Goal-directed conceptions are 'mistaken for the things themselves' (Durkheim, 1964, p. 17), and the character of social reality as essentially refractory to the will is forgotten. Only sociology can grasp the objectivity of social reality by treating social facts as things, distinguishing between cause and function, and adhering to the other precepts of *The Rules*. It follows, of course, that only sociology can comprehend the real processes through which modern societies develop and the real problems to which they are subject.

A scientific analysis of the conditions of modernity makes it possible to address questions of social development in a new way. Durkheim insists that 'our constant preoccupation has been to orient [sociology] so that it might have practical results' (Durkheim, 1964, p. 143), and he has in mind more than that sociology should advise on the best means to attain an ideologically given end. The scientific differentiation of 'normal' from 'pathological' phenomena is the new basis on which 'should be settled all controversial questions . . . such as those concerning the normality of the decline in religious belief or of the development of state powers' (Durkheim, 1964, p. 62). Durkheim's various proposals for the abolition of inherited wealth, for the development and promulgation of 'moral individualism', for the establishment of 'occupational groups', and the rest, are intended as scientific solutions to problems which science has identified, solutions which will remove obstacles to the development of 'organic solidarity' and modernity.

To re-state the general point, Marx's historical materialism and Durkheim's sociology are *radical* projects which set out to revolutionise both social theory and social practice, and which insist on the necessary unity of these twin revolutions. They are *modernist* projects to the extent that they insist that only through the twin revolutions which they accomplish can social modernity be understood and completed. The question remains whether these defining claims of modernist radicalism are to be taken at face value. One problematic aspect of the claims, which is taken up in the postmodernist critique, concerns the alleged 'break' which modernist radicalism makes with metaphysics. With the hindsight which a century or so can give, the continuities which link Marx to Hegel and the German critical tradition, or Durkheim to Renouvier and French rationalism, are as visible as the breaks which divide them. On this basis, Giddens (1982, Ch. 4) has warned against complicity in the 'myth of the great divide' when discussing 'classical' social theory while Bauman (1987) has underlined the links between the legislative pretensions of enlightenment philosophy and social science.

These associations facilitate postmodernist claims that modernist social theory is just the continuation of metaphysics.

Foucault is able to claim that 'at the deepest level of Western knowledge, Marxism introduced no real discontinuity; it found its place without difficulty' (Foucault, 1970, p. 261). In a less sober spirit, Glucksmann polemicises against the notion that Marxism as a 'revolutionary science' is 'a quite *extraordinary* because unprecedented reality. "That quite unheard of reality" was for nineteenth-century Germany the commonest of common places – what was *The* theory or *The* science . . . that did not claim to be an unprecedented "algebra", and the algebra of "revolution"' (Glucksmann, 1980, p. 122).[2] The way in which continuities with metaphysics render modernist radicalism chronically susceptible to postmodernist critique can usefully be linked to the problem of 'foundationalism'.

Margolis (1986, p. 38) offers a concise definition of foundation-alism in the theory of knowledge as 'the belief that we possess a privileged basis for cognitive certainty'. So, Descartes' assertion that the *Cogito* provides a basis of certainty on which the edifice of knowledge can be constructed is archetypically foundationalist, but so too are phenomenalist claims that sense-data are privileged building blocks of knowledge. As Hamlyn (1970, Ch. 1) has pointed out, foundationalism typically emerges in response to sceptical critiques of knowledge, and turns on the dubious metaphor of knowledge as a building to which storeys are constantly added, so that 'if the foundations are not secure the whole building will come crashing to the ground' (Hamlyn, 1970, p. 10). This is not the place for an extended discussion of foundationalist epistemologies, but they are suspect on a number of grounds. The most germane of these for present purposes is that they seek to guarantee the validity of substantive enquiries in *a priori* formulae. Most variants of foundationalism exert a constant pressure to displace empirical questions to the *a priori* level of epistemological or ontological presuppositions.[3]

Foundationalist social theories, such as those which Marx and Durkheim attack as metaphysical, proceed from epistemological or ontological principles to privileged and speculative accounts of the nature of social reality, the direction of social change, and the role of social practice. For Marx and Durkheim, the foundationalist quest for *a priori* certainties in social theory is transcended by their respective projects. But these claims are haunted by a pervasive sense of either naivety or bad faith. Marx and Durkheim do not simply practice science, they produce programmes which load their sciences with metaphysical significance: in 'transcending' metaphysics they 'realise' its rational potential. Moreover, historical materialism and sociology are both the subject of foundationalist guarantees: both establish what social reality is like, and how it is to be known, prior to enquiry itself.

The crux of the claim to have moved 'beyond' foundationalism and metaphysics lies in the inauguration by modernist radicalism of a new constellation of theory and practice. As the earlier quote from Kilminster indicated, for Marx it is 'practice' which transcends (and 'realises', of course) philosophy. Adorno (1973, p. 144), who prefigured many postmodernist themes, once remarked, 'practice itself was an eminently theoretical concept': the demand for a rational, or revolutionary, practice reformulates, but does not go beyond, the traditional demand for the 'realisation' of philosophy. As social reality stubbornly declines its standing invitation to realise philosophy, the modernist radicalisms of the twentieth century come to stand more and more visibly in a direct line of continuity with metaphysics. Lukács, Marcuse, Habermas and the rest are soft targets for postmodernist critique because of their patent foundationalism.[4] Their projects become a series of reflections on the epistemological and ontological foundations of the kind of knowledge which might *really* guarantee that 'unity of theory and practice' which, in turn, will redeem the promises of philosophy and modernity.

## 3. Postmodernism and Metaphysics

Postmodernism aims to show that modernist claims to have moved beyond metaphysics are bogus. Lyotard's *The Postmodern Condition* develops a critique which is aimed primarily at Habermas. Lyotard identifies three main lines of continuity which fatally link modernist theory to metaphysics and foundationalism. First, and most generally, modernism 'legitimates itself with reference to a meta-discourse ... making an explicit appeal to some grand narrative' (Lyotard, 1984, p. xxiii). Two such 'grand narratives' are later distinguished according to whether they present 'the hero of the narrative as cognitive or practical, a hero of knowledge or a hero of liberty' (Lyotard, 1984, p. 31). The vocabulary may be unfamiliar, but the basic argument is less so: modernism remains metaphysical because it seeks a foundation in the image of history as the working out of a purpose (enlightenment or emancipation). Lyotard's postmodernism moves beyond this foundationalist teleology, defining itself in terms of 'an incredulity towards metanarratives' (Lyotard, 1984, p. xxiv).

Second, Lyotard repeatedly asserts that modernism is tied to the anachronistic pursuit of a 'unity' in which contradictions will be reconciled. Habermas's consensual theory of language is represented as an impossible attempt to impose unity on the diverse range of language games (see Lyotard, 1984, p. 14). Again, the 'aesthetic of the beautiful' which Lyotard ascribes to Habermas is said to require that art overcome 'the gap between cognitive, ethical and political discourses, thus opening the way to a unity of experience' (Lyotard, 1984a, p. 72). Finally, modernism remains attached to a metaphysical conception of the human subject which infects its view of the function of knowledge. In the light of 'post-industrial' developments in computerisation and information science, 'the old principle that the acquisition of knowledge is indissociable from the training (*Bildung*) of minds, or even of individuals is becoming obsolete' (Lyotard, 1984, p. 4). These charges that modernism is founded on teleological metanarratives, pursues essentialist syntheses, and deploys humanist conceptions of the subject, have close affinities with other strands in French social theory. Versions of them can be found in Althusser's critiques of ideology, in Deleuze's pursuit of difference, in Derrida's deconstructions and in Foucault's genealogies.

If it is allowed that critiques of this type find their mark, the question arises of whether postmodern projects evade their own strictures against modernism and 'really' break with metaphysics and foundationalism. The argument that they do not can begin with the observation that French postmodernisms are chronically one-eyed in equating metaphysics with the German critical tradition. Kantian, Hegelian or phenomenological themes are relentlessly pursued and exposed, while the critique of evolutionism, postivitism and physicalism is, to say the least, underdeveloped. This lacuna becomes crucial when postmodernism attempts to define just what its 'postmodern' status entails. It has already been noted that postmodernism gains its particular flavour by linking questions about theoretical and epochal thresholds, a feature which it is now clear that it shares with early modernist radicalisms. This linkage imposes a difficult task on the self-definition of postmodernism, as Hassan's remarks on the idea of a 'period' in literature make clear. 'A period is generally not a period at all; it is rather both a diachronic and synchronic construct. Postmodernism is no exception; it requires both historical and theoretical definition' (Hassan, 1985, p. 122).

Postmodernism is required, then, to show that it is both 'historically' and 'theoretically' distinct from modernism in ways which are more than accidentally related. Further, it must do this without falling back on foundationalist formulae. The difficulties involved in the performance of this trick help to explain the paradox, which Honneth (1985, p. 147) notes, that the 'suggestiveness' of the idea of the postmodern has increased as its 'technical and temporal clarity' has decreased. The 'clarity' of the idea of the postmodern might reasonably be expected to be greatest in those debates about *aesthetic* postmodernity which are the home turf of postmodernism, and which are a useful starting point for an examination of postmodernism's difficulties.

In fact, the label 'postmodernist' has been used for virtually all major developments since the 1940s or fifties which have sought to distance themselves from aesthetic modernism, from Pollock to Warhol, from Stockhausen to Glass. If postmodernisms, in the plural, have in common only that they are constituted in varying degrees after and against the modernist 'school', the historical-cum-theoretical concept of the postmodern seems lost.[5] Attempts by Jameson and Lyotard to save the concept illustrate two strategies which set a pattern for more general claims. Jameson (1983, p. 113) regards postmodernism as 'a periodising concept whose function is to correlate the emergence of new formal features in culture with the emergence of a new type of social life and a new economic order'. His difficulty lies in squaring this claim with the evident internal diversity of postmodernism. He identifies four constitutive features of postmodernism: a reaction against high-modernism, the erosion of disciplinary boundaries, a tendency to pastiche, and a 'schizophrenic' isolation of the present and immediate.[6] Jameson allows that these features may also be present in modernist work, and asserts that 'radical breaks between periods' turn on a shift in the arrangement of elements,

rather than a transformation of the elements themselves. This nuanced account of the postmodern lacks the clarity and unity which an historical-cum-theoretical concept requires. In the end, Jameson saves the unity of the concept through a reductionist appeal to socio-economic developments. The 'reality' of post-modernism, in a later formulation, is 'a third great expansion of capitalism around the globe' (Jameson, 1984, p. 88). Its constitutive features are 'closely related to' or 'extraordinarily consonant with' consumerism, advertising, suburbanism and so on (Jameson, 1983, pp. 123–5). Postmodern culture is not so much correlated with a new socio-economic order as defined by it. The 'given' unity of capitalism is the only principle of unity which Jameson can offer to the postmodern.

Lyotard's account of aesthetic postmodernity begins by drawing on Kant's distinction between 'beauty' and 'sublimity': 'The beautiful in nature is a question of the form of the object, and this consists in limitation, whereas the sublime is to be found in an object even devoid of form ... [as] a representation of limitless-ness, yet with a super-added thought of its totality' (Kant, 1952, p. 90). An alignment of postmodernism with an aesthetic of sublimity is in tune with the postmodern rejection of the modernist quest for unities. However, modernism cannot directly be aligned with an aesthetic of beauty, since it clearly offers its own critique of traditionally beautiful representations. Rather, modernism approaches the sublime in an attempt 'to represent the fact that the non-representable exists' (Lyotard, 1984a, p. 78), and thereby becomes 'nostalgic'. Postmodernism breaks with this final illusion, and 'denies itself the solace of good forms' in its intimations of the sublime. Drawing on Kant again, Lyotard formalises the distinction: postmodernism refuses to apply 'determining' judge-ments which subsume the particular under a 'given' universal or form.[7]

Modernism and postmodernism are both very close and very far apart: 'the nuance which distinguishes these two modes may be infinitesimal; they often coexist in the same piece ... and yet they testify to a difference (*un différend*) on which the fate of thought depends' (Lyotard, 1984a, p. 80).[8] The paradox here is that Lyotard differentiates an anti-formalist postmodernism from a formalist modernism in a manner which is definitively formalist. The 'unity' of postmodernism is that of a shared formal relation to the sublime. This formalism achieves its clarity by excluding any historical dimension, and reinforces the suspicion that postmodernism can be defined clearly only through the resources of the modernism it claims to supersede. A similar case should be made against related attempts to define postmodernism, such as Lash's juxtaposition of a postmodernism of 'desire' against formalist modernisms (Lash, 1985, *passim*).

Jameson's 'reductionism' and Lyotard's 'formalism' can stand for the options facing attempts to define a more general theoretical postmodernism. Each strategy constitutes postmodernism as a form of metaphysical monism. A third 'ism' contributes to this outcome: many postmodern projects draw their historical dimension from an 'evolutionism' in which the periodising schemes of positivist philosophy constantly reappear. So, Lyotard's distinction between a modernism which depends on 'metanarratives' and a postmodernism which manages without them seems close to that between the 'metaphysical' and the 'positive' stages of Comte's triad. Lyotard's entire attack on Habermas's 'critical' concept of modernity draws quite uncritically on the most problematic periodisations of 'post industrialism' and the 'information revolution' in American sociology (Lyotard, 1984, pp. 3–6). In a powerful assault on this aspect of postmodernist thinking, Rose has noted that Foucault's 'bio-history' also recapitulates the 'law of three stages' while the concept of 'disciplinary power' 'merely adds a third stage to Durkheim's two laws of penal evolution' (Rose, 1984, pp. 169, 176). Postmodernism might equally well be seen as a pre-critical modernism.

The reductionist strain in postmodernism urges a form of materialist social analysis which frequently degenerates into an overt physicalism. This is clearly the case for the concept of 'intensity' developed by Deleuze and deployed by Guattari, who asserts that 'with both nature and signs, we are concerned with the same type of machinism and the same semiotic of material intensities' (Guattari, 1984, p. 120). Baudrillard (1983) represents the most florid case of a postmodernism dominated by physicalism, urging the impossibility of any social theory, be it sociological, Marxist or Foucauldian. The argument is carried entirely by a series of physicalist tropes. Its basic theme is that 'the mass', the material which composes the putative object 'the social', behaves in a way which debars it from forming the object of a science. The mass is 'an opaque nebula whose growing density absorbs all the surrounding energy and light rays, to collapse finally under its weight. A black hole which engulfs the social' (Baudrillard, 1983a, p. 4).

Baudrillard's theme of the growing invisibility of the mass, and hence of the social, is linked to a metaphor for change: modern society was once based on a principle of expansion, or explosion, but having reached a certain 'critical mass' it has begun to implode. 'The notion of critical mass usually associated with the process of nuclear explosion, is reapplied here with reference to nuclear *implosion*. What we are witnessing in the domain of the social . . . is a kind of inverse explosion through the force of inertia' (Baudrillard, 1983, p. 88n). *Any* attempt to save the principle of expansion, even Guattari's model of 'molecular revolution' or Foucault's hope for 'resistance' to power, is now 'archaic, regressive or nostalgic' (Baudrillard, 1983, p. 60).[9] The reality of the social, in an inversion of Durkheim's realism, can only be 'hypersimulated' in an imaginary 'pataphysics of the social'. Physicalism is the beginning and end of Baudrillard's models of the social and of social change, forming the basis of an explicit rejection of the possibility of any radical social theory. But physicalism traps the argument in a curious loop. If a physicalist model of the social is valid, there is no reason why there cannot be a science of the social. 'Black holes' are objects of scientific enquiry. But if the parallel between nuclear and social processes is not valid, Baudrillard's argument collapses entirely. This oddity adds to a sense that despite Baudrillard's enthusiasm for metaphors drawn from natural science, his project is *meta*physical. The idea of the physical is a formal one, designating some wholly 'other' postmodern 'object = X'.[10]

It is unsurprising, then, that appeals to what Rose has termed a 'transcendent principle of the physical' have an analogue in formalist postmodernisms. For example, Lash draws on Foucauldian themes to identify a 'fold' in language which 'is the space of a non-discursive "literature", where language takes on an opacity, an "ontological weight". It is in this *pli*, this fold, that the postmodern is constituted' (Lash, 1985, p. 4). In the attempt to mark out this 'space', the only alternative to a critical metaphysics of *constitution* must be a naturalistic metaphysics of *givenness*. Indeed, Lash sees no problem in the claim that postmodernists 'subscribe to a (more or less weak) form of foundationalism' (Lash, 1985, p. 29) since it enables him to suggest a convergence between Habermas and postmodernism: 'communicative rationality' and the 'problematics of desire' both mark a gratifying break with relativism, for Lash.

Many of the themes of formalist postmodernism were introduced into anglophone social theory through the form of analysis which Hindess, Hirst and their associates developed in the 1970s. Their critiques of Althusserian rationalism issued in a model of 'discourse' as the medium of theoretical and practical knowledge, where discourse is conceived as a grid of concepts linked by 'logical' relations. In this formalism 'the entities specified in discourse must be referred to solely in and through the forms of discourse, theoretical, political, etc., in which they are constituted (Hindess and Hirst, 1977, p. 19). The 'etc.' here links 'forms of discourse' with Lash's 'fold' and, beyond that, with the physicalisms of 'intensity' and 'implosion'. For all the emphasis which they place on 'rigour', Hindess and Hirst's analysis rests on a covert and *ad hoc* assumption of the 'givenness' of discourses.

The submerged link between those postmodernist strategies which have been termed 'reductionist' and 'formalist' is a metaphysical monism (whether of 'intensity' or 'discourse') which serves as the foundation for critiques of modernist radicalism. Modernism requires 'metanarratives', searches for 'unities', emphasises the role of subjectivity because it is searching for ways to reconcile contradiction. Contradiction is seen to pervade a world constituted in a whole series of dualisms: mind and body, knowledge and reality, potential and actuality, theory and practice. The postmodern critique undercuts the problem of contradiction by dissolving dualisms in some single world-constituting substance. The disputes between postmodernisms of 'discourse' and those of 'intensity' parallel pre-Socratic debates about whether fire, air, or water is the primary element. Monisms of various types have an honourable place in the history of metaphysics,[11] but they can hardly be represented as the abolition of metaphysics.

## 4. Postmodernism and Nihilism

Social theory becomes 'radical' in taking up the responsibility of giving reasons why change is required, of making the demand for change accountable in terms of some standards of judgement. Modernist radicalisms attempt to carry out this task through the foundationalist integration of the two dimensions of theoretical and social change, this integration portrayed as the completion of modernity. This response to the requirements of radicalism may not be acceptable, but at least it represents a serious attempt to grapple with the problem. When radical social theory loses its accountability, when it can no longer give reasons, something has gone very wrong. But this is precisely what happens to postmodern theory, and it seems appropriate to use the over-stretched term 'nihilism' as a label for this degeneration. The nihilism of post-modernism shows itself in two symptoms: an inability to specify possible mechanisms of change, and an inability to state why change is better than no change.

The first symptom afflicts a wide range of projects. Most notoriously, Foucault's model of 'Power/Knowledge' seems able to articulate 'resistance' only as an embodiment of the power which it is supposed to resist. Jameson concludes his account of the new age of postmodernity with the remark that it is an open question whether any sources of opposition to the new age will be found (Jameson, 1983, p. 125). His later hopes for 'the invention and projection of a global cognitive mapping' scarcely solve the problem (Jameson, 1984, p. 92). Baudrillard offers a vision of a 'one dimensional' system impenetrable to change, of 'all secrets, spaces and scenes abolished in a single dimension of information' (Baudrillard, 1983a, p. 131). The only paradoxical hope he offers is of a hopeless 'challenge' which is both 'unremitting and invisible' (Baudrillard, 1980, p. 107).

This difficulty is clearly related to the monistic foundations of postmodernisms. To divide 'intensity' or 'discourse' into two moments, one of which is the foundation of opposition, or to posit some external foundation, is to reintroduce dualism and with it the modernist problems of contradiction and reconciliation. In resisting this kind of relapse into modernism, postmodernisms exclude that sense of 'tension' which is critical for radical theory. This issue will be taken up again in the final section of the paper. For now, it will suffice to show that the monistic slackening of the tension of theory induces the second of two symptoms of nihilism, an inability to justify the demand for change. Examples taken from Guattari, from Hindess and Hirst, and from Lyotard can make the point.

For Guattari, the conditions of postmodernity call for a 'micro-politics' which will set loose: 'a whole host of expressions and experimentations – those of children, of schizophrenics, of homo-sexuals, or prisoners, or misfits of every kind – that all work to penetrate and enter into the semiology of the dominant order' (Guattari, 1984, p. 184). Opposition is a natural force to be unleashed, a quantitative rather than a qualitative phenomenon. But if this naturalisation cures the first symptom of nihilism, it induces the second. There can be no *reason* inherent to Guattari's argument why the 'experimentations' of rapists, or child murderers, or racist fanatics should be excluded from the carnival. Any qualitative principle of differentiation, any sense of tension be-tween 'is' and 'ought', would undermine Guattari's naturalism and pitch him back into some modernist 'grand narrative'. The choice of 'experimentations' is instructive, clearly being shaped by some view of which 'misfits' Guattari's readers will sympathise with. But that choice could be made accountable only with reference to a continuous and developing progressive *tradition* which Guattari's reductionism is quite unable to articulate.

In the formalism of Hindess and Hirst the collapse into nihilism flows from the exclusion of any sense that the significance of discourse results from a production, or movement. 'A rigorous separation should be maintained between problems concerned with the logical properties of the order of concepts of a discourse and those concerned with its process of production' (Hindess, 1977, p. 190). Significance becomes a function of a single principle of logical order in a strategy which is as nihilistic as Guattari's naturalism. The political implications of this model are presented as a Nietzschean emancipation: the fantasy that Marxism is a science of practice can be dispensed with as socialists face the reality that 'there are no "socialist" issues and areas of struggle per se assigned as "socialist" by class-interests and experience' (Cutler et al., 1978, p. 261). 'Socialism' can no longer 'evade questions about the objectives of its practice and the content of its political programmes' (Hirst, 1979, p. 6). But the rethinking of socialism which is put in train issues in an instrumentalisation, rather than a revaluation, of political values. The constraints of discourse theory tie political theory and practice to a logic of 'calculation'. While theory can 'begin to investigate the conditions and limits of forms of political calculation . . . [it] can never itself step outside of the conditions of calculation' (Hirst, 1979, p. 11). Forms of discourse, governed by one-dimensional 'logics', are treated as givens which cannot be coherently assessed in other than their own terms. The accountability of theory is transformed into a self-enclosed form of 'calculation', and a formalist monism produces the same incapacity to give reasons as a physicalist monism. No reasons can be adduced for engaging in socialist rather than, say, fascist discourse.

Lyotard draws on concepts of system performance developed by writers such as Luhmann, and also on the Austin/Searle account of linguistic performance, to construct a model of 'performativity' as the dominant, and questionable, value of postmodernity. Opposition to performativity cannot be founded on Habermas's attempt to homogenise language in a consensus. Instead, opposition should celebrate the irreducible diversity of language games, limited only by a rejection of 'terror', defined as 'the efficiency gained by eliminating, or threatening to eliminate, a player from the language game one shares with him' (Lyotard, 1984, p. 63). The rejection of terror is suspect on several grounds. First, even if Lyotard's argument is conceded, he has not excluded terror against third parties (barbarians, *Untermenschen*, women) whom the participants in a game deem to be excluded from their *agon*.[12] Only by stretching the concepts of 'game' and 'rules of the game' to an extent that would constitute a new 'grand narrative' ('all rational beings are potential members of the game', for example) could Lyotard exclude such terror. Even in relations between mutually acknowledged participants, the exclusion of terror seems arbitrary and external. It is plausible only for a game constituted between two players, so that the elimination of one player destroys rather than wins the game, and is in that sense contradictory. But if games are constituted by institutionally embedded rules which outlive any players, or even by a large number of players, the sense of contradiction dissipates. The 'game' of gladiatorial combat can survive the 'elimination' of any number of players.

Lyotard must exclude terror because it represents a denial of the 'heteromorphy', or diversity, of language. If he does not, a potentially terrorist opposition to performativity cannot be preferred to performativity itself, which also represents a denial of the diversity of language in the name of globalising 'efficiency'. The problem is similar to that facing Foucault's concepts of 'power' and 'resistance'. But in order to make the exclusion, Lyotard must either stretch the 'rules of the game', or restrict the concept of 'game' itself, in a way that transforms them into normative principles of the modernist type. The reflections on 'justice' in the final pages of *The Postmodern Condition* suggest that, in the end, Lyotard prefers an accountable modernism to a nihilistic postmodernism. He seeks to rehabilitate the concept of 'justice' by cutting its ties with 'consensus', so that 'justice as a value is neither outmoded nor suspect' and has a place in 'a politics which would respect both the desire for justice and the desire for the unknown' (Lyotard, 1984, pp. 66, 67). In contrast, Baudrillard's discussion of terrorism opts for the other arm of the dilemma. Terrorism 'represents' nothing, and between terror and the masses there passes a 'reverse energy ... of absorption and annulment of the political' (Baudrillard, 1983, p. 56). Terror is naturalised by Baudrillard (1983, p. 56) so that in its 'defiance of sense', terror is 'akin to the natural catastrophe'.

In summary, postmodernism's reliance on either reductionist or formalist monisms renders it nihilistic in the sense discussed at the beginning of this section. The identifications of language and social life with some single principle of proliferation generate images of bad totality which must absorb all apparent opposition. Attempts to find some natural ground for oppositional critique and practice are either unable to give any reasons for preferring opposition to compliance, or are able to do so only through a reversion to modernist regulative principles.

## 5. An Alternative: the Idea of Radical Enquiry

Straightforward endorsements of postmodernist claims apart, there have been two major types of response to the modernism/ postmodernism debate. The first suggests that postmodernism is incoherent and that its critiques of modernism have no force, so that the latter can be rehabilitated. Habermas's equation of post- with pre- modernism offers a version of this strategy (see Habermas 1981, 1985, 1987), as does Rose's (1984) argument that postmodernism cannot evade the 'antinomy of law'. A number of defences of Marxism against postmodernist critiques, such as

Callinicos's (1982) and Eagleton's (1985), offer stronger forms of the same response. The second response is to construct some kind of synthesis between selected modern and postmodern themes. Ryan's (1982) image of 'deconstruction' as the cultural counterpart of Marxist social analysis is a straightforward example. Smart (1983) offers a more nuanced view of the continuities between Foucault and the Marxist tradition, while O'Neill (1986, 1986a) reviews Foucault's relation to the mainstream of sociological theory. Lash's (1985) account of a convergence between modernism and postmodernism has already been noted.

While many of these contributions to the debate are of great interest and importance, the strategies which they represent fall short of an adequate response to the dilemma of radical social theory. The first response fails to acknowledge the extent of the convergences between modernism and postmodernism, while the second fails to recognise how fatal those convergences are to the pretensions of radicalism. On the analysis sketched above, the prospects of radical social theory are gloomy in the extreme. Its only options are a modernism which locks it into a metaphysical programme for the 'realisation' of philosophy and modernity, or a postmodernism which pitches it into a speculative and nihilistic monism. The possibility that the idea of 'radical social theory' as such is beyond repair must be entertained seriously.

The shared commitment which locks modernism and post-modernism into a degenerative circuit of metaphysics and nihilism is foundationalism, in the sense discussed in section 2, above. Postmodernism can offer no alternative to the metaphysics of modernist radicalism because it fails to become a 'postfoundation-alism'. The difficult, and somewhat paradoxical, task facing this final stage of the argument is to indicate the directions in which a 'post foundational radicalism' might develop, and the resources on which it might draw. The task is difficult because there is no space to do more than outline possibilities, and it is paradoxical because such an outline risks being read as a specification of the 'foundations of postfoundationalism'. The argument can usefully be broken down into three stages, each of which relates to a problem which has emerged in earlier sections of the paper. These are, the 'unity of theory and practice', and the problem of 'accountability', and the problem of thresholds and transitions.

*(a) Theory and Practice*

Foundationalism in social theory is a doctrine about the relations between different 'levels' of discourse. Most obviously, it asserts that the discourse of empirical social enquiry, in a broad sense, depends on claims (epistemological, ontological) secured within a meta-discourse. It is a corollary of this doctrine that the 'radicalism' of social theory requires a similar foundation. The discourses through which people conduct and reflect upon their ordinary affairs are held to be incapable of a level of self-reflection which could generate radical practice. Foundationalist radicalism, then, invokes two claims for discursive privilege: a claim on behalf of meta-discourse against the discourse of enquiry, and a claim on behalf of the discourse of theory against the discourse of practice.

An important first step in the direction of postfoundational radicalism will be to disentangle and withdraw from these claims. On the latter claim, the principle of a linkage between theory and practice cannot differentiate radical from non-radical theory. That 'theory' is itself a social practice, and that all social practices are, to a degree, articulate are principles common to a wide range of traditions in social science. If such a 'double hermeneutic' is the condition of all social enquiry, the distinction between theory and practice, and therefore the demand for a privileged unity between the two, loses some of its magic. The demand for a 'unity of theory and practice', translated into non-foundationalist terms, becomes the problem of the appropriate relations between 'expert' and 'lay' discourses of social life. This is not, of course, a single problem which admits of a single solution, and any suggestion that the distinction between the two orders of discourse might be 'overcome' in some higher unity is actively unhelpful.

The utility of any particular articulation between the two will vary with circumstances, but broadly speaking two types of articulation can be distinguished. In the first, the concerns of expert and lay discourse are recognisably of the same order. Academic and saloon bar reflections on social problems of various kinds, from unemployment to child abuse, will vary widely on many dimensions, but they are in some sense reflections on the 'same' problem. On this pattern, expert discourses and enquiries become 'radical' to the extent that they place their expertise at the service of movements and programmes which are established as 'radical' in the wider culture and society. Radical enquiry reflects on the causes, consequences and cures of what it takes to be social problems, discusses the relative salience of competing values, and generally participates in the 'conversation' of a culture, as Oakeshott or Rorty would term it. Rorty's advice to expert theorists is to 'relax', to recognise the continuities between their concerns and those of other members of a culture, and to contribute to the 'traditional humanist task' of 'enlarging a linguistic and argumentative repertoire, and thus an imagination' (Rorty, 1982, p. 222).[13]

This type of 'relaxed' articulation between expert and lay discourses has much to commend it, but it cannot be quite the whole story. Given the condition of the 'double hermeneutic', another articulation is possible in which the task of the expert is to approach lay discourses orthogonally, as it were, and to enquire into how those discourses routinely accomplish their 'unities' of theory and practice. The concerns of expert and laity are clearly not of the same order here: what is a resource for the latter becomes a topic for the former, in the familiar formula. One paradigm for such 'orthogonal' enquiries is provided by the tradition of conversation analysis. Themes drawn from this tradition might inform enquiries into the mechanisms through which salient social and political issues, and the 'space' within which they are salient, are jointly constituted.[14] A second paradigm is provided by one model of Foucault's 'genealogies', in which these are glossed as a de-transcendentalised continuation of the Kantian project. Critique 'is no longer to be practiced in the search for formal structures with universal value, but rather as an historical investigation into the events that have lead us to constitute ourselves as subjects of what we are doing, thinking, saying' (Foucault, 1984, p. 46). If this genealogical project can be turned from its attachment to a metaphysics of Power/Knowledge, it might join conversation–analytic themes in a postfoundational account of the 'constitution' of constellations of theory and practice, which would reject both the syntheses of modernism and the monistic proliferations of postmodernism. Finally, a postfoundational radicalism would dispense with the pervasive belief of modernist radicalism that radical enquiries into the constitution of the social world are of necessary and direct relevance to radical concerns within that world.[15] If this illusion of a guaranteed unity between the two different types of articulation of expert and lay discourses is rejected, the question of how radical enquiry maintains its accountability becomes a pressing one.

*(b) Accountability*

It has been suggested above that it is the monistic tendency of postmodernism to reduce the movement of theory to the effect of a single principle (in nature or in language) which generates its nihilistic loss of 'accountability', of the capacity to give reasons why change is possible and desirable. On the other hand, it is the demand that the accountability of theory be guaranteed in advance by a series of asserted 'unities' which pitches modernist radicalism into foundationalism and metaphysics. The maintenance of accountability in postfoundational enquiry requires that a 'gap' be opened within these metaphysical reductions and syntheses. Projects of social theory can be thought of as constituted 'between' a context from which they emerge (considered as 'history', perhaps, or 'discourse'), and the goals to which they are directed. Accountability is lost if this distinction collapses. If goals are reduced to effects of their context, purpose and deliberation are mere illusions, or reflexes. If contexts are reduced to goals, the world becomes the product of an unconditioned will, which can be under no obligation of accountability. Projects of postfoundational radicalism must maintain and explore the constitutive tension between their 'relation-to-context' and their 'relation-to-goals', considering them as the irreducible poles between which discourse and enquiry move.[16] In order to sketch the main features of an accountability constituted in this tension, it will be necessary to rehabilitate three concepts which postmodernism regards as hopelessly metaphysical: reflexivity, judgement and teleology. Each concept requires a pragmatic and anti-foundationalist twist if the pattern of modernist radicalism is not to be recapitulated.

The equation of 'reflexivity' with rationality itself generates a concern with the auspices, or grounds, of enquiry and provides a model for accountability.[17] It imposes on enquiry the obligation to account for where it has come from and where it is going to, and the literature of 'reflexive sociology' is an important resource for a post-foundational radicalism. However, it is important to resist the notion that auspices stand in a foundational relation to enquiry itself: the practice of reflexivity is not a metanarrative to the first-order narrative of enquiry, nor does it guarantee some desirable outcome. Rather, reflexivity (or its absence) should be seen as a property of the way in which enquiry is conducted and reported. Mulkay's (1985) experiments in the textual forms of sociology, and the 'sociological invention' on health economics by Mulkay, Ashmore and Pinch (1987) exemplify the ways in which a refusal of the standard rhetorics of the scientific text can open up to deliberation many of the taken for granted auspices of enquiry.

An insistence on the necessity of a moment of 'judgement' in enquiry helps to keep open the gap between 'context' and 'goal'. The relations between these two poles should be seen as accomplished in an act of judgement, rather than as given in some logic of discourse. So, the salience of specific values to, or the appropriateness of particular strategies within, social and political debates can only be established in a judgement. Their status is not guaranteed by some logic of immanence, such as those associated with 'raised consciousness', or 'undistorted communication'. The irreducibility of judgement marks radical projects as always provisional and contingent, without firm foundations and unable to guarantee outcomes. Suspicion of the concept centres on its connotations of a subjectivity which constitutes its own experience, but there is no reason why 'judgement' should not be reformulated as part of a sociological account of enquiry. The conditions under which judgements are generated and sustained in enquiry can itself become a topic of 'orthogonal' enquiry. Developments within the sociology of science which draw on conversation analytic themes have moved in this direction.[18] Equally, the ways in which judgement is accomplished in non-expert discourses can become the topic of enquiries which are both reflexive and empirical.

'Teleology' has long served as the whipping-boy of Althusserian and postmodernist theory. Hindess offers a typical critique of the 'teleological postulate' which regards 'distinct forms as the realisation of their respective inner principles' (Hindess, 1977, p. 159). He has no difficulty in establishing the links between this postulate, the 'rationalist conception of action' and 'theoretical humanism', nor in showing that they are all equally 'incoherent'. However, this kind of exclusion of any 'relation-to-goals' from social theory runs the risk of falling into paradox. A denial that goals play a role in shaping and directing enquiry actually increases the temptation to gloss enquiry as the product of some single principle of power, or logic, or whatever. Any sociologically reflexive, adequate account of organised enquiry must recognise the formative role of the processes through which the goals of enquiry are debated, set and pursued. Equally, of course, that account must recognise that such processes do not determine the outcomes of enquiry. An important dimension of the accountability of a post-foundational radicalism must be a capacity to reflect on the contingencies which relate the contexts, goals and outcomes of enquiry.

In the anti-foundational twist to which the concepts of reflexivity, judgement and teleology must be subjected the three concepts operate as organising features of enquiry itself, within the normal discursive resources of enquiry. There are no other resources with which accountability could be maintained, it cannot be imported from some more profound order of foundational discourse. Approaching the problem from the other end, the meta-discourse which traces the movement of enquiry is closer to an ethnography, or a rhetorics, than to a classical philosophy or sociology of science.

### (c) Thresholds and Transitions

The problem of the articulation between history and theory haunts the modernist/postmodernist debate. Modernism requires a unity between the two in order to legitimate its promise to complete modernity, while postmodernism requires an 'historical and theoretical' definition which will legitimate its break from modernity and modernism. The dilemma facing postmodernism is that it must either allow that modernism was once valid, but is no longer, in which case it begins to look like an orthodox historicism, or it must insist that modernism (and pre-modernism) were always false, in which case it seems to be advancing claims to represent a timeless truth.[19] This problem arises because postmodernism makes only half a break with modernism. To draw on a theme of Blumenberg's, postmodernism breaks with modernist answers, but not with the (equally modernist) questions which prompt them.

Postmodernism claims that modernism is 'illegitimate' because it recapitulates an anachronistic metaphysics. The very similar claim which Blumenberg sets out to contest is that modernity is 'illegitimate' because its typical figures are secularisations of the theology of an earlier period. Two elements of the argument are pertinent here. First, the continuities between pre-modernity and modernity are not to be thought as the secularisation of themes, the transformation of some 'ideal substance'. They lie, rather, in a 're-occupation of answer-positions that had become vacant and whose corresponding questions could not be eliminated', and the way to avoid such regressive re-occupations is shake free of the view that theory must address 'a firm canon of "the great questions"' (Blumenberg, 1983, p. 65). Postmodernism may not have shaken quite free enough of the 'great questions' of modernism, questions about the potential of modernity, the relations between theory and practice, the articulation between historical and theoretical thresholds, and so on. Sometimes the postmodernist answers are also very close to modernism, as on the question of thresholds. In other cases, postmodernism achieves its *succès de scandale* by simply negating the modernist answer: there is no 'meaning' in history, there is no guarantee that 'resistance' will succeed, there can be no 'science' of the social. In all cases, as its title suggests, postmodernism is parasitic upon the defining problems of the modernism it contests. It makes no breakthrough into new questions.

The second of Blumenberg's themes is precisely that the most important historical transitions are those concerned with the emergence of new questions. So, he argues that the legitimate meaning of the idea of 'progress' does not come from a 're-occupation' in which progress is seen as the 'meaning of history'. It derives, rather, from the appearance in the late medieval period of the programming of human 'self-assertion'. Here man (sic) 'indicates to himself how he is going to deal with the reality surrounding him, and how he will make use of the possibilities that are open to him' (Blumenberg, 1983, p. 138). For Blumenberg, this programme finds a level of self awareness in the Nietzschean claim that there is no necessary relation between 'truth' and human purposes. It might be added that the pursuit of necessary negative relations should also fall under this ban. This argument suggests that both modernism and postmodernism misunderstand the challenges which social enquiry is called upon to meet. Neither can break an obsession with necessary unities between knowledge and some medium in which it proliferates. The evolutionism, physicalism and formalism of postmodernism, as much as the historicism, essentialism and humanism of modernism, are symptoms of the continued scratching at old questions. To adapt a favourite figure of Rorty's, they both scratch where it does not itch, but fail to scratch where it does. If radical social enquiry is to have any continuing salience within the conversations of contemporary cultures it must end its romance with ends. The 'ends' which radical theory continually makes and re-makes with metaphysics and modernity (or pre-modernity) always turn out to be something other than an end: a transcendence, perhaps, a negation. A post-foundational radicalism which insisted that the relations between enquiry, context and temporal thresholds were wholly contingent and pragmatic might be able to make an end of the ends. By simply ceasing to address the old questions it may be able to pose new ones about contemporary realities and possibilities.

## Notes and References

1. The classic statements such as Bell (1973) and Touraine (1971) are exemplary in this respect. Lyotard (1984), for example, enthusiastically embraces the 'post-industrialism' theme, but presses it into the service of a more radical critique of social theory.

2. The immediate target of both of these attacks is not so much Marx as Althusser, and particularly his doctrine of an 'epistemological break' in Marx's work which enables Marxism to enter the register of science.

3. This would be particularly the case with rationalism, of which Althusser's Marxism and Habermas's critical theory are very different examples, and with currently fashionable realist doctrines, less so with phenomenalism.

4. It must be said that Habermas is aware of the problem of foundationalism, holding that while there may have been difficulties with the 'quasi-transcendental' status of 'knowledge constituting interests', no such problems arise in his model of communication, which is an example of 'reconstructive theory'. For a discussion of this concept see 'What is Universal Pragmatics?' in Habermas, 1979. See also Habermas, 1982, pp. 229–250 and Habermas, 1984, pp. 66–74. To the sceptic, Habermas does not seem to have drawn back from classically foundationalist figures, seeking an 'immanent' principle of 'transcendence' in the structures of communication.

5. A number of attempts to 'save' the concept do so by splitting it in two. Thus, Butler (1980, p. ix) distinguishes between a 'rule-dominated' and an 'irrationalist, indeterminate or aleatory' postmodernism, while Foster (1983, p. xii) separates 'a postmodernism of resistance and a postmodernism of reaction'. Huyssen (1984) places a similar 'radical/reactionary' split within a useful chronology of US postmodernism.

6. In Jameson, 1984 (p. 58), which articulates the idea of postmodernism as a 'cultural dominant', the four 'constitutive features' are given rather differently as a new depthlessness, a weakening of historicity, a

return to theories of the sublime, and a relation between cultural, technical and social change at the global level.

7. As opposed to a 'merely reflective' judgement in which only the particular is 'given' (Kant, 1952, p. 18). Lyotard's distinction between the modernist and postmodernist approaches to sublimity is very close to that which Kant (1952, p. 94) makes between the 'mathematically' and the 'dynamically' sublime. The former exercises the faculty of cognition, the latter that of desire. Lyotard makes no direct reference to the distinction, however.

8. Lyotard gives no example of a single work which is both modern and postmodern. He suggests that the German Expressionists and Proust, for example, are 'nostalgic', while Picasso and Joyce take a postmodern attitude to the sublime.

9. So, Foucauldian 'power' remains a structural concept. 'Power is an irreversible principle of organisation because it fabricates the real . . . nowhere does it cancel itself out, become entangled in itself, or mingle with death' (Baudrillard, 1980, pp. 100–1).

10. The term 'object = X' is used by Kant to refer to the noumenal 'thing in itself' which is a condition of phenomenal knowledge, but which cannot be known 'in itself'. For a more sympathetic account of Baudrillard's 'anti-theory' which construes it as a 'tracing out of the Nietzschean regression in Marx', see Kroker, 1985 (quote from p. 69).

11. The most significant modern figure is Spinoza, who posited a single substance, *'Deus sive Natura'* (God or Nature). Spinoza's monism provides the pattern for Althusser's early 'system', and Althusser, in turn, pre-figures a number of postmodernist themes.

12. Lyotard's equation of 'game' with *agon*, or contest, might itself be seen as an attempt to pre-empt and subordinate the specificity of other types of game (games as play, games of chance, games as ritual, etc.). It certainly sits uneasily with his Wittgensteinian references to 'language games'.

13. On the tasks of social science, Rorty (1982, p. 187) specifies 'two distinct requirements' for a social scientific vocabulary. '(1) it should contain descriptions of situations which facilitate prediction and control. (2) It should contain descriptions which help one decide what to do'.

14. It should not be necessary to add that this does not imply that social outcomes are to be analysed as effects of a 'conspiracy' between agents. As Atkinson and Heritage (1984, p. 1) insist, in conversation analysis 'the analyst is . . . not required to speculate on what the interactants hypothetically or imaginably understood'.

15. Thus, in Marxism the 'forces and relations of production' constitute the social world as it is, and are to be the object of revolutionary change: to know how the world 'really is' is to know how it *should* be. For Habermas, to know how language *does* work is to know how it *should* work.

16. An important version of this point is made in Rosen's (1969) diagnosis of nihilism as the result of a reduction of rationality either to a moment of vision (*noesis*) or to the mere proliferation of speech (*dianoia*).

Reason and value are constituted only in the mediation of vision by speech and speech by vision.

17. Gouldner (1976, p. 49), for example, urges that 'rationality as reflexive about our groundings premises an ability to speak about our speech and the factors that ground it'. Important contributions to the reflexive sociology of the seventies include Blum, 1974; O'Neill, 1972 and and Sandywell et al., 1975. For more recent reflections on the problem see Mulkay, 1985 and Woolgar, 1987.

18. Examples include the comparison of laboratory interaction with the production of scientific texts in Knorr-Cetina, 1981, and the study of the ways in which scientists make error 'accountable' in Gilbert & Mulkay, 1984.

19. Foucault's periodisation of the mutations of power faces a version of this dilemma. The problem is whether *any* regime ever operated on the basis of 'sovereign power' as defined by Foucault: were there *no* 'micro powers' at play in medieval Europe? If there were not, the conjunction of historical and theoretical thresholds looks suspiciously neat, and savours of historicism. If 'disciplinary power' does have an existence prior to the emergence of the 'disciplinary matrix' in its modern form, Foucault has produced an a-historical typology of power in the manner of Weber.

## Bibliography

ADORNO, T. (1973), *Negative Dialectics*, London, Routledge & Kegan Paul.

ATKINSON, J. M. and HERITAGE, J. (eds) (1984), *Structures of Social Action*, Cambridge, Cambridge University Press.

BAUDRILLARD, J. (1980), 'Forgetting Foucault', *Humanities in Society*, 3.1, pp. 87–111.

BAUDRILLARD, J. (1983), *In the Shadow of the Silent Majorities*, New York, Semiotext(e).

BAUDRILLARD, J. (1983a), 'The Ecstasy of Communication', in Foster (ed.), op. cit.

BAUMAN, Z. (1987), *Legislators and Interpreters*, Cambridge, Polity Press.

BELL, D. (1973), *The Coming of Post-Industrial Society*, New York, Basic Books.

BERNSTEIN, J. (ed.) (1985), *Habermas and Modernity*, Cambridge, Polity Press.

BLUM, A. (1974), *Theorizing*, London, Heinemann.

BLUMENBERG, H. (1983), *The Legitimacy of the Modern Age*, Cambridge, Mass., MIT Press.

BUTLER, C. (1980), *After the Wake*, Oxford, Oxford University Press.

CALLINICOS, A. (1982), *Is There a Future for Marxism?*, London, Macmillan.

CUTLER, A. et al. (1978), *Marx's 'Capital' and Capitalism Today*, Volume 2, London, Routledge & Kegan Paul.

DURKHEIM, E. (1964), *The Rules of Sociological Method*, New York, Free Press.
EAGLETON, T. (1985), 'Capitalism, Modernism and Post-modernism', *New Left Review*, 152, pp. 60–73.
FOSTER, H. (1983), 'Post-Modernism: a Preface', in Foster (ed.), op. cit.
FOSTER, H. (ed.) (1983), *The Anti-Aesthetic*, Port Townsend, Bay Press.
FOUCAULT, M. (1970), *The Order of Things*, London, Tavistock.
FOUCAULT, M. (1984), 'What is Enlightenment?', in Rabinow (ed.), op. cit.
GIDDENS, A. (1982), *Profiles and Critiques in Social Theory*, London, Macmillan.
GILBERT, N. and MULKAY, M. (1984), *Opening Pandora's Box*, Cambridge, Cambridge University Press.
GLUCKSMANN, A. (1980), *The Master Thinkers*, Brighton, The Harvester Press.
GOULDNER, A. (1976), *The Dialectic of Ideology and Technology*, London, Macmillan.
GUATTARI, F. (1984), *Molecular Revolution*, Harmondsworth, Penguin.
HABERMAS, J. (1979), *Communication and the Evolution of Society*, London, Heinemann.
HABERMAS, J. (1981), 'Modernity versus Postmodernity', *New German Critique*, 22, pp. 3–14.
HABERMAS, J. (1982), 'A Reply to My Critics' in Thompson & Held (eds), op. cit.
HABERMAS, J. (1984), *Reason and the Rationalization of Society*, London, Heinemann.
HABERMAS, J. (1985), 'Neoconservative Cultural Criticism: etc', in Bernstein (ed.), op. cit.
HABERMAS, J. (1987), *The Philosophical Discourse of Modernity*, Cambridge, Polity Press.
HAMLYN, D. (1970), *The Theory of Knowledge*, London, Macmillan.
HASSAN, I. (1985), 'The Culture of Post Modernism', *Theory, Culture & Society*, 2.3, pp. 119–31.
HINDESS, B. (1977), *Philosophy and Methodology in the Social Sciences*, Brighton, Harvester Press.
HINDESS, B. and HIRST, P. (1977), *Mode of Production and Social Formation*, London, Routledge & Kegan Paul.
HIRST, P. (1979), *On Law and Ideology*, London, Macmillan.
HONNETH, A. (1985), 'An Aversion against the Universal: etc', *Theory, Culture & Society*, 2.3, pp. 147–56.
HUYSSEN, A. (1984), 'From Counter Culture to Neo-Conservatism and Beyond: Stages of the Post Modern', *Social Science Information*, 23, pp. 147–56.
JAMESON, F. (1983), 'Post-Modernism and Consumer Society', in Foster (ed.), op. cit.

JAMESON, F. (1984), 'Post-Modernism, or the Cultural Logic of Late Capitalism', *New Left Review*, 146, pp. 53–92.

KANT, I. (1952), *The Critique of Judgement*, Oxford, Oxford University Press.

KILMINSTER, R. (1982), 'Theory and Practice in Marx and Marxism', in Parkinson (ed.), op. cit.

KNORR-CETINA, K. (1981), *The Manufacture of Knowledge*, Oxford, Pergamon Press.

KROKER, A. (1985), 'Baudrillard's Marx', *Theory, Culture & Society*, 2.3, pp. 69–83.

LASH, S. (1985), 'Postmodernity and Desire', *Theory & Society*, 14, pp. 1–33.

LYOTARD, J.-F. (1984), *The Postmodern Condition*, Manchester, Manchester University Press.

LYOTARD, J.-F. (1984a), 'Answering the Question: What is Postmodernism' in Lyotard (1984), op. cit.

MARGOLIS, J. (1986), *Pragmatism Without Foundations*, Oxford, Blackwell.

MARX, K. (1973), *Grundrisse*, Harmondsworth, Penguin.

MARX, K. (1975), *Early Writings*, Harmondsworth, Penguin.

MULKAY, M. (1985), *The Word and the World*, London, Allen & Unwin.

MULKAY, M., ASHMORE, M. and PINCH, T. (1987), 'Measuring the Quality of Life: etc', *Sociology*, 21, pp. 541–64.

O'NEILL, J. (1972), *Sociology as a Skin Trade*, London, Heinemann.

O'NEILL, J. (1986), 'Sociological Nemesis: Parsons and Foucault on the Theraputic Disciplines', in Wardell and Turner (eds), op. cit.

O'NEILL, J. (1986a), 'The Disciplinary Society: from Weber to Foucault', *British Journal of Sociology*, 37, pp. 42–60.

PARKINSON, G. (ed.) (1982), *Marx and Marxisms*, Cambridge, Cambridge University Press.

RABINOW, P. (ed.) (1984), *The Foucault Reader*, New York, Random House.

RORTY, R. (1982), *The Consequences of Pragmatism*, Brighton, Harvester Press.

ROSE, G. (1984), *Dialectic of Nihilism*, Oxford, Blackwell.

ROSEN, S. (1969), *Nihilism*, New Haven, Yale University Press.

RYAN, M. (1982), *Marxism and Deconstruction*, Baltimore, Johns Hopkins University Press.

SANDYWELL, B., et al. (1975), *Problems of Reflexivity and Dialectic in Sociology*, London, Rouledge & Kegan Paul.

SMART, B. (1983), *Foucault, Marxism and Critique*, London, Routledge & Kegan Paul.

THOMPSON, J. and HELD, D. (eds) (1982), *Habermas: Critical Debates*, London, Macmillan.

TOURAINE, A. (1971), *The Post-Industrial Society*, New York, Random House.

WARDELL, M. and TURNER, S. (eds) (1986), *Sociological Theory in Transition*, Boston, Allen & Unwin.
WHITEBOOK, J. (1982), 'Saving the Subject: etc.', *Telos*, 50, pp. 79–102.
WOOLGAR, S. (ed.) (1987), *Knowledge and Reflexivity*, London, Sage.

# Chapter 3

# Postmodernism and Language

Jean-Jacques Lecercle

## 1. Postmodernism and Linguistics

If we accept Lyotard's (1979) argument that the advent of post-modernism is marked by a shift from truth to fiction and narrative, by a change from the world of experience to that of language, and by the demise of the three great metanarratives of science, religion and politics with their replacement by local language-games, then the science of linguistics finds itself in an irreducible quandary, yet in a privileged position. As a science it must submit to the general fate of metanarratives, and at least change its concept of truth. On the other hand, however, it is *the* science whose subject matter is at the centre of the postmodern critique. It might hope therefore to survive relatively unscathed, with the result that there still could be something like a postmodern linguistics. It is my intention to explore this profoundly ambiguous situation, even though it might be said of me as a linguist, that I am attempting to have my cake and eat it too.

It is clear that modern structural linguistics does belong to the allegedly exhausted paradigm of science. It has all the character-istics of Galilean science. It can be argued that Saussure's founding concepts constitute an epistemological break, as Althusser might say, opening up the continent of language for science. Saussure's 'langue' would thus be seen as a scientific object, constructed, through exclusion and separation out of the formless reality of language, by applying the typical scientific operations of abstraction and generalisation. As Milner shows (1978), Saussurean linguistics follows the same dual operation as all the other forms of Galilean science: (i) *closure* – *langue* is construed as something real,[1] postulating, in other words, that it has no cause other than itself. This corresponds to the arbitrary character of the sign; and (ii) *formalisation* – *langue* can be described by a formal calculus, so that *langue* is made up of signs, with the users of language reduced to the position of simple agents in this calculus. These language users are pure abstractions, angels or speaking subjects. They have no past or future, neither consciousness nor an unconscious, neither body nor soul. They are the addressor and the addressee in the well-known diagram of communication.[2]

Even if linguists make the modest claim to be descriptive rather than prescriptive, even if they restrict their pretensions to the lowest level of adequacy (Chomsky is a case in point, for he distinguished between observational, descriptive and explanatory levels of adequacy, and claimed only to be operating at the lowest level, that of observational adequacy), even when their outlook is determinedly and solidly empiricist[3] and without any aspiration to philosophical profundity or psychological insight, *still* they find themselves right in the centre of the paradigm of truth. The most timid attempt to claim adequacy for a linguistic description is equivalent to a statement of truth. There is no doubt therefore that Saussure's concept of *langue*, as a *real* constructed out of reality, purports to state the truth about language, and may thus be seen to be marked by that hubristic character denounced by the postmodern critique.

It comes as no surprise, then, that linguistics fits within what Lyotard calls the pragmatics of scientific knowledge, and that it is, like other sciences, 'legitimised through its performativity' (Lyotard, 1979: pp. 69–78). The power and influence of linguistic science is considerable. It continues to provide a model for the social sciences. Its university departments, with their professoriate, attract research funding. Furthermore, and most importantly, linguistics has technological implications – to see a computer scientist rediscover the basic concepts of structural linguistics, in the course of work on machine translation or speech synthesis or speech interpretation, is really quite touching.

Overall, if the 'postmodern revolution' is an effect of the explosion of communication techniques, linguistics appears to be right in the middle of it. Here we come to the second, and contradictory, aspect of my account, because linguistics is even closer than this to postmodernism. The reason for this is that even while it is caught up in the technological revolution in communications, its field of study is at the centre of the post-modern crisis. This contradiction means that linguistics cannot be just like other sciences. And indeed it is not.

Linguistics is indifferent to the great story of science, whose main narrative device is, as we know, the idea of progress. Now, in linguistics, as in philosophy, there is no progress. Or, rather, claims to progress coexist with evidence of its absence, and this amounts to the same thing. Saussure's epistemological break could have been a sign of progress in linguistics. Did it not found structural linguistics after all? But one of the masterpieces (this is no metaphor) of structural linguistics is Panini's grammar of Sanskrit, written 4000 years ago. Taking another example, Chomsky's revolution-ary work turns out to be at the same time a return to the Cartesian grammar of Artaud and Nicole. This situation is normal in philo-sophy, but, to say the least, infrequent in science (Democritus' theory of atoms, for example, is hardly an integral part of contemporary atomic physics). The reason for this ambiguous relation to progress is not hard to find: the object of linguistics is too close to the scientist for it to be mastered with instruments.

The paradox of metalanguage – the simultaneous necessity and impossibility of it – is central to linguistics. One's mother tongue is not easily turned into an object of study, for it is first an object of desire, a bearer of desiring cathexes. Some spheres may witness a ruptural emergence from a magical to a scientific vision of the world, but in the case of language one must doubt the possibility of fully achieving this. This is not just a question of difficulty, which would explain the late development of linguistics as compared, for example, with physics. It is a question of *reflexivity*. Linguistics cannot be fully inserted into one of the great narratives, because its very object is that of which narratives are made. The post-modern philosophising of Lyotard's *Le Differend* is a case in point, for this work is based on a *linguistic turn*, on the description of language games and the pragmatics of sentence types.

It is the phenomenon of reflexivity in linguistics which helps to explain its perpetual cycle of progression and regression, its undulation between fashion and neglect (ten years ago, linguistics was 'in'; two years ago, it was 'out'; now, if the postmodern critique is sustained, it may well come to be central again, albeit in an almost unrecognisable form). This is not the first time that such things have occurred, and that similar alternations mark the history of philology casts a rather dubious light on what I have referred to as Saussure's epistemological break.

This ambiguous position points to a recurrent and even constitutive problem. It is already embodied in the personality of the founder of linguistics. I refer, of course, to the famous issue of the two Saussures, to the Dodgson-Carroll type of schizophrenia (etymologically speaking) which has afflicted linguistics since its inception. We might, in fact, go a little further than usual, and talk of three Saussures: not only the demented seeker of anagrams constantly threatening to destroy the rather staid social scientist by speaking through and instead of him like Judge Schreber's voices, but also the revolutionary social scientist who succeeded in possessing and silencing the old-fashioned but extraordinarily gifted philologist, whose greatest work was a reconstruction of the vowel system of Indo-European. In Saussure, the epistemological break separates the linguist from the philologist; but it becomes compulsive – a source for repetition and symptom – and the mad seeker of anagrams soon comes up with his break to overcome the linguist.

The postmodern crisis is already prefigured in this situation. The energy which establishes the rule of truth is not thereby exhausted; it impels us toward the destruction of the very paradigm of truth for which it was responsible. In Saussure's case, the anagrams deny the rules which circumscribe the arbitrary sign, ruling out any possibility of consistency and completeness. Their disquieting proliferation eventually condemned him to silence. In science, there are fixed rules, determinate units and closed sequences; with anagrams, there are no fixed rules, no single site of operations (a phrase, a line, a stanza: these are equivalent loci for the anagrammatic operation), and a multiplicity of results. In science, we find the two structural operations of analysis and synthesis. In the case of anagrams, we find that these operations are subverted to produce multiple analyses and incalculable syntheses.

This schizophrenic legacy is not merely a question of historical happenstance. The ambiguity is constitutive and is related to the paradox of metalanguage. Every construction of a linguistic object, every *langue*, leaves a remainder. While it is true that all sciences have to go through the arduous process of separating the relevant from the irrelevant phenomena, in the case of linguistics the process is unstable. For in the science of language the remainder, like the Freudian repressed, must always return. This repression and return arise because, due to the identity between the analytical tool and the object of analysis, the 'initial' separation must be arbitrary and violent. This paradox of metalanguage goes further than the difficulties of the hermeneutic circle which are common to all of the social sciences (one has only to think of Vico's theorisation of history to see that the latter can have a liberating effect). It produces at least two major weaknesses in the study of language. First, the basic concepts remain unstable and uncertain. The concept 'word', for example, cannot be given a clear and unique definition; and a detour through a scientific construct such as 'morpheme' does not avoid the issue because *word*, *sentence*, and so on remain units of language even though they cannot be satisfactorily defined. Second, the history of the subject is a *fuite en avant*, in which each new linguist compulsively attempts to integrate the previous remainder into the object of the science, inevitably creating a 'new' remainder in the process. The history of linguistics is, indeed, the history of the extension of *langue*: from syntax to semantics, and latterly, with the advent of pragmatics, to discourse and context. This history is also the story of a phoenix-like remainder, forever reborn from its ashes at the very moment when linguists proclaim that it has finally disappeared. Chomsky's latest solution is modular linguistics. Here, grammar is seen as an assemblage of more or less independent modules. There is a transformational module, a phonological module and so on. This strategy relies on the faith in scientific progress, assuming that the remainder will either be dealt with through a more refined combination of the existing modules, or through the elaboration of module $n+1$ (not described yet, but certainly describable). This is a modern version of the story of Achilles and the tortoise: when module $n+1$ is constructed, a new remainder will be found, requiring the construction of module $n+2$, and so on indefinitely. This 'solution' is, in fact, a denial of the appearance, long delayed by the *fuite en avant* mentioned above, of the postmodern crisis within linguistics. It is based on the idea of progress in science. But, as we know, we can no longer believe in the old narratives, impressive though they are. The only solution is to welcome the crisis, and take advantage of its positivity. Postmodernism in language is the crisis of the return of the remainder. It is the contemporary crisis in linguistics.

## 2. Two Aspects of the Crisis in Linguistics

A full account of the crisis would have to assess the situation of Chomskyan linguistics today. It would have to describe its involution, its loss of dominance, the flight of linguists into philosophy or psychology, the return of older theories, and much more. This would however be far beyond the limits of this paper. I shall be content, therefore, with evoking two texts, one in which the crisis is faced, the other in which the crisis is overcome, but also, in a way, denied.

The first 'text' comprises the works of J. C. Milner. His work exemplifies the crisis of contradiction within linguistics, because while being a Chomskyan linguist of the first order, whose study of the grammar of insults and exclamations is perhaps the most important contribution to French linguistics since Benveniste, he is also, if not a practising psychoanalyst, at least a disciple of Lacan. Two of his works (1978, 1983) are built on this contradiction. They originated in seminars given in the department of psychoanalysis at the University of Vincennes.

The contradiction here is not in the linguist's head (nor was it in Saussure's head: neither he nor Carroll were, in the vulgar sense of the phrase, divided selves), but we do approach it with the opposition between *langue* and *lalangue*. The contradiction is within the object, in language; in other words, the contradiction is *real*. We must define this term *real*. Milner uses it in the Lacanian sense, where the real is opposed to the imaginary and to the symbolic.[4] Controversially, let me say that the difference between linguistics and the other social sciences is that linguistics is not only an imaginary construction, but that it touches on something real. It comes up against the fact that language is outside the control or power of the speaking subject. To an extent, this is captured by the formula 'not everything can be said'.[5] This real character of language, that it is beyond rational control or analytic grasp, accounts for the timelessness of linguistics. Grammar will always be with us, and has always been with us (as the example of Panini indicates), unlike sociology which, as Milner cattily reminds us, has not always existed.

For the linguist, then, the contradiction arises because in the sphere of language science never has the last word. It must always leave a remainder because of the *real* character of language. As Milner says, '*La science vient à manquer*'. The science of linguistics postulates that the real character of languages can be grasped through a calculus, a system of fixed units and syntactic rules. But an artificial language is not a natural language. There is no *suture* (Miller, 1977; Laclau and Mouffe, 1985) in natural languages, where rules are neither complete nor coherent. Beyond the frontiers of the calculus, subverting the well-formed sequences calculated by grammar, there lies *lalangue*, the best embodiment of which is the mother-tongue – an apt metaphor, for it shows that desire is present in language. Now we are no longer in the domain of the linguist but rather in that of the language-lover: a dubious name for a dubious practice. The language lover does not analyse but *makes* language. This is no longer a question of theory, as with linguistics; it is now a matter of practice. The angels in the diagram of communication are no longer transparent and sexless ghosts. They become subjects in the psychoanalytic sense: desiring subjects, endowed with an unconscious.

Saussure's *langue* was based on the exclusion of the desiring subject from language. This subject returns with *lalangue*. The disguises of this language-loving, logophiliac (the allusion to the realm of perversions is quite intentional) subject are many: the purist defending language against change and corruption with the weapons of good taste rather than those of science; the polyglottal linguist who cannot desist from learning more languages (every student of languages suffers from a mild case of this mania); the hopeful esperantist, seemingly striving after universal peace but actually pursuing a fantasy of total power over language, who seeks an impossible transference of language from the field of the real to that of the imaginary; the philologist, an esperantist of the origins, whose glory lies in writing the grammar of a language – Indo-European – which has never existed; the delirious patient, whose symptom, as in the case of Wolfson, Brisset, or perhaps even Saussure, is an inordinate interest in the workings of language; and lastly, the poet, who etymologically *makes* language, and whose playful activity sometimes borders on delirium, as in the cases of Roussel and Artaud. The points in language where *lalangue* asserts itself are equally numerous. Milner calls them, for reasons which should now be clear, 'points of subjectivity' or 'points of poetry'. The refractory and destabilising power of *lalangue* can be appreciated by considering the principle of homophony. This principle, in fact, ruins the thesis of the arbitrary character of the sign: why should words be related by sound, rather than by, say, meaning or syntax? Homophony introduces relationships which threaten the whole system, bringing with it the poetic and delirious consequences of an ambiguity of meanings that shift and slide along the formless ranks of signifiers.

Milner's position has the extraordinary advantage of recognising the existence and importance of, what I have called, 'the remainder'. Furthermore, it allows this remainder to escape the connotation of negativity, and to be seen positively as a constitutive aspect of language, perhaps more important than grammar itself. It is true that Milner will not go that far. In attempting to mark out frontiers, and to establish a division of labour in which the determinate function of grammar would be quite secure, he betrays his concern to 'save grammar', in much the same way as philosophers have been concerned to 'save truth'. But the postmodern crisis questions the necessity of 'saving truth', and perhaps also of 'saving grammar'.

Milner's text might be seen, if I may put it this way, as pre-postmodern. It reintroduces the desiring subject within language, but it sets limits which preserve linguistics as a form of Galilean science. This is not the case for Deleuze and Guattari in Plateau No. 4 of their *Mille Plateaux* (1980). Their plan is to destroy structural linguistics and replace it with a version of pragmatics (although they do this at the cost of a gross misprision of the concept [Lecercle, 1988]). Their demolition of linguistics is quite comprehensive, and, leaving aside for the moment the question of what is to succeed it – we can be certain that it will not be another *scientific* praxis, although a form of praxis it must surely be – it will be instructive to examine their critique.

In fairly uncontentious fashion, Deleuze and Guattari ascribe the following characteristics to linguistics: (1) The function of language is to provide information and allow communication. (2)

Language is an abstract machine without any cause exterior to itself. (3) Language is a homogeneous system. (4) The standard version of language is the only one worth studying.

Against the first postulate, it can be argued that language does *not* inform and communicate, but rather one *does* things with words. Instead of the speech act model of performativity, however, Deleuze and Guattari point to the command and the slogan as the model for language. Words do not inform, they command. They ascribe to each and every participant in a speech-situation a place in a hierarchy. Their maxim is that 'Syntactic markers are markers of power'. One is reminded here of Barthes' epigram, '*La langue est fasciste*' (1978: p. 14).

It can also be said that it is not in the power of speaking subjects to express their thoughts and exchange whatever information they have. One does not speak language as one uses a tool, rather one is spoken by it: language is a social practice not an individual faculty. Returning to the subject of the command and the slogan, these are not the product of a single speaking subject, but rather originate in a 'collective arrangement of utterance'. Pessimistic references to a kind of linguistic Big Brother are perhaps apposite, and Deleuze and Guattari are very near to Orwell's para-marxist critique of language at this point.

Against the second postulate, far from being an abstract machine closed in on itself, language is material in at least two senses. First, it is produced by bodies and therefore caught up in their violent passions (this is the hidden meaning of Chrysippus' apparent paradox: 'when you talk of a chariot, a chariot goes out of your mouth'). Second, it is a social product, material in so far as it is required by institutions and used within institutional relations. In other words, we must go against the current of both linguistics and Marxism, rejecting the thesis of Stalin's *Considerations about Marxism in Linguistics* (that we now know that Stalin did not write this piece that bears his name provides an ironic demonstration that language as expression of a subject *is* dependent on institutions and power).

The postulation that language is a homogeneous system is patently false. *Parole* always returns within *langue*. Our language, as we actually use it, is a multiplicity of dialects (we do not address our butcher as we do our beloved), of styles, and of sequences completed and otherwise (anacoluthon is a constant feature of actual speech, as every conversation analyst knows).

Lastly, against the fourth postulate, we must argue that standard language is hardly an innocent construct. L. J. Calvet (1974) has coined the term *glottophagy* to refer to the consumption of one language by another. Deleuze and Guattari show that such linguistic colonialism operates within any language: the major dialect always attempts to repress the minor dialects, with the latter engaged in a perpetual struggle against this oppression. The history of the Welsh or Breton language testifies to all of this; nor is this just a geographical or national question, as feminist studies of the language of women have shown. Deleuze and Guattari point to the creative side of such unstable combinations. Their book on Kafka treats a Czech Jew writing in Austrian German; Babel is within his head. This is not a case where language speaks, but where languages speak. Furthermore, when minorities of this sort are added up, they end up forming the vast majority. As a teacher of English, of necessity imposing on my students the standard dialect, I know that I am passing on a version of the language that most English speakers would laugh at.

This concept of language as minor is of particular importance to my point: linguistics is only possible if it concentrates on the major dialect (even dialectology, which describes other dialects, operates negatively, by comparison with the standard version; unsurprisingly, it is reduced to a minor place within the discipline). Once linguistics is seen as not accounting for the whole, or even for most of the language, there is a certain sense of liberation. New aspects, denied by science, come to the foreground: the subjective, but also the social, the violent, but also the desiring aspects of language are given free rein. Deleuze and Guattari embody this conception in their twin metaphors of the tree and the rhizome. On the one hand, we can see language as an ordered hierarchic structure, the image of which (as notably in Chomsky) is the tree. On the other hand, we can conceive of it as a proliferating organism without structure or origin, the image for which is the rhizome, a subterranean root branching out in all directions.

There is a certain facility in Deleuze and Guattari's critique of linguistics. There is also scope and a breath of fresh air. The regrounding of language in the desiring body or the body politic is certainly an advantage, as is the account of the sheer instability and violence of an object in which the minor constantly subverts the major. But one has the feeling that, contrary to Milner's

ascetic account of the achievement of linguistics, certain aspects –
those which pertain to grammar as *real* – are too quickly dismissed.
Nevertheless, they provide us with the crucial break with the
narrative of science, and with a way of abandoning theory for
practice. Learning from Deleuze and Guattari, we should forget
about the constraints and the constructions, and, for a while at
least, explore the rhizome of language.

## 3. From Theory to Practice

Language in action is not a strikingly Saussurean sight. It is much
more plastic than grammar would allow it to be, bearing the same
desultory attitude towards its own rules as Deleuze and Guattari
have towards the structures of linguistics. It seems to be simultaneously rule-bound and rule-transcendent, as if caught in its own
version of the liar paradox. In order to investigate this further, I
shall proceed in two steps. First, we will examine linguistic
*practice*, and produce a ragbag of linguistic phenomena which
apparently do not conform to the rules of Saussurean linguistics.
Second, we will seek *theoretically* to produce other 'rules', aware
from the beginning that these are unlikely to be of the same type as
the rules of grammar.

The contents of the ragbag will not be accumulated through a
search for ordered sets of propositions or well-defined examples.
Rather, we will find what is required through a joyous drifting
through language, through a leisurely exploration while on holiday
in the rhizome. Indeed, the playful aspect will be central. It will
appear, for instance, that many of the phenomena mentioned will
be games one plays with language (reversing the phrase, we might
think that the concept of language-game provides a better basis for
approaching language than the idea of structure; at any rate,
Lyotard's (1979) extensive references to Wittgenstein might point
us in that direction). It is important to note, however, that such
games will not be the only contents of the ragbag: alongside the
intentional attacks on the structure of language, that we find in, for
example, jokes, we will also encounter linguistic devices to which
language itself and not the individual speaker has recourse.

The general idea is that it is language, and not the subject, that
speaks. Scientific linguistics assumes, in Cartesian fashion, the
subject of its science to be the speaking subject, seen as a centre

for mastery and control over language; but we must dissolve this controlling subject. There is no master of language. Its speakers are only travellers along pathways that have emerged in the course of what is a collective and organically developing phenomenon. So, I do not deny the existence of the speaking subject, but I do dispute the role of such subjects as a source of meaning and sometimes even as a source of speech. The speaking subject is the surface effect of a process of Freudian compromise or struggle for meaning, in the course of which I emerge as a subject from a background of possession by language and liberation from it (this is the 'violence of language' to which I referred earlier). Overall, then, the phenomena in my ragbag will be *at the same time* highly intentional (the linguistic joke is the highest form of mastery over language) and totally unintentional (language jokes in its own right, as in homophony. Such effects can possess and even create subjects; as I have discussed elsewhere [Lecercle, 1985], a logophiliac like Wolfson is a prime example). Inside the ragbag, then, we no longer find the competent subject, the abstract system, and the formal operations of analysis and synthesis (i.e., within structural linguistics, the formation of, respectively, paradigms and syntagms). Instead, we have multiple analysis, the *Brissetising* of language, if I may coin the phrase, and we have dubious synthesis, what we might call the *Wolfsonising* of language. I will expand upon these categories.

Jean-Pierre Brisset, a delirious French linguist, claimed that he could prove, by purely philological means, that humanity descends from the frog. He did this by turning every word in the French language into a multiple source of etymological puns. Thus, to the question, 'Where were our ancestors lodged?', the answer is given by an analysis of the French for 'lodged'. The word is *logé*, which can be heard as *l'eau j'ai*, meaning 'I have water'. Before concluding, however, that our ancestors were amphibians, it is relevant to consider that *logé* may also be heard as *l'haut j'ai*, which means 'I have the height'. Perhaps, then, our ancestors lived in houses built on posts, in marshes, for instance. Without going into any more detail, at the end of the entire process, it becomes clear that our true ancestor was the frog.

Now, it is not really the content of the delirium that is interesting, but the form. There are a number of points to make about this form. First of all, Brisset's etymologies are no more delirious than

official etymologies were for centuries: Isidore of Seville, or even
Horne Tooke, are rich sources of inventive madness of this kind.
In fact, Brisset's deliriums are no more delirious than language
itself. Consider, in this respect, the etymology of the word
'grammar.' Predictably, Brisset asserts an etymological link with
'grandma' (*grammaire/grand mère*); but 'true' etymology tells us
that 'grammar' is the etymological source of 'glamour', and the
historical chain of meaning that goes from the book of grammar
(which was, in the Middle Ages, a euphemism for a book of magic,
hence grammar came to mean 'obscure power', then 'charm') to
the glamour girl is no more far fetched than the possible chain of
meaning between grandma and grammar – a semantic link which
at least has the advantage of showing the relationship between
family structure, the desires it channels, and language. A further
point which should be made is that Brisset's technique applies the
same operations as grammar, i.e. the analysis of the word mor-
phemes (considered diachronically in the case of etymology). It
does, however, apply the operation *more than once*, thus turning it
into an instance of delirium. This may seem like just a small
change, but it has tremendous consequences. For if an already
analysed sequence can be re-analysed, the result is an endless
proliferation of interpretations. Such a proliferation offers no fixed
units for the construction of any determinate structures.

I do not have to go very far with this to realise that not only does
ordinary language allow or induce or impel me to proceed in this
delirious way, but that it is also the case that language does it itself.
Changes of meaning and etymological relationships are beyond
the control of the individual subject. Take puns for instance. My
nephew sometimes consumes a particularly long lollipop, which
answers to the proud name of *So long sucker*. As with all good
puns, which more often than not are groups of words rather than
single words, the amazing thing here is not that 'so long' and
'sucker' can each have more than one meaning, but that these
meanings combine to form at least two entirely different, but
coherent, phrases. If Brisset is delirious, at least we must grant
him extenuating circumstances. There is provocation; for homophony induces the speaker to use the multiple possibilities of
meaning that it creates.

What is more, the feeling is always pleasurable. The object of
the exercise is to convince, to influence, in a word, to act, to exert

power: punning is no more innocent than the other jokes analysed by Freud (see Todorov, 1970). It is caught in the same structure of alliance and domination. We should not be surprised, then, about the extensive use of punning jokes in advertising or in politics. Here is an example dating from the 1981 French presidential election: *un mythe errant, ça trompe énormément* (Mitterrand/a wandering myth is grossly deceptive). This is actually a pun on a pun, based on an old children's joke: *un éléphant, ça* (sa) *trompe* (an elephant deceives/an elephant's trunk). The political efficacy of the Mitterand pun depends upon a purely arbitrary combination of meanings arising out of homophony. It is not that the joke gained Giscard d'Estaing thousands of voters, as, by the same token, I would not claim that the appearance of the loveliest of Persian kittens on my television screen will persuade me to buy one brand of toilet paper rather than another. What I do claim, however, is that the joke had an effect. To begin with, it had an effect on me, since I remember it some seven years later (even as we probably all remember 'I like Ike!' long after we have forgotten most of Eisenhower's deeds and pronouncements, perhaps even what he looked like). The effect is social, and even political: a new possibility opened out by language has been taken up. A further branch of the rhizome has sprouted, adding a new text to the collective corpus of language. Let me provide another instance, which I hope will underline the point. E. P. Thompson (1968: p. 733) quotes one of the Luddite slogans: 'Long live the levelution'. Here homophony lets the Luddite militant interpret the new political ideas of the French Revolution in the terms of the older native tradition of the Levellers. It is language which allows this incorporation of the two traditions into a new political construct.

Such associations may be interlingual, as in Wolfson's device of transforming the hated words of his mother tongue into similar sounding words in French, German, Hebrew or Russian. It can also be intralingual, as in plays on proper names which ascribe meaning to what only has reference. This latter device is a favourite with advertisers. I recently read on the walls of the London underground (the kind of place where modern linguists do their fieldwork): 'Foiled again? Try Dillon's'. Is there not a certain amount of injustice in the fact that you can re-semanticise the names of your competitors, to their detriment? This injustice is part of the violence exerted by language. It is the violence of bad luck and of arbitrariness, which has nothing to do with Saussure's characterisation of the sign as arbitrary.

We can investigate the complexities of all this by looking at one of the slogans used in recent French student demonstrations. Monsieur Devaquet, the Secretary of State for Universities, was responsible for a series of reforms. His name became targetted in the protests against the proposed changes. The best of the slogans was probably, *un vacquet, ça va, deux vaquets, bonjour les dégâts*. The point of the joke (and it does not really matter that *vacquet* is not a word, for it easily could have been) is that it was based on a successful slogan for the anti-alcohol campaign on French television: *deux verres, ça va, trois verres, bonjour les dégâts* ('two glasses, allright, three glasses, there's trouble coming'). In its turn, this slogan employs a popular French turn of phrase – *bonjour* + noun phrase – which probably had its origin with Françoise Sagan's best seller of the fifties, *Bonjour Tristesse*. This title was itself borrowed from a poem by Paul Eluard. The whole process is a good example of the way that language, as a social organism, works; and it has nothing to do with structural linguistics. First, a poet coins a phrase – an intentional act if ever there was one, but an act set against a background made up of the rules of an already existing organism, in which, strictly speaking it would be illicit to *personify* sadness. Next, a novelist makes use of a frequent tactic in the rhetoric of titles, and uses a quotation for a title. Again, the act is intentional: attributable to the decision of one single individual. But the phrase soon becomes popular; it becomes common linguistic property. In the following stage, the phrase becomes productive: any noun phrase can be substituted for *tristesse*. This step cannot be ascribed to an individual speaker: language has taken over (that trope of personification again!). Next, a clever advertising copy-writer uses the phrase for a euphonic slogan – an intentional move again. Lastly, the slogan fits, by pure chance, part of the name of a minister, and someone successfully parodies it. But who? In the first demonstration, the joke already appeared on a dozen different banners. The only answer can be that the students as a *whole* did it, that it was a collective arrangement of utterance.[6]

Let us now move on from multiple analysis[7] to the second half of my ragbag, to what I have called the Wolfsonising of language.

Louis Wolfson was an American-Jewish schizophrenic who wrote his memoirs in French because he could not bear to hear the sounds of his mother tongue. There was more to him than this, however, and his particular art was that of *dubious synthesis*, putting together words that did not fit. He did this across several languages at once, giving us the ultimate translator's nightmare, by breaking with the logical principle of identity as it applies to language. Of course, language itself ignores this rule that language A is not language B. The peculiar mixture of French and Saxon that is English provides a typical illustration of the borrowings and blendings which are the norm; and didn't language itself incite Joyce to write Finnegan's Wake? Still, Wolfson's device remains shocking, as we can see from his Franco-Germanic-Hebraic translation of the sentence, 'Don't trip over the wire', into '*Tu nicht trébucher Über eth he zwirn*'.

Such practices of illicit synthesis are by no means limited to delirious logophiliacs. Another example is provided by Portmanteau words (even if the phrase comes from Lewis Carroll, hardly the sanest of Victorian academics). They point to an old practice: my etymological dictionary tells me that 'to scurry' (of a mouse) is to scatter in a hurry; and morphologists use a Sanskrit term, *bahuvrihi*, to refer to those compound words where the head noun is missing, as in *paperback*, which is not a back made of paper. There are also exocentric compounds, where there appears to be no relation at all between the words making up the compound and the compound itself – what has a cocktail got to do with the tail of a cock?

Such dubious syntheses occur not only at the level of words, but also at the level of sentences. In the famous lines by e. e. cummings:

anyone lived in a pretty home town
with up so floating many bells down

even after we realise that the 'anyone' is to be treated as a proper name, and that the second line places the right words in the wrong order, the rest of the first line still has to be interpreted. Taking my lead from Ruwet (1975), it can be treated as a portmanteau construction as follows: 'Anyone lived in a big town – how big? – pretty big': a pretty how town'. Such ellipsis is a version of what is known as multiple syntax, as in the following lines from *The Wasteland*, where 'the typist' is *at the same time* both subject and object of different verbs:

> At the violet hour, the evening hour that strives
> Homeward, and brings the sailor home from sea,
> The typist home at tea-time, clears her breakfast, lights
> Her stove, and lays out food in tins.

The main lesson to be drawn from my ragbag was stated at the beginning: while language provides the ground for a calculus, it also allows and even induces the breaking of every rule within that calculus. As a final demonstration of this, consider the first rule of syntax, that a sentence is composed of a noun phrase and a verb phrase, or a subject and a predicate. Then take the well-known phrase 'A poem is a poem is a poem'. It is a perfectly respectable pattern, and a productive one, since pretty much anything can be substituted for 'poem'. It has two recognised uses: as an intensive (in the example quoted) and as a marker of equality, the linguistic equivalent of a double use of the mathematical 'equals' sign (e.g. 'Crime is money is consideration'). Yet it breaks the first rule of any syntax, and cannot be accounted for within the rules of syntax. Perhaps we should change our theory!

## 4. An Alternative View of Language

The paradox is inescapable. Having sought to undermine *any* theory of language, I am tempted to formulate an alternative view of it. Even if I base my alternative view on the notion of the rhizome, which is something without fixed structure and with no determinate rules of ordering, doesn't the endeavour remain theoretical? Such conundrums are the very element in which postmodernism thrives, and my response has to be that any new rules for language will themselves be paradoxical.

I want to put forward four such rules[8]:

1. The first rule is the rule of excess (or lack, which is the same thing). A structural grammar is based on the idea that a language can be calculated using a limited number of rules. The rule of excess states that whatever the number of rules arrived at, one can always add rule $n+1$, or cancel one of the rules and arrive at the delirium of an $n-1$ grammar, or apply a non-recursive rule once

too often. An example of the n+1 case would be Perec's *La Disparition*, a lipogram whose additional rule is never to use the letter 'e'; an example of the n−1 condition would be Freud's joke: '*j'ai voyagé avec lui tête à bête*', which cancels out a generally accepted phonemic distinction; and an example of the multiple application of a rule meant to be applied once only can be seen in the 'illegitimately' double grammatical role of 'the typist' in the lines by Eliot which were quoted earlier. This rule of excess is, in fact, another version of the Grician principle of exploitation: language is built in such a way that there is not one of its rules which cannot be breached and thereby exploited.

2. The second rule is the rule of paradox, and it follows from what has just been said. The rule of paradox states that the *n* rules of any language must always be supplemented by rule n+1 which allows any or all of the *n* rules to be broken. This is actually how language works, and an inventory of tropes reads like a list of instances of this rule. Chomsky had a similar intuition when he formulated his paradox of nonsense: an ungrammatical sequence of words can always be made into a grammatical English sentence, by embedding it as an object completive within the frame, 'It is nonsense to say that . . .' (Chomsky, 1965: pp. 157–8).

3. The third rule is that of rhizome-work. It states that language is not organised like a mathematical structure, but (as with Freud's dream-work, which this rule imitates) that it is organised in accordance with the laws of condensation, displacement and compromise. One of Jakobson's most perceptive insights was his comparison of the linguistic opposition between syntagm and paradigm with the rhetorical opposition between metonym and metaphor. Developing that here, we can say that language is more plastic than the rules of grammar allow, and this is because it is based on the operation of metaphor (which accounts, for instance, for the device called conversion, when a word changes its paradigm: 'But me no but nor uncle me no uncle!', as the irate uncle says to the traitorous nephew in *Richard II*). Language, then, is no mathematical set. Language is a badger sett.

4. The fourth rule is the rule of corruption. It has been said that the founding moment for 'scientific linguistics' was the separation of synchrony from diachrony. Now, however, we must step backwards to the first Saussure, to the philologist. As my insistence on etymology has shown, language is not a timeless synchronic

structure. It is historical through and through, a treasury of words, phrases, constructions, and temporary rules, all, as Frederic Jameson (1981: pp. 140–1) would say, *sedimented* within language. From this diachronic point of view, an unstable and violent language constantly seeks to impose meaning upon a social subject which must equally resist and accept such imposition in the name of freedom of thought and expression. The result, of course, is compromise.

## 5. Afterword

Before these rules are consigned to the dustbin of history, where like all theory they belong, and we go back to enjoying our language, some clarification of that Heideggerian phrase, 'language speaks', is called for. I have used the phrase in an ambiguous way. On the one hand, it might mean that language is so powerful that it determines all meaning, making the speaker or writer a mere linguistic puppet. On the other hand, language may be seen as talking to us and offering us the freedom to explore innumerable paths within the rhizome. I believe that this opposition between constraint and creativity must somehow be overcome. The important act is that of playing with language, which is to say not only negotiating one's meaning with the language, but also taking and deploying the strategies of the language games within the concrete situations which exist in the context of a whole culture.

It has recently been reported that learning nursery rhymes helps develop intelligence and language skills. This confirms me in my view that Lewis Carroll was right to hold that nonsense has a prophylactic value, and, more than this, that it provides a privileged access to language since it mirrors its workings. Nonesense rather than the science of language: my alternative, postmodern view of language turns out to be not so new after all. This is another paradox, and a welcome one. It tells us why this postmodern view reaches parts of language that other theories fail to reach.

## Notes and References

1. There is an implicit opposition here between reality and the 'real'. This Lacanian notion will be explained in the second part of this paper.

2. Deleuze and Guattari ascribe different postulates to 'scientific linguistics' (of which more later); but the principle is the same, that linguistics is based on a number of postulates within the Galilean paradigm.

3. That they can only describe what they hear or read.

4. Alan Sheridan's glossary entry for these three terms, in his translation of Jacques Lacan, *The Four Fundamental Concepts of Psychoanalysis* (Penguin, 1977, pp. 279–80), is helpful:

[at first] Lacan regarded the "imago" as the proper study of psychology and identification as the fundamental psychical process. The imaginary was then the world, the register, the dimension of images, conscious or unconscious, perceived or imagined. In this respect, "imaginary" is not simply the opposite of "real": the image certainly belongs to reality . . . The notion of the symbolic came to the forefront in the Rome Report [1953]. The symbols referred to here are not icons . . . but signifiers . . . differential elements, in themselves without meaning, which acquire value only in their mutual relations . . . Henceforth it is the symbolic, not the imaginary, that is seen to be the determining order of the subject . . . The "real" emerges as a third term . . . it stands for what is neither symbolic nor imaginary . . . It began, naturally enough, by presenting, in relation to symbolic substitutions and imaginary variations, a function of constancy: "the real is that which always returns to the same place". It then became that before which the imaginary faltered, that over which the symbolic stumbles, that which is refractory, resistant . . . It is in this sense that the term begins to appear regularly . . . to describe that which is lacking in the symbolic order, the ineliminable residue of all articulation, the foreclosed element, which may be approached but never grasped . . . [eds]

5. When a student asks me why something cannot be said in a particular way, I know that the answer is 'because it is like this, and that is all there is to it'. Future tense and modal auxiliary cannot be combined in a formulation such as 'I'll can,' because *c'est comme ça et pas autrement*. The best proof of this is that in the language of Stevenson's highlanders in *Kidnapped* or *Catriona*, you *can*, or if you prefer, *you'll can*, combine them.

6. The link between advertising and student protest, apparent in the way that the best slogans in the recent demonstrations were travesties of advertising catch-phrases or of the titles of popular films and novels, supports Deleuze and Guattari's view of language. Slogans are of prime importance, as every old Leninist knows (Lenin, 1917). They make apparent the workings of that unstable and violent entity which we call language, and far from deriding the language of advertising, we should pay attention to it, for it shows language at work.

7. I have only given some examples of multiple analysis. Others that might be mentioned are: *false analysis* which presupposes a duality of correct and incorrect analysis; *folk-etymology*, what etymologists call metanalysis, which examines the historical changes undergone by words

or phrases (an *eke name* becomes a *nickname*, the old English *naedre* becomes *adder*); and all those innumerable linguistic games like *daft definitions* (What is the definition of 'dehydrate'? The answer is 'proportionally excess tax you are charged with for concealing your true income.') and *alphabet games* (here is one of George Perec's: dadedidodu. The interpretation of this sequence of vowels combined with the single consonant 'd' runs as follows: 'My father, an Englishman, is said to be rather plump.' In French: *dad est did dodu*).

8. The very fact of numbering them seems to testify to a continued, even if artificial, relationship with the narrative of science.

## Bibliography

BARTHES, R. (1978), *Leçon*, Paris, Seuil.

CALVET, L. J. (1974), *Linguistique et colonialisme*, Paris, Payot.

CHOMSKY, N. (1965), *Aspects of the Theory of Syntax*, Cambridge, Mass., MIT Press.

DELEUZE, G. and GUATTARI, F. (1980), *Milles plateaux*, Paris, Minuit.

DELEUZE, G. and GUATTARI, F. (1975), *Kafka*, Paris, Minuit.

JAMESON, F. (1981), *The Political Unconscious*, Cornell, Cornell UP.

LACLAU, E. and MOUFFE, C. (1985), *Hegemony and Socialist Strategy*, London, Verso.

LECERCLE, J.-J., (1985), *Philosophy Through the Looking-Glass*, London, Hutchinson.

LECERCLE, J.-J., (1988), 'Répétition et vérité dans *Caleb Williams*', *Tropismes*, No. 5, Paris.

LECERCLE, J.-J., (1988), 'The misprision of pragmatics' in A. Phillips Griffiths (ed.), *Contemporary French Philosophy*, Cambridge, CUP.

LENIN, V. I., (1917), *On Slogans*.

LYOTARD, J. F. (1979), *La condition postmoderne*, Paris, Minuit.

LYOTARD, J. F. (1983), *Le différend*, Paris, Minuit.

MILLER, J. A. (1977), 'Suture, elements of the logic of the signifier', *Screen*, Vol. 18, No. 4.

MILNER, J.-C. (1978), *L'Amour de la langue*, Paris, Seuil.

MILNER, J.-C. (1983), *Les noms indistincts*, Paris, Seuil.

RUWET, N. (1975), 'Parallelismes et déviations en poésie' in J. Kristeva, J.-C. Milner and N. Ruwet (eds), *Langue, Discours, Société*, Paris, Seuil.

THOMPSON, E. P. (1968), *The Making of the English Working Class*, Harmondsworth, Penguin.

TODOROV, T. (1970), 'Freud sur l'énonciation', *Langages*, No. 17, Paris.

# Chapter 4

# Reactionary Postmodernism?

Alex Callinicos

What is postmodernism? What political implications does it have? These were the two questions which I set out to answer in this essay. As I went on, it became increasingly clear that they were inseparable. Determining the referent of the word 'postmodern', a word suddenly, in the mid-1980s, on everyone's lips, turned out to depend on understanding one aspect of politics in the Reagan–Thatcher era.

## For and against the Enlightenment

The politics of postmodernism has already been the subject of considerable debate. One, only slightly caricatured, way of stating the central issue, as it seems to present itself to many of those involved is: Was the Enlightenment a Good Thing? By 'Enlightenment' I mean, roughly speaking, the project on which the *philosophes* of eighteenth-century France and Scotland, and their followers elsewhere, embarked. Its basis was the belief that the development of scientific knowledge along lines opened up by Galileo and Newton would lead to the rational control by human beings of their natural and social environment. It was a view epitomized by Condorcet's conception of history as 'the progress of the human mind'.

Although 'modern' is an old word, the *philosophes* seem to have set a permanent stamp on what we think of as modernity, so that it is identified with the kind of society produced by the realisation of the Enlightenment project. Thus sociological definitions of modern society tend it to treat it, by contrast with its traditional predecessors, as charcterised by constant innovation arising in particular from the systematic practical application of the physical and mathematical sciences in order to increase human control of nature. An early instance of this approach is the sketch of industrial society offered by Condorcet's disciple Saint-Simon.

Lyotard defines '*postmodern* as incredulity toward metanarratives'.[1] Whereas hitherto knowledge has required legitimation in terms of the kind of grand narrative offered, for example, by Hegel and Marx, today it does not. The main reason Lyotard gives for this shift is 'the failure of the modern project'. The *philosophes*' 'idea of progress as possible, probable or necessary was rooted in the certainty that the development of the arts, technology, knowledge and liberty would be profitable to mankind as a whole.' But this certainty has collapsed in the course of the 'sanguinary last two centuries'. 'What kind of thought is able to sublate (*Aufheben*) Auschwitz in a general ... process towards a universal emancipation?'[2] Rather than seek to weave the individuality of events into some comprehensive scheme of human liberation, 'let us wage a war on totality; let us be witnesses to the unpresentable; let us activate the differences and save the honour of the name.'[3]

Somewhat similar sentiments were expressed with unparalleled force and eloquence by Adorno and Horkheimer in the masterworks of Frankfurt Marxism: *Dialectic of Enlightenment, Eclipse of Reason, Minima Moralia*, and *Negative Dialectics*. Yet it is Habermas, the social theorist generally identified as their intellectual heir who has emerged as the chief defender of the Enlightenment against postmodernism. He argues that theorists of modernity have tended to operate with a one-sided conception of rationality, according to which the subject seeks to understand nature as part of the effort to control it. This view of reason as instrumental is, according to Habermas, closely associated with the differentiation in recent centuries of the social 'lifeworld', constituted by unarticulated traditions underpinning everyday life, into autonomous economic and political sub-systems which are no longer intelligible to the agents caught up in them. This rationalisation of social life is, however, selective: a broader, *communicative* reason implicit in every speech act is also at work in modernity – present, for example, in the development of universal normative structures such as law and morality, and in the evolution of representative democracy. Those who fail to grasp the fundamentally communicative nature of reason must either treat the colonization of the lifeworld by market and state as the inevitable price of modernisation or, like Lyotard, treat modernity and reason itself as fatally compromised by the selective forms they have taken under the reign of instrumental rationality.[4]

Habermas has given these arguments a political inflection by associating the kind of critique of modernity offered by Lyotard with the ideas of the neo-conservative right. This has, I suspect, caused some puzzlement in the English-speaking world, where Lyotard, along with Foucault, Derrida, Deleuze et al., is associated with the intellectual avant-garde and the political Left. This bemusement has much to do with the decontextualised way in which German thought is received in Anglophone intellectual culture. It may be a healthy reaction to the idiot Germanophobia which distorted discussion of Hegel and Nietzsche by English-speaking philosophers in the first half of the century that Heidegger is now thought of as a precursor of Derrida and the Yale Deconstructionists rather than as an apologist for Nazism, but it does make one less sensitive to the political resonances of Habermas's polemic with postmodernism.

This political dimension, however, seems to me crucial to understanding Habermas's writings on modernity. Their passion and directness (not always the kind of qualities that first come to mind when reading him) reflect the fact that Habermas is writing within a culture where the critique of the Enlightenment has been as much the property of the Right as of the Left. He believes that Lyotard's celebration of fragmentation creates a vacuum in which the demand for the restoration of an 'organic' pre-modern social order can take shape. In Germany this demand has all too definite a political meaning – fascism. Hence there is a necessary connection between Habermas's critique of postmodernism and his attacks on the various strands of conservative thought in German society. One position can, he believes, all too easily pass over into the other. Thus Habermas is suspicious of the vogue in some circles for the reactionary legal theorist Carl Schmitt, denouncing 'those left-wingers in the Federal Republic, and above all Italy, who drive out the Devil with Beelzebub, by filling the gap left by the non-existent Marxist theory of democracy with Schmitt's fascist critique of democracy'.[5]

For Habermas, then, postmodernism is the latest episode in the Counter-Enlightenment. The problem with this approach is that it tells us little about what distinguishes postmodernism from what, on this view, are its predecessors. In what follows I shall try to explore postmodernism's politics by considering what, in the past few years, has provoked such an explosion of discourse on modernity and its putative successor. The conference for which this paper was originally written is merely one instance of the vast proliferation of *talk* about postmodernism – of symposia, articles, collections, conferences, even a series in the *Guardian* newspaper. The concept of modernity as, in Habermas's words, 'the rational organization of everyday social life'[6] has been with us for a good two centuries. Why now, in the 1980s, this garrulous certainty about its exhaustion?

**Defining Postmodernism**

One characteristic of this discourse is the desire to define post-modernism. While trying not wholly to succumb to this desire, I think it is necessary to draw some distinctions. Three separate intellectual trends have been brought together under the general heading of 'postmodernism'. The first is post-structuralism, the somewhat heterogeneous group of French thinkers who have nevertheless participated in the common effort of subverting the notions of truth, meaning and subjectivity held to be defining features of Western metaphysics. The most important names associated with this project are those of Foucault, Derrida and Deleuze. Secondly, there is what might be called the theory of postmodernity, and more particularly the idea that the advanced countries are entering a new, post-industrial phase, in which the production of goods is supplanted in social and economic import-ance by the development and dissemination of scientific knowledge. Daniel Bell and Alain Touraine are perhaps the best-known proponents of this analysis. Finally, there is what I shall call for simplicity's sake cultural Postmodernism, apparently the oldest claimant to the name (and therefore distinguished in what follows by being capitalised), originating in the reaction against abstraction in painting and the International Style in architecture that has gathered force in the past twenty years.

While the three kinds of postmodernism, philosophy, social theory and aesthetic, developed according to what seem to be irreducibly different dynamics, connections can be, and of course have been, made between them. Indeed Lyotard's significance lies less in the originality or penetration of his writings than in their identification of a common logic. One could put it this way. According to Lyotard, the kind of science which prevails in post-industrial society resembles discourse as it is conceived in post-structuralist thought, dispersed and heterogeneous, making no claim to truth, a plurality of games pursuing their course in a manner identical to Postmodern art, which also refuses the whole and delights in fragmentation. Post-structuralism and cultural Postmodernism do not so much reflect the structure of post-industrial society as actively participate in its inner being.

This construction does not hold together very well under examination, leaving behind the discourse which seeks to weave them together into aspects of the postmodern. More specifically, the claim of the post-structuralists to have achieved a radical insight into the nature of being and language, of the theorists of post-industrial society to have discovered a new stage of historical development, of the aestheticians of the Postmodern to have distinguished a major cultural sea-change – all these claims cannot be sustained. Thus, in the first place, none of the different variants of post-structuralism seem to me tenable for reasons that I shall only sketch out here, having developed my arguments at length elsewhere.[7] A mistaken philosophy of language developed from Saussure's writings encourages post-structuralists to conceive of discourse as a proliferation of signifiers denying us any access to an independent reality or (in the more extreme versions) placing in question the very existence of such a reality – a conception which also renders problematic post-structuralist discourse itself. Further difficulties arise from the tendency to borrow from Nietzsche a conception of power so all-embracing as to incorpoate every aspect of human life – including, once again, the discourse which claims to trace the genealogies of forms of domination. Take, finally, perhaps post-structuralism's most distinctive claim, its denial of any identity, coherence, or continuity to the individual human agent. Only Deleuze and Guattari have had the philosophical courage to develp the kind of metaphysics required to make out this claim. The result, on display in *Mille Plateaux*, is a bizarre if often entertaining neo-Romantic *Naturphilosophie*. Prudently wishing to avoid committing himself to such a position, Foucault nevertheless sought to employ concepts such as power and resistance, despite their evident dependence on some kind of theory of human nature. He was therefore forced into a series of hesitations, silences, ambiguities, and plain ambiguities well captured by Charles Taylor when he accused Foucault of 'talking . . . out of both sides of his mouth'.[8]

At least post-structuralism gave birth to grand, original, exciting ideas. The social theory of postmodernity is, like them, false, but lacks their brilliance. To read Bell's *The Coming of Post-Industrial Society* (1974), perhaps the most systematic version of this theory, is to sample most of the characteristic fallacies of post-war Anglo-Saxon social science. Typically enough, the US is treated in isolation from the world-system into which it is inserted, and its condition conceived teleologically as the end-state towards which all industrial societies are evolving. The emerging post-industrial society is a 'knowledge society' both because of the 'centrality of *theoretical* knowledge' in technological innovation and because a growing proportion of the workforce are employed in knowledge-related activities. Many of the features of the managerial revolution which supposedly occurred in the early twentieth century are projected onto post-industrial society. Thus corporations are increasingly oriented towards the welfare of their employees, while '*today ownership is simply a legal fiction*'.[9]

One does not have to be a Marxist to find in this little more than a compendium of errors.[10] Bell was unfortunate in that his book appeared at the very onset of a succession of worldwide crises of overproduction. One aspect of the consequent stagnation of industrial production in the West has been the emergence now of good, old-fashioned speculative money capitalism on a gargantuan scale: the best illustration is provided by the take-over booms, and their sleazy concomitant, the insider-trading scandals, on Wall Street and in the City of London during the bull market which ended so abruptly on 19 October 1987. Contrary to Bell's crass optimism, the 'legal fiction' of ownership proved very important indeed to the victims of takeover bids and greenmail scams. The one trend to have lent some plausibility to the idea of a post-industrial society, the decline in the proportion of output and employment taken by manufacturing production in most OECD countries is best seen as part of a global reorganisation of capital, the emergence of a 'world manufacturing system', sited in various parts of the Third World as well as in the Western metropolis.[11] The extent of these changes should not, however, be exaggerated: the less developed countries had a slightly smaller share of world industrial production in 1984 than they had in 1948.[12]

Finally, Bell's prediction that 'the class of knowledge-workers is becoming predominant'[13] has not been borne out. Take California, the prototypical post-industrial society, where services accounted for 70 per cent of employment in 1985. While the recessions of 1979–80 and 1981–3 wiped out much of the state's heavy industry – autos, steel, tyres – new jobs have been concentrated in low-tech, low-productivity sectors, Californian costs in that arche-typical sweated industry, textiles, now match those of Hong Kong and Taiwan, while the *Financial Times* reports that even 'Silicon Valley companies typically combine a small highly-paid white-collar workforce with a pool of low-skilled and relatively low-paid production workers'.[14] Hardly the 'knowledge-society' anticipated by Bell and Lyotard.

Beyond these empirical objections is the more fundamental point that the concept of post-industrial society is, as Krishan Kumar has noted, an inflection of the problematic of modernity.[15] Modernity is characterised by the systematic application of science to control the natural and social environment. The difference between industrial and post-industrial society revolves, according to Bell, around a change in the source of innovation, in which theoretical inquiry replaces piecemeal tinkering. The concepts of the two kinds of society share a common technological determinism, according to which the social structure can be read off from the nature of technological innovation. It is characteristic of Lyotard's casual attitude towards consistency that he should so readily employ a concept whose intelligibility depends on the original Enlightenment project.

Theorising about cultural Postmodernism might at first glance seem more robust, inasmuch as it is less ambitious, claiming to identify the emergence of a cluster of new artistic movements. Indeed, Charles Jencks, one of the originators of the term 'Post-modern', seeks to restrict its extension to a limited set of cases. He denounces 'Nothing Post-Modernism', the promiscuous use of 'Post-Modern' to refer to '*everything* that was different from High Modernism'. Lyotard, in particular, is taken to task for confusing 'Post-Modernism with the latest avant-gardism, that is Late Modernism'. Rather it should be understood as '*double-coding: the combination of Modern techniques with something else (usually traditional building) in order to communicate with the public and a concerned minority, usually other architects*'. Although intended originally to apply to architecture, this definition is extended to cover other media which have experienced in the past decades a 'return to the larger Western tradition'.[16]

Perhaps this does identify accurately certain shifts – the revival of ornament in architecture, and of figuration and expression in painting. But the idea that 'double-coding' distinguishes the Post-modern from the Modern in art (understood all-embracingly) seems on the face of it extraordinary. The master-works of Modernist writing – think of *The Wasteland* or *Ulysses* – are characterised precisely by their conscious relation to, as well as discontinuity with tradition. Thus Stephen Spender writes that T. S. Eliot was

> a poet who brought into consciousness and into confrontation with one another, two opposite things: the spiritually negative character of the contemporary world and the spiritually positive character of the past tradition ... The past and the modern co-exist in his poetry as an imagined present of conflicting symbols to which are attached values of spiritual life or death.[17]

One might argue that while Eliot uses Modernist techniques to explore the disintegration of tradition, modernity's distance from the past, the Postmodern represents, as Jencks puts it, a *return* to tradition. But even if one accepts this contrast, the Modern and the Postmodern still share, on this account, the fundamental feature of 'double-coding', the consciously achieved co-existence and interaction in the same text of different discourses. (One could be less kind about the form this takes in Postmodern art. '*Punk* bricolage' is how Peter Fuller describes it). Jencks's narrow definition of cultural Postmodernism does not, therefore, seem to

provide grounds for treating the artistic developments he describes
as a break with Modernism. Fuller suggests that they 'make sense
only in terms of *reaction* to the Modernist art that went before.
The pendulum has swung, but it has done so only within that ever
narrowing, and ever more restricting, funnel of Modernist art
history'.[18]

Jencks' identification of the Postmodern with 'double-coding' is
interesting because it is characteristic of much discussion of the
subject in claiming as exclusive to Postmodernism the reflexive
properties that were normally thought of as peculiar to Modernism.
Sometimes the results of this approach verge on the absurd. Thus
Umberto Eco, to whom Jencks owes the notion of double-coding,
gives as an example of the 'postmodern attitude' a man saying to a
woman: 'As Barbara Cartland would put it, I love you madly'. Eco
comments: 'He loves her, but he loves her in an age of lost
innocence'. Postmodernism is a matter of 'irony, metalinguistic
play, enunciation squared'.[19] But if we are to take this kind of
word-play as definitive of the Postmodern, then the English upper
and upper-middle classes have been practising it for much of this
century, or, if not they, then their humourists. Is P. G. Wode-
house, then, to become a precursor of Postmodernism? We should
not let such absurdities blind us to the strength of the urge, of
which the discourse of postmodernism is the symptom, to discover
some great, and recent socio-cultural transformation. It is this urge
which requires analysis.

## Jameson on Postmodernism

While Frederic Jameson defines cultural Postmodernism very
differently from Jencks and Eco, he too claims to have detected a
major change. Jameson, in a widely discussed and highly stimul-
ating essay, treats Postmodernism as a particular form of *mimesis*,
a particular way of representing the world. He identified various
features of the Postmodern which, he contends, distinguish it from
the Modern. Contemporary works of art, Jameson argues, are
particularly depthless, and drained of real emotion, filled instead
with an euphoric celebration of the disintegration of the self,
relating to other works only in the form of pastiche, a fake nostalgia
taking the place of any real connection with the past, while any

critical distance from the present is cancelled. While, in all these
respects, Postmodernism might seem to mark a degeneration from
the achievements of High Modernism, Jameson wishes 'to reject
moralizing condemnations of the Postmodern and of its essential
triviality'. He prefers to discuss it in the spirit of the *Communist
Manifesto*, where Marx advocates 'a type of thinking that would be
capable of grasping the demonstrably baleful features of capitalism
along with its extra-ordinary and liberating dynamism simultaneously, within a single thought'. Postmodern art must be seen as
'so many different approaches to the representation of (a new)
reality', namely the new phase of capitalist development which
Jameson calls 'multinational capitalism' and Ernest Mandel late
capitalism, 'a third great expansion of capitalism (after the earlier
expansions of the national market and the older imperialist system
. . .)'. Just as Realism corresponded to the first phase, competitive
capitalism, and Modernism to the second, monopoly capitalism, so
Postmodernism seeks to represent contemporary, multinational
capitalism.[20]

Jameson's suspicion of the snobbery implicit in some dismissals
of Postmodern art, and his insistence on understanding and
explanation, rather than condemnation, are admirable. Nevertheless, his own treatment of Postmodernism is highly problematic. As
Mike Davis observes in a perceptive critique of Jameson's essay,

> like all imposing totalizations (modes of thought that Althusser,
> among others, has taught us to be wary of), Jameson's Post-
> Modernism tends to homogenize the details of the contemporary
> landscape, to subsume under a master-concept too many contra-
> dictory phenomena which, though undoubtedly visible in the
> same chronological moment, are nonetheless separated in their
> true temporalities.[21]

Davis makes the fundamental point that Jameson's periodisation
of the 'cultural logic of late capitalism' is at odds with his main
economic authority. For Mandel, late capitalism emerged after
1945, while Jameson identifies the changes which gave rise to
cultural Postmodernism with the 1960s. No explanation is given of
this apparent time-lag. One has the impression that the sense of a
fundamental change which has altered our modes of thinking and
feeling is more important to Jameson than any precise historical
analysis of the actual transformations the capitalist world-system

has undergone. Thus, in *Marxism and Form* (1971), he drew a similar contrast, this time between pre-war capitalism and 'post-industrial monopoly capitalism', which has 'brought with it an increasing occultation of the class structure ... since the onset of the Cold War', so that 'our experience is no longer whole', and 'the products with which we are furnished are utterly without depth'. Jameson used this contrast brilliantly in his analysis of Surrealism as peculiar to a semi-industrialised economy, in which the traces of human labour are still to be detected in its products. Nevertheless, one cannot help having doubts about the facility with which different dates, and accounts of capitalist development (Mandel's recently, Baran's and Sweezy's in *Marxism and Form*) are employed to support Jameson's sense of 'a cultural trans-formation of signal proportions, a historical break of an unex-pectedly absolute kind'.[22]

There are more specific difficulties of detail and interpretation. Jameson has on several occasions given as a prime example of Postmodern art what he calls 'nostalgia film',

> a formal compensation for the enfeeblement of historicity in our own time, and as it were a glossy fetish in the service of that unsatisfied craving. In nostalgia film, the image – the surface sheen of a period fashion reality – is consumed, having been transformed into a visual commodity.[23]

Bertolucci's *The Conformist* is, for Jameson, a case in point. I doubt whether this is an adequate judgement of this complex film, but Jameson's entire discussion of 'nostalgia films' is unsatisfactory. Thus we are asked to believe that what he regards as the recovery of the Eisenhower era in *American Graffiti* (the film is in fact set in 1962, on the very edge of the Vietnam years), released in 1973, permitted the 'stylistic recuperation' of the 1930s in such films as *The Conformist*, released in 1970! *Body Heat* is supposedly 'set in some eternal Thirties', even though its dialogue, not to speak of its treatment of sex, the police, and the legal system bear the unmistakable stamp of the 1960s. Nor is the handling of the past in perhaps the greatest of the 'nostalgia films' which Jameson discusses, Polanski's *Chinatown*, the presentation of 'a glossy mirage'. Indeed, Polanski's use of *film-noir* techniques to uncover the dark secrets behind the creation of modern Los Angeles seems to be a masterly demonstration of the capacity of at least some contemporary art to transcend the superficiality and affectlessness to which Jameson claims it is condemned.[24]

Jameson's honourable attempt to continue the tradition of Hegelian Marxism leads him in this instance not merely to reductionism, but to the fallacy of *tout comprendre, c'est tout pardonner*. Thus he takes up the notion of the sublime, which Lyotard has transplanted from Burke's and Kant's aesthetics in order to characterise Postmodern art as seeking to present the unpresentable, in its very construction displaying the impossibility of representing certain Ideas.[25] Jameson tries to give this claim a 'moment of truth' by arguing that multinational capitalism is peculiarly 'unrepresentable', though he is careful to stress that this is not the same as being 'unknowable': the 'global world system' may be grasped conceptually, but no sensuous image can reveal its nature. His argument for saying that late capitalism is peculiar in this respect is highly unconvincing. It turns on the claim that while steam-engines and motor cars (the technologies supposedly characteristic of the earlier, competitive and monopoly phases of capitalist development) can be pictorially represented, computers, their postmodern counterpart, cannot.[26] But why should this be so? And what is a Marxist doing believing that the nature of particular phases of historical development can be captured by the prevailing technique?

Marx himself thought, of course, that capitalism necessarily involved a systematic difference between its surface appearance and underlying character, such that its nature could only be understood through the construction of a body of theoretical abstractions. If this is right, then it is of capitalism's essence to be an instance of the sublime (in the sense in which Lyotard and Jameson use the term), and the latter concept's particular association with the Postmodern collapses. Lyotard unintentionally makes the same point when he argues that various Marxian concepts, for example, those of labour-power and of the proletariat, are cases of the sublime.[27] It is not clear to me that he is doing anything more than pointing to a general feature of modern science since the seventeenth century, namely that it constructs theoretical concepts referring to unobservable entities. The passages in *Capital* where Marx justifies his own scientific practice by appealing to the model of classical physics are well known.[28]

Lyotard's identification of the sublime with so long-established a feature of theoretical enquiry as the explanation of the observed in terms of the unobservable is an instance of what the otherwise sympathetic Richard Rorty describes as his 'casual and anecdotal attempts' to justify his theory of the postmodern by claiming to have discovered 'a recent change in the nature of science'.[29] The effect is to deprive the notion of the sublime of the specific content given it by Burke and Kant. Thus for Kant the sublime involves 'a representation of *limitlessness*, yet with a super-added thought of its totality'. It arises when 'the mind has been incited to abandon sensibility, and to employ itself upon ideas involving higher finality'.[30] Clearly the sublime thus conceived has nothing to do either with the procedures of modern science or with Postmodern art which, according to Lyotard, 'wage(s) war on totality' rather than seeking to represent it. It is unfortunate that Jameson's desire dialectically to weave every phenomenon into an integrated whole should have permitted Lyotard thus to lead him up the garden path.

The criticism I have made of Jameson's analysis of cultural Postmodernism should not be allowed to obscure its real strengths. In the first place, his definition of the Postmodern certainly captures some cases of contemporary art: it fits Andy Warhol and his entourage, for example, like a glove. Secondly, and more fundamentally, his treatment of this art as a form of *mimesis* does pose the question of what changes in our experience of the social world might have given rise to the current discourse of post-modernism. It is on this discourse, the claim that we live in a postmodern epoch, that I shall concentrate in the rest of this essay; the three intellectual phenomena which it attempts to weave together – post-structuralism, the social theory of postmodernity, and cultural Postmodernism – emerged, in my view, for reasons largely distinct from those responsible for the proliferating discourse of postmodernism.

**Fragmentation and Late Capitalism**

Jameson tries to capture the distinctive nature of our experience of late capitalism when he writes of

the extraordinary surface of the photorealist cityscape, where

even the automobile wrecks gleam with some hallucinatory
splendour ... How urban squalor can be delight to the eyes,
when expressed in commodification, and how an unparalleled
quantum leap in the alienation of daily life in the city can now be
experienced in the form of a strange new hallucinatory exhilara-
tion – these are some of the questions that confront us ...[31]

To me at least this description rings true.

Lyotard seems to be getting at a similar point when he says that
Postmodern art lacks Modernism's 'nostalgia of the whole and the
one'.[32] Certainly Eliot's poetry is a clear case of such a nostalgia.
What makes him a Modernist is the way in which his yearning for
an organic social order is married to techniques which convey an
intensely felt experience of fragmentation. Spender indeed calls
Eliot 'a poet of fragments' and writes of *The Wasteland*:

> The poem is about a fragmented culture, so the fragmentariness
> seems suited to it. Fragmentariness when projected onto many
> scenes, with shifts of centre of attention and mood, lends force
> to the obsession, gives the poem its apocalyptic visionary
> force.[33]

One might then say that where Modernism experiences fragmentation as loss, Lyotard and other prophets of the postmodern
celebrate it.

As reference to Eliot should make clear, there is nothing new
about this experience of fragmentation. Nowhere has it been
analysed more brilliantly than by Adorno and Horkheimer in the
1930s and 1940s, above all in the former's literary masterpiece,
*Minima Moralia*. For Adorno, this experience was to be understood in terms of the various ways in which the mechanisms of
commodity fetishism in the era of monopoly capitalism reduced
human subjects to passive and isolated consumers. When all
appropriate qualifications have been made for the Frankfurt
School's tendency to underestimate the underlying economic
contradictions, and to overestimate the normative integration of
the masses into the existing order, a fundamental kernel of truth in
their analysis remains.[34]

There have been various attempts to characterise the changes in
the quality of social experience to which the early Frankfurt school
pointed. One of the most interesting, by Richard Sennett, focuses

on the erosion of public life, its transformation into a domain where the mass of citizens play at best a passive role, and the valorisation of personal relations as both a refuge from a harsh social world and the realm in which individuals can achieve genuine self-realisation.[35] Sennett traces the development of this culture of intimacy in the nineteenth-century European city, but emphasises also its extension and consolidation in the twentieth century. Arguably the turning-point in this process was the emergence in the inter-war era and consolidation after 1945 of what Michel Aglietta calls 'Fordism', combining *'semi-automatic assembly-line production'* with the *'mass consumption'* of the products of these processes. Aglietta argues:

> With Fordism ... the generalization of commodity relations extended to their domination of practices of consumption. This was a mode of consumption restructured by capitalism, because the time devoted to consumption witnessed an increasing density in the individual use of commodities and a notable impoverishment of non-commodity interpersonal relations.[36]

We could see, then, the penetration of mass commodity production into the sphere of consumption as underlying the spreading privatisation of social life analysed by Sennett and others.

Recent decades have taken the process of fragmentation further. Habermas aptly summarised these developments when he spoke recently of the 'really existing surrealism' of contemporary urban life.[37] It is open to question, however, whether the post-war epoch has seen a qualitative change in this respect rather than the quantitative expansion of economic practices whose effect is the disintegration of any public sphere, and the privatisation of social life. Bell, otherwise all too eager to detect epochal change in the past generation, observes:

> In terms of *daily life* of individuals, more change was experienced between 1850 and 1940 – when railroad, steamships, telegraph, electricity, telephone, automobile, radio and airplanes were introduced – than in the period since when the future is supposed to be accelerating. In fact, other than television, there has not been one major innovation which has affected the daily life of persons to the extent of the items enumerated.[38]

What, in any case, might lead one to draw comfort from our

experience of the social world as fragmented? The answer might lie less in any change in this experience than in a diminished sense of possible alternatives. High Modernism's 'nostalgia of the whole' involved some belief in the existence of a feasible alternative – whether the alternative take a reactionary form, as in Eliot's dreams of a Coleridgean clerisy, or a revolutionary one, in the shape of the communism of Mayakovsky and Brecht. Perhaps it is the apparent loss of any reasonable hope in a desirable alternative to the present which gives rise to the idea that we live in a postmodern world.

## The Moment of Postmodernism

If this thought is along the right lines, then one might develop it by trying to identify the historical conjuncture in which this fore-closure of perceived possibilities occurred. A clue is provided by Perry Anderson's '*conjunctural* explanation of the set of aesthetic practices and doctrines subsequently grouped together as "Modernist"'. He identifies 'three decisive co-ordinates' present in Europe *circa* 1914. First, 'the codification of a highly formalized *academicism* in the visual and other arts, which itself was institutionalized within the official régimes of states and society still massively pervaded, often dominated, by aristocratic or land-owning classes.' Secondly, 'the still incipient, hence essentially *novel* emergence within these societies of the key technologies or inventions of the second industrial revolution: telephone, radio, automobile, aircraft and so on'. Thirdly, 'the imaginative proximity of social revolution'.

> European Modernism in the first years of this century thus flowered in the space between a still usable classical past, a still indeterminate technical present, and still unpredictable political future. Or, it arose at the intersection between a semi-aristocratic ruling order, a semi-industrialized capitalist economy, and a semi-emergent, or -insurgent, labour movement.[39]

Anderson argues that these three conditions disappeared after 1945, with the stabilisation throughout Western capitalism of advanced liberal democracy and a Fordist regime of accumulation permitting the incorporation of the organized workers' movement.

'What marks the typical situation of the contemporary artist in the West, it might be said, is . . . the closure of horizons: without an appropriate past, or imaginable future, in an interminably recurrent present'. [40] Persuasive though this analysis is in many respects, it requires extension in order to explain why the discourse of the postmodern has emerged in the past decade or so rather than in the 1950s and 1960s.

Two factors seem crucial here. First, the end of the post-war boom undermined the faith in an enlightened liberal technocracy of which Bell is such a prominent exponent. Secondly, this economic change, in the late 1960s and early 1970s, was accompanied by the sharpest upturn in the European class struggle for fifty years – the events of May–June 1968 in France, the Italian 'Hot Autumn' of 1969, the strikes against the 1970–4 Heath government in Britain, the Portuguese revolution of 1974–5, and the struggles surrounding the end of Francoism in Spain during 1975–6. Even the US experienced the most militant strikes and the biggest political crisis since the 1930s. These conditions drew a generation into radical political activity, often in the form of a commitment to one of the far-left organisations which grew enormously in size and influence during these years. But the euphoria of '68 and after was followed in the late 1970s by the widespread collapse of revolutionary hopes, arising from a variety of factors – the success of the various reformist parties in containing the genuine working-class radicalisation which occurred at the height of this upturn, the shift of the Western workers' movement from offensive to defensive in the face of mass unemployment and a new and aggressive militancy on the employers' part, and the rise of the 'new social movements' (feminism, black nationalism, gay liberation etc.), which challenged the revolutionary left's often highly reductionist preoccupation with class antagonisms. There followed a massive exodus from the far left, and the collapse of many *groupuscules*. [41]

There has emerged from the ruins a generation, now in its thirties and forties, of intellectuals and quasi-intellectuals who derive from their past leftist sympathies and present experience considerable scepticism about the rationality and justice of the existing order, but who have also lost any belief in a desirable and feasible alternative. At the same time, the rapid expansion of posts in the 'new middle class' of highly-paid professional, managerial, and administrative employees, a social layer that in America and

Britain has done well out of the Reagan–Thatcher era, has offered
the disillusioned children of '68 the prospect of social mobility and
constantly increased consumption.[42] Who could be better qualified
to provide a rationale for lying back and enjoying late capitalism
than Lyotard, himself an ex-militant of the semi-Trotskyist *Socialisme ou Barbarie* group?

That this is what Lyotard effectively does seems to me beyond
question. One might put it this way. The central political concept
of classical Marxism is that of socialist revolution, the conquest of
state power by the working class. In the 1970s Foucault and
Deleuze argued that we must abandon this objective: to pursue it
could only lead to a new version of the Gulag Archipelago. In
place of revolution they set the notion of resistance – of contesting
the existing apparatus of power–knowledge in a decentralised,
fragmented fashion, women, gays, prisoners, mental patients,
gypsies all fighting in their own separate ways. One might wish to
quarrel with this notion – I certainly would – but it is part of a
recognisably political theory and strategy. Lyotard's talk of 'acti-
vating the differences', however, represents a depoliticisation, one
might also say an aestheticization, of resistance. The production –
no, even the consumption – of Postmodern art counts as resistance. The term has ceased to possess any connotation of political
struggle – a convenient enough shift for the readers and auditors
of this discourse, who may now sample the benefits of commodity
fetishism without a twinge of guilt.

Lyotard often compares his position to Adorno's. And indeed
the latter's *Aesthetic Theory* does treat reflection on Modernist art
as the highest form of cognition. But what makes it so is the fact
that, according to Adorno, this art conceals in its structure the
aspiration to an unalienated, emancipated existence, a world beyond
class exploitation, commodity fetishism, and the domination of
nature. In Lyotard's terms, Adorno suffers from the characteristic
Modernist 'nostalgia of the whole'.[43] Short-circuiting the need for
any serious analysis of Stalinism and fascism, and collapsing into
the traditional liberal critique of 'totalitarianism', Lyotard claims
that 'the price to pay for such an illusion is terror'.[44] It is here that
postmodernism does seem reactionary – in its attempt to repress
our sense of other possibilities, of different ways of living, of a
change that goes beyond piecemeal modification, the aspiration,
shared not simply by Marx and his followers, but by Fourier and

the other Utopian socialists, to an emancipated society. A social theory which denies that there are other possible social worlds thereby gives up any pretension to be critical.

The discourse of postmodernism is therefore best seen as the product of a socially mobile intelligentsia in a climate dominated by the retreat of the Western labour movement and the 'overconsumptionist' dynamic of capitalism in the Reagan–Thatcher era. From this perspective, the term 'postmodern' would seem to be a floating signifier by means of which this intelligentsia has sought to articulate its political disillusionment and its aspiration to a consumption-oriented lifestyle.[45] The difficulties involved in identifying a referent for this term are therefore beside the point, since talk about postmodernism turns out to be less about the world than the expression of a particular generation's sense of an ending.

Having reasons for holding fast against the current to the goal of 'human emancipation', as Marx called it, requires several things. I shall conclude by mentioning just two. First, a frontal challenge must be made to the idea of the 'death of the subject', the reduction effected by post-structuralism of the human organism to a cluster of subindividual drives and desires collected together according to the requirements of supra-individual apparatuses. The aporias of Foucault's account of power and resistance, mentioned above, indicate that no critical theory can fail to treat human beings as centres capable of initiating actions. Contrary to the claims of both post-structuralists and Althusserians, there is no relation of necessary entailment between a theory of human nature and a teleological conception of history in which events subserve some overarching purpose. Indeed, it is impossible to account for historical struggles and transformations without an understanding of the powers which human beings have, by virtue of both their shared nature and their position in social structures, to change the course of events. It is in part because agents have the ability to choose between different courses of action that historical processes do not follow an inevitable path of progress.[46] Lyotard, rightly recognising that there are no guarantees of human emancipation of the kind the *philosophes* sought to give, wrongly concludes that we must therefore abandon the goal of emancipation itself, and the conception of human nature which it presupposes.

This brings us, secondly, to the question with which I began, of the Enlightenment and its promise of 'a rational organization of

... social life'. Habermas was speaking for himself as well when he said that Adorno 'remains true to the idea that there is no cure for the wounds of Enlightenment other than the radicalized Enlightenment'.[47] It is open to question whether either managed to strike the kind of balance implied by this formulation. Habermas has diagnosed the one-sided nature of Adorno's view of modernity as the unqualified triumph of alienated instrumental reason. But Habermas has himself veered towards the opposite extreme, seeing what he characterises with some exaggeration as the consensual character of speech as underpinning the gradual expansion of normative structures of law and morality which make possible the rational regulation of the autonomised sub-systems of money and power. He consequently vastly underestimates the scale of the economic contradictions to which contemporary capitalism is subject – an error also made by Adorno, though he saw post-war economic stability as an aspect of the 'totally administered society' rather than as a stage in the slow progress of communicative reason.

The aspiration towards the 'radicalised Enlightenment' is nevertheless fundamentally sound. It is the stance taken by Marx towards capitalism – open to the potential for human self-realisation implied by the development of the productive forces, but equally aware of its ever-present destructiveness and irrationality and its roots in class exploitation. But, as Marshall Berman has recently reminded us, this attitude to modernity is far from unique to Marx.[48] Even Marx's greatest opponents – Nietzsche and Weber – display an acute awareness that the Enlightenment can be neither uncritically endorsed nor simply rejected. And Foucault, the most important recent inheritor of this tradition, seems to have come to a similar view at the end of his life.[49] Critical social theory can continue only in this vein, as both the heir and the critic of the Enlightenment.

## Notes and References

1. J.-F. Lyotard, *The Postmodern Condition* (Manchester, 1984), p. xxiv.

2. Id., 'Defining the Post-Modern', *ICA Documents* 4 (1986), p. 6.

3. Id., 'Answering the Question: What is Postmodernism?', appendix to *Postmodern Condition*, p. 82.

4. See especially J. Habermas, *The Philosophical Discourse of Modernity* (Cambridge, 1987).

5. Id. 'Sovereignty and the *Führerdemokratie*', *Times Literary Supplement*, 26 September 1986, p. 1054.

6. Id., 'Modernity – an Incomplete Project', in H. Foster, ed., *Postmodern Culture* (London, 1985), p. 9.

7. A. Callinicos, *Is There a Future for Marxism?* (London, 1982), and 'Post-Modernism, Post-Structuralism, Post-Marxism?', *Theory, Culture & Society* 2:3 (1985). See also P. Dews, *Logics of Disintegration* (London, 1987).

8. C. Taylor, 'Foucault on Freedom and Truth', in D. C. Hoy, ed., *Foucault: A Critical Reader* (Oxford, 1986), p. 102 n. 46.

9. D. Bell, *The Coming of Post-Industrial Society* (London, 1974), pp. 212, 294.

10. See R. Heilbroner, *Business Civilization in Decline* (Harmondsworth, 1977), and K. Kumar, *Prophecy and Progress* (Harmondsworth, 1978).

11. See N. Harris, *Of Bread and Guns* (Harmondsworth, 1983), and *The End of the Third World* (London, 1986).

12. D. Gordon, 'The Global Economy', *New Left Review* 168 (1988), pp. 30–8.

13. Bell, op. cit., p. 343.

14. *Financial Times*, 15 October 1986. See also the analysis of contemporary Los Angeles in M. Davis, '*Chinatown* Part Two?', *New Left Review*, 164 (1987).

15. Kumar, *op. cit., passim.*

16. C. Jencks, *What is Post-modernism?* (London, 1986), pp. 33–4, 42, 14–15, 43.

17. S. Spender, *Eliot* (London, 1975), p. 9.

18. P. Fuller, *Images of God* (London, 1985), pp. 13–14.

19. U. Eco, *Reflections on 'The Name of the Rose'* (London, 1984), pp. 66–7.

20. F. Jameson, 'Postmodernism, or the Cultural Logic of Late Capitalism', *New Left Review* 146 (1984), pp. 85, 86, 88, and *passim*.

21. M. Davis, 'Urban Renaissance and the Spirit of Postmodernism', ibid. 151 (1985), p. 107.

22. F. Jameson, *Marxism and Form* (Princeton, 1971), pp. xvii–xviii, 105, 95–106, 105.

23. Id., 'On Magic Realism in Film', *Critical Inquiry* 12:2 (1986), p. 303. See also the rather longer definition of 'nostalgia film' on p. 310. Compare the analysis of *The Conformist* in R. P. Kolker, *Bernardo Bertolucci* (London, 1985), pp. 86–104.

24. Id., 'Postmodernism', pp. 66–8.

25. See Lyotard, 'Answering the Question'.

26. Jameson, *op cit.*, pp. 76–80, 91.

27. Lyotard, 'Complexity and the Sublime', *ICA Documents* 4 (1986), p. 10. It is a pity (and also rather surprising) that Terry Eagleton's critical remarks at an ICA conference on postmodernism, to which this text was a response, were not published along with it.

28. See, for example, Marx, *Capital*, I (Harmondsworth, 1976), p. 433.

29. R. Rorty, 'Habermas and Lyotard on Post-Modernity', in R. Bernstein (ed.), *Habermas and Modernity* (Cambridge, 1985), p. 163.

30. I. Kant, *Critique of Judgement* (Oxford, 1973), I, pp. 90, 92.

31. Jameson, 'Postmodernism', p. 76.

32. Lyotard, 'Answering the Question', p. 81.

33. Spender, *op. cit.,* p. 106.

34. See D. Held, 'Crisis-Tendencies, Legitimation and the State', in J. Thompson and D. Held, eds, *Habermas: Critical Debates* (London, 1982).

35. R. Sennett, *The Fall of Public Man* (New York, 1977).

36. M. Aglietta, *A Theory of Capitalist Regulation* (London, 1979), pp. 117, 154, 158. Aglietta's concept of Fordism does not, however, provide an explanation of the post-war boom: see C. Harman, *Explaining the Crisis* (London, 1984), pp. 141–7.

37. J. Habermas, *Autonomy and Solidarity* (ed. P. Dews, London, 1986), p. 179.

38. Bell, p. 318 n. 30. Many would see television as responsible in large part for the emergence of what they believe to be a postmodern epoch. But while television has certainly contributed to the atomisation of social life, it arguably places the viewer in a less passive position than does cinema. Its effects are in any case complex, and require more careful analysis than they have received at the hands of most theorists of postmodernity.

39. P. Anderson, 'Modernity and Revolution', *New Left Review* 144 (1984), pp. 104–5.

40. Ibid., p. 107.

41. See C. Harman, *The Fire Last Time* (London, 1988).

42. See A. Callinicos and C. Harman, *The Changing Working Class* (London, 1987), esp. ch. 1.

43. See P. Dews, 'Adorno, Post-Structuralism and the Critique of Identity', *New Left Review* 157 (1986).

44. Lyotard, 'Answering the Question', p. 81.

45. See M. Davis, *Prisoners of the American Dream* (London, 1986), Ch. 5, for a provocative analysis of the US economy which places great emphasis on the notion of 'overconsumptionism'. Raphael Samuel painted a brilliant social portrait of the lifestyle and outlook of the new middle class in *New Society*, 22 and 29 April 1982.

46. See A. Callinicos, *Making History* (Cambridge, 1987).

47. Habermas, *Autonomy*, p. 158.

48. See M. Berman, *All that is Solid Melts into Air* (London, 1983).

49. See M. Foucault, 'What is Enlightenment?', in P. Rabinow, ed., *A Foucault Reader* (Harmondsworth, 1986).

# Chapter 5

# Lost in the Funhouse: Baudrillard and the Politics of Postmodernism

Christopher Norris

## I

'Forget Foucault' was Baudrillard's title for a nifty piece of polemics which, in the current French manner, staked his claim to be 'post-', just about everything, post-structuralism and Foucault included.[1] I think we would do well to forget Baudrillard, though not without treating his texts to more in the way of argued critique than Baudrillard sees fit to provide when dealing with his own precursors and rivals on the intellectual scene. Baudrillard is undoubtedly the one who has gone furthest toward renouncing enlightenment reason and all its works, from the Kantian–liberal agenda to Marxism, Frankfurt Critical Theory, the structuralist 'sciences of man', and even – on his view – the residual theoreticist delusions of a thinker like Foucault. The nearest equivalents are Richard Rorty's brand of postmodern neopragmatist anti-philosophy and the strain of so-called 'weak thought' (not unaptly so called) that has lately been canvassed by Gianni Vattimo and other Heideggerian apostles of unreason.[2] But one suspects that Baudrillard would reject these comparisons, regarding them as moves in a pointless game whose rule-book has been endlessly re-written and should now be torn up for good and all.

Mark Poster's introduction to a recent collection of Baudrillard's writings[3] raises certain doubts as to his style ('hyperbolic and declarative, often lacking sustained, systematic analysis when appropriate'), his tendency to extrapolate far-reaching conclusions from limited evidence, and his habit of ignoring any hopeful signs that might complicate the otherwise dire prognosis for civilization and its discontents. All the same, Poster takes it as read that Baudrillard has important things to say and that his work engages the most salient features of our current 'postmodern' situation. More specifically, it offers new bearings in an age when 'the instant, worldwide availability of information has changed human society forever, probably for the good' (p. 8). No longer can we fall back on those old 'metanarratives' or enlightenment myths of information, grounded as they were (or as they claimed to be) in a capacity to distinguish truth from falsehood, progress from reaction, knowledge from the various kinds of pseudo-knowledge (or mere 'ideology') that passed themselves off as the genuine thing. Of course other thinkers (among them Rorty and Lyotard) have argued to similar effect.[4] But none of them has maintained such an extreme oppositional stance toward every last truth-claim, every form or vestige of enlightened critical thought. In Lyotard's case there has been a marked shift of emphasis, from a work like *The Postmodern Condition* where Enlightenment values are seen as the source of manifold errors and evils, to those recent texts where a certain (albeit heterodox) reading of Kant is applied to questions of history, politics and interpretation.[5] But with Baudrillard the movement is in an appropriate direction, starting out from the critique of Marxism and other such 'foundationalist' or 'epistemo-logical' paradigms, and then – as the very notion of critique becomes suspect – embracing a wholesale postmodernist creed where the ideas of truth, validity or right reason simply drop out of the picture.

This is where Poster locates the significance of Baudrillard's work: in the way that it 'shatters the existing foundations for critical social theory, showing how the privilege they give to labor and their rationalist epistemologies are inadequate for the analysis of the media and other new social activities' (p. 8). Thus, despite his detailed reservations, Poster accepts the basic claim that we have moved into a new (and as-yet unthinkable) stage of postmodern evolution; that the old paradigms (whether Kantian, Marxist, structuralist or whatever) are of no use at all in grasping this emergent phase; and that therefore we had best help the process along by not putting up any kind of misguided theoretical resistance. Philosophers and political theorists since Plato have taken it as axiomatic that thought must at some point distinguish between truth and faslehood, reason and rhetoric, essence and appearance, science and ideology. One way of grasping Baudrillard's project is to see it as a species of inverted Platonism, a discourse that systematically promotes the negative terms (rhetoric, appearance, ideology) above their positive counterparts. It is no longer possible to maintain the old economy of truth and representation in a world where 'reality' is entirely constructed through forms of mass-media feedback, where values are determined by consumer demand (itself brought about by the endless circulation of meanings, images and advertising codes), and where nothing could serve as a means of distinguishing true from merely true-seeming (or ideological) habits of belief. Such is the world we now inhabit, according to Baudrillard, and such are the governing conditions for any project of thought that hopes to make sense of the postmodern epoch.

Hence Baudrillard's quarrel with Marxism, developed most fully in *The Mirror of Production* (1973). Here he sets out to deconstruct the opposition between use-value and exchange-value, the one conceived in terms of 'genuine' needs and productive resources, the other identified with a late-capitalist or consumer economy which invades and distorts every aspect of human existence. But this is to get the matter backward, Baudrillard argues, since any definition of use-value will have to take account of the socialised desires, needs and expectations which constitute the sphere of values in general. Thus the positive terms of Marxist theory – labor-power, production, use-value, needs – are still caught up in a form of essentialist or metaphysical thinking which in effect reproduces the discourse of eighteenth-century political economy. That is to say, they are subject to an 'anthropological postulate', one that starts out from the Marxian premise that 'men begin to distinguish themselves from animals as soon as they begin to produce their means of subsistence' (p. 98). In a just social order, needs would be satisfied through a system based on use-values alone, or on the capacity of human individuals to create and enjoy the fruits of their own labour. It is only with the advent of exchange-value – of an artificial system created and sustained by capitalist market forces – that workers become 'alienated' from their real conditions of existence, thus falling victim to various forms of ideological false consciousness. It is this line of argument that Baudrillard rejects, since he sees it as just another version of the classical (Platonist) doctrine that holds out for truth against the snares of illusion and false seeming. More specifically, Marxism invests concepts like 'need', 'labour' and 'production' with an abstract generality or universal value which places them beyond further question. And to this extent it betrays its own critical imperative, the will to demystify naturalised, commonsense modes of perception (like those of classical free-market doctrine) by showing them to rest on stipulative values derived from some particular class-interest or ideological world-view.

There are close parallels to be drawn between Baudrillard's *Mirror of Production* and Richard Rorty's *Philosophy and the Mirror of Nature* (published some seven years later).[6] Rorty rejects the idea of philosophy as a foundational or first-order discipline, one that explains how knowledge comes about by working to achieve an accurate match between real-world experience and concepts of pure understanding. Such was the decisive wrong turn that philosophy took when, with Descartes and Kant, it seized upon certain privileged metaphors – centrally those of the mind as a 'glassy essence' or 'mirror of nature' – and allowed these tropes to determine its entire future project. The result was a discourse that increasingly specialised in the discovery of unreal 'solutions' to unreal 'problems', a narrative whose chief episodes would include the entire history of post-Kantian debate on the powers and limits of knowledge, along with much of the modern analytical tradition (where, according to Rorty, these topics are merely recast in linguistic as opposed to idealist or metaphysical terms). The exchange of one technical vocabulary for another brought nothing in the way of improved understanding or enhanced social relevance. What should now be apparent, after so much wasted ingenuity, is the fact that no solutions will ever be forthcoming, that epistemology was a pointless endeavour from the outset, and that therefore philosophers should give up this deluded quest and rejoin the cultural 'conversation of mankind' on equal terms with sociologists, literary critics, and others who never entertained such high-flown ambitions. And this would mean dispensing with a whole set of pseudo-solutions ('clear and distinct ideas', a priori concepts, sense-data, transcendental arguments and so forth) which have hitherto managed to exert such a spell-binding power.

Rorty sees nothing to regret in this mood of postmodern disenchantment with Enlightenment reason in its various forms. On the contrary, he hopes that it will bring philosophers around to the belated recognition that there is no ultimate truth to be had, no language that would 'cut nature at the joints' or achieve an ideal, one-to-one match between concepts and sensuous intuitions. 'True' can then be redefined for all practical purposes as 'good in the way of belief', a label of convenience attached to those ideas that currently enjoy widespread approval, or which make good sense in the context of this or that language-game, discipline or cultural 'form of life'. Of course we can carry on using those old conceptual idioms – Kantian, Hegelian, Marxist or whatever – in the hope that they might come up with some argument proof against time and change. But really they amount to nothing more than a range of alternative 'final vocabularies', styles of talk that serve well enough to keep the conversation going, but no longer possess much persuasive power in an age of neo-pragmatist (or 'postmodern bourgeois liberal') culture. In fact we should do better – so Rorty argues – to give up these outworn habits of thought and instead make every effort to multiply the language-games and thereby create as many conversational openings as possible. Philosophy to date has been hooked on a handful of metaphors masquerading as concepts, poetic ideas that were taken as absolute truths, thus losing whatever they once possessed of imaginative vigour and force. On the Nietzschean view that Rorty adopts, this process started out with the victory of Socratic ration-alism and achieved its bad apotheosis with Descartes, Kant and their successors. Its last major episode was the rise of Anglo-American analytical philosophy, a movement that has now lost its way among various competing (and wholly undecidable) claims and counter-claims. So our best option is to drop the old meta-phors – especially those that still trade on ideas of privileged epistemic access, or the mind as a mirror of nature – and try out whatever promising substitutes now come to hand.

Baudrillard is arguing a similar case with regard to the concepts and categories of Marxist theory. Like Rorty, he denounces such thinking as just another variant on the old, self-deluding Enlightenment theme, the idea that one can criticise existing beliefs from some superior vantage-point of truth, reason or scientific method. Marxism compounds this error, according to Baudrillard, by basing its critique on a series of essentialist or anthropological concepts, among them the privilege accorded to economic use-value and the notion of 'man' as a creature defined by *needs* on the one hand and *productive capacity* on the other. It is in this sense that the Marxist 'mirror of production' takes its place among the governing metaphors of modern (post-Kantian) thought. When Marx set out to stand the Hegelian dialectic back on its feet – to invert the terms of idealist philosophy by restoring the material forces of production to their rightful primacy over everything pertaining to the social and cultural spheres – he provided just one more delusive variation on the old metaphysical theme. And this applies all the more to those latter-day exponents who argue, like Althusser, for a reading of the Marxian text that would separate the elements of a dialectical-materialist 'science' from the residues of a humanist or 'ideological' project that persists into the early ('pre-Marxist') writings.[7] For it is a mark of their historical obsolescence that such arguments cling to the old Enlightenement paradigm, the idea that we might yet come up with some *theory* – some infallible method or technique – for separating truth from the various currencies of true-seeming ideological belief.

    What these thinkers fail to grasp – as Baudrillard sees it – is the fact that we have now moved on into an epoch where no such distinctions hold, where truth is entirely a product of consensus values, and where 'science' itself is just the name we attach to certain (currently prestigious) modes of explanation. Marxism especially invites this charge since it holds out the prospect of a liberating break with earlier paradigms (e.g., those of idealist metaphysics and eighteenth-century political economy) while in fact reproducing the selfsame structures of thought through its appeal to use-value, labour-power, forces of production etc. For these categories still pay homage to a certain residual 'essence of man', one that is defined precisely in terms of *natural productive capacities* on the one hand and *elemental human needs* on the other. They are thus caught up in a specular relation or a pattern of unwitting dialectical reprise that ends up by confirming every last theorem of the 'false' sciences that Marx set out to controvert. And so it happens that, according to Baudrillard,

> the weapon Marx created turns against him and turns his theory into the dialectical apotheosis of political economy . . . The concept of critique emerged in the West at the same time as political economy and, as the quintessence of Enlightenment rationality, is perhaps only the subtle, long-term expression of the system's expanded reproduction . . . Perhaps, under the guise of producing its fatal internal contradiction, Marx only rendered a descriptive theory. The logic of representation – of the duplication of its object – haunts all rational discursiveness. Every critical theory is haunted by this surreptitious religion, this desire bound up with the construction of its object, this negativity subtly haunted by the very form that it negates (p. 116).

And if critical theory is thus fated to undo itself – to fall straight back into the errors and delusions of some antecedent discourse which it aims to criticise – then we might as well give up on the whole attempt to get beyond existing consensus-values in the name of some better, more 'enlightened' or adequate understanding. This project would at best be a mere waste of time, and at worst a form of repressive instrumental reason that reduces all history to its own metanarrative system of concepts and categories. For, in Baudrillard's view, such arguments must always be deluded, based as they are on an outworn (epistemological) paradigm which still thinks to distinguish *truth* or its various surrogates – 'science', 'the real', 'objectivity', 'use-value' 'need' or whatever – from the ideological representations which currently lay claim to that title.

It is for this reason that Marxism stands squarely within the line of mainstream Western intellectual descent, a line that begins with the Platonic distinction between *doxa* (mere opinion) and *episteme* (genuine knowledge), and which then comes down via Descartes and Kant to the present-day human sciences. Such is the fate of all critical concepts as soon as they claim any kind of explanatory power beyond the historical context that produced them or the circumstances that gave rise to their first elaboration. In short, theories can only be of use in so far as we apply them reflexively to the material or socio-political conditions under which they came into being. To suppose otherwise – to credit (say) the Kantian or

Marxist critiques with any kind of ultimate validity – is to lapse into a form of 'metaphysical' thinking which persistently ignores this lesson.

So Marx may have managed to 'transform the concepts of production and mode of production at a given moment', and thus brought about a 'break in the social mystery of exchange-value' which helps to understand the conditions prevailing at that moment. But Marxism goes wrong when it attempts to universalise such insights, building them up into a full-scale critical theory or 'science' that claims some kind of ultimate truth. At this point, Baudrillard writes, such concepts

> become canonical and enter the general system's mode of representation ... They set themselves up as expressing an 'objective reality'. They become signs: signifiers of a 'real' signified. And although at the best of times these concepts have been practised as concepts without taking themselves for reality, they have nonetheless subsequently fallen into the *imaginary of the sign*, or the *sphere of truth*. They are no longer in the sphere of interpretation but enter that of *repressive simulation* (p. 114).

This passage is clearly much indebted to Nietzsche. It repeats his genealogical account of how 'truth' came about through a process of forgetting its own formative prehistory; how certain originary metaphors were subsequently mistaken for concepts, and philosophy was thereby launched on its quest for ideas and essences that never existed outside this jargon specialised for the purpose of systematic self-deception.[8] It is an argument – or a piece of enabling background narrative – that unites Baudrillard with other thinkers like Foucault, Lyotard and Rorty, all of them committed to a postmodern-pragmatist or anti-enlightenment viewpoint. But it is Baudrillard, more than anyone, who has pushed this kind of rhetoric as far as it will go and used it as a weapon against every last claim of truth, validity and critical reason. For if Baudrillard is right – setting aside the question of what 'rightness' could amount to, given this degree of epistemological scepticism – then it is hard to envisage any way forward other than a total abandonment of all such ideas and a willing embrace of the so-called 'postmodern condition'.

**II**

His case therefore rests on the following propositions: 1) that theory is a discredited enterprise, since 'truth' has turned out to be a fictive, rhetorical or imaginary construct; 2) that this prevents (or ought to prevent) our engaging in activities of 'rational' argument or *Ideologiekritik*; and 3) that we must henceforth drop all talk of 'the real' as opposed to its mystified, distorted or 'ideological' representation, since such talk continues to trade on old assumptions that no longer possess any force or credibility.

Now one could hardly deny that Baudrillard's diagnosis does have a bearing on our present situation in the 'advanced' Western democracies. That is to say, it speaks directly to a widespread sense that we are living in a world of pervasive unreality, a world where perceptions are increasingly shaped by mass-media imagery, political rhetoric and techniques of wholesale disinformation that substitute for any kind of reasoned public debate. This process has undoubtedly intensified in recent years, as anyone will know who took more than a passing interest in the latest British and American election campaigns. In which case it might seem that Baudrillard's arguments are amply borne out by the evidence nearest to hand. Any notion that people are at liberty to think for themselves on the most important issues – that this is indeed what distinguishes the 'free world' from its 'totalitarian' counterpart – is surely belied by the extent to which their ideas, attitudes and voting behaviour are thus programmed in advance. Saturation coverage in the mass media has the effect, not of creating a better-informed electorate, but of reducing the whole business to a dead level of mindless slogans, trivialised issues and a near-total absence of genuine debate on substantive policy issues. Bush's victory in 1988, like Thatcher's the previous year, was a melancholy lesson in the way that elections can be stage-managed so as to distract attention from anything that might create problems for the party (or the cross-party nexus of interests) currently in power. 'Public opinion' is relentlessly monitored through a system of polls and so-called 'random sampling' which can always be adjusted – by suitably framing the questions or the method of statistical analysis – so as to produce the desired results. As a result, it becomes neither necessary nor desirable for candidates to engage in serious discus-

sion on matters of public concern. The imbecile performances of a
Reagan or a Quayle may cause some occasional embarrassment –
even a short-term dip in the polls – but are soon enough forgotten
with the next round of mass-media polemics.

In short, it is hard to argue with Baudrillard's contention that
ours is an age of postmodern 'hyperreality' where truth is merely
what counts as such according to the latest media consensus, or as
defined through the various loops and circuits of a highly evolved
feedback mechanism. And from here it might seem a very short
distance to the standpoint that renounces all competence to judge
in questions of reality and illusion, truth and falsehood, reasoned
argument and rhetorical or suasive efect. Baudrillard's systematic
inversion of these concepts – his treatment of 'truth' as the mere
by-product of a generalised fictive economy, or of use-value as
determined through and through by the currencies of exchange-
value – would then be nothing more than a fair extrapolation from
the evidence of an epoch that has at last witnessed the definitive
collapse of those old, self-deluding ontologies. If 'simulation' is the
postmodern name of the game, it is not some misfortune that has
lately overtaken us, but a condition that was always already in
force despite the best efforts of truth-seeking theorists, from Plato
onwards, to pretend otherwise.

Baudrillard develops this case in his essay 'Simulacra and
Simulations', which again follows Nietzsche in its genealogical
undoing of truth as an effect of multiplied errors and illusions.
'These would be the successive phases of the image: 1) It is the
reflection of a basic reality. 2) It masks and perverts a basic reality.
3) It masks the *absence* of a basic reality. 4) It bears no relation to
any reality whatever: it is its own pure simulacrum.' (p. 170). Thus
the story starts out, in Hegelian fashion, with primitive sense-
certainty; goes on to a principled mistrust of appearances that
unites idealists like Plato with critical thinkers like Kant, Hegel and
Marx; arrives (item 3) at the Nietzschean stage of a thoroughgoing
epistemological scepticism; and finally comes round to the postmodern viewpoint that everything is appearance, that 'truth' was
always a species of self-promoting fiction, and that scepticism
misses the point since it still makes a big dramatic scene of this
belated discovery. For Baudrillard, it is not a question of our now
having lost the old confidence in reason and truth as a result of fairly
recent upheavals or mutations in the socio-political sphere. Nor is

it the case that these changes could be treated as a form of widespread pathological affliction, a loss of the capacity to discriminate truth from falsehood, or the will to exercise reason in matters of political judgment. What we are experiencing now is an ultimate stage of disenchantment with the concepts and categories of Enlightenment thought. And it is pointless to deplore or to criticise this process, since it represents not only an accurate diagnosis of our present condition but, beyond that, a readiness to cope with the absence of all 'metaphysical' guarantees, all those old self-deluding appeals to reason, truth, reality and so forth.

In fact, Baudrillard goes out of his way to block any reading of his work that would still find solace in traditional (Enlightenment) notions of truth as arrived at by criticising false appearances. Like the Marxist distinction between use-value and exchange-value, these ideas betray not only a false nostalgia – false because premised on a purely imaginary difference – but also a desire to pass themselves off as the real thing, and thus to perpetuate what Baudrillard calls the regime of 'repressive simulation'. This effect comes about through a kind of perverse compensatory mechanism, a process whereby the perceived loss of truth (or the sheer unreality of present-day experience) goes along with an hysterical desire to prove otherwise. 'When the real is no longer what it used to be', Baudrillard writes,

> nostalgia assumes its full meaning. There is a proliferation of myths of origin and signs of reality; of second-hand truth, objectivity and authenticity. There is an escalation of the true, of lived experience ... And there is a panic-stricken production of the real and of the referential, above and parallel to the panic of material production. This is how simulation appears in the phase that concerns us: a strategy of the real, neo-real and hyperreal, whose universal double is a strategy of deterrence (p. 171).

And it is clear from what he says elsewhere on this topic that Baudrillard 'believes in' nuclear deterrence.[9] It is something that has demonstrably worked, he thinks, at least to the extent that it has produced a continuing strategic stand-off, a situation where the exchange of 'simulated' threats and counter-threats is so unthinkably unreal – so far beyond the grasp of any rational decision-making power – that we have managed to survive thus far through the waging of a purely rhetorical warfare. But this effect depends entirely on the refusal of each side to call the other's bluff, or on the way that deterrence is confined to a realm of simulation or 'hyperreality' where nobody (nobody in their right mind) would think to try conclusions in a practical way. 'In its orbital and ecstatic form warfare has become an impossible exchange, and this orbitalness protects us' (p. 191). So we had much better stick to the crazy 'logic' of deterrence, make believe that nuclear weapons have indeed 'kept the peace' these past forty years, and not get too worried when each new stage of rhetorical escalation creates a new threat, a new endgame scenario and – most often – a new weapons system to give it 'credible' force. For the only alternative, as Baudrillard sees it, is to think these questions through to a 'rational' or 'realistic' conclusion. And the upshot of this would be to undermine deterrence, substitute serious (war-fighting) plans for simulated (war-game) scenarios, and thus bring about the very catastrophe that we have so far managed to avoid. From which he draws the lesson that any critique of nuclear double-think – any attempt to get at the truth behind appearances, or to lay bare the sophistries that maintain this illusion – is necessarily a mistaken and dangerous endeavour. [10]

Baudrillard offers various examples of the way that criticism is played off the field by this 'hyperreality' that supposedly extends to every aspect of postmodern life. One of them is Disneyland, often treated (as by demythologising commentators like Louis Marin)[11] as 'a digest of the American way of life, panegyric to American values, idealized transposition of a contradictory reality' (p. 172). But such analyses take for granted what Baudrillard is out to deny: namely, the possibility of drawing a line between real and fictive, or authentic and inauthentic modes of knowledge. Thus 'Disneyland is presented as imaginary in order to make us believe that the rest [i.e. the world outside Disneyland] is real, whereas in fact all of Los Angeles and the America surrounding it are no longer real, but of the order of the hyperreal and of simulation' (p. 172). To think otherwise – like critics who locate the 'truth' of Disneyland in its power to legitimise a world elsewhere, a real world of pressing 'contradictions' which are here resolved in imaginary form – is to fall straight back into the old Enlightenment trap. In short, 'it is no longer a question of a false representation of reality (ideology), but of concealing the fact that the real is no longer real, and thus of saving the reality principle' (p. 172). Thus the Marxists go wrong – in company with the Platonists, Kantians and culture-critics like Marin – when they claim to strip away the accretions of mythology (or commonsense belief) and expose the truth that has hitherto sheltered behind these saving appearances. The effect of such thinking would then be precisely to *endorse* the Disneyland myth, the idea that there exists an alternative world where the reality-principle reigns, where illusions come up against hard fact and theory will inevitably have the last word. For, according to Baudrillard, there is nothing to choose between this kind of self-deceiving attitude on the part of left-wing intellectuals and the other, more 'naive' or spontaneous kind that simply enjoys Disneyland and never gives a thought to its 'ideological' function. In fact he strongly implies that the latter is preferable in so far as it avoids the theoreticist mistake of constructing just one more alibi for truth, and thus reinforcing the selfsame mythical message.

Another case-in-point (as Baudrillard reads it) is the Watergate affair and the way that this episode gave rise to a wholesale media campaign of 'public morality' versus the lies, intrigues and abuses of state power. Here again, the basic trick was to represent Nixon's behaviour as if it were a scandalous departure from the norm, a criminal folly that could then be brought to light by the courageous detective-work of two *Washington Post* journalists, inspired (as their book and the subsequent film made clear) by a dogged belief in truth, good reporting and the virtues of American democracy. Baudrillard sees this as a prime instance of the way that 'capitalism' can turn anything to advantage, even in the case of a political scandal that would seem to strike directly at its own vested interests. For such events help to confirm the idea that there is nothing wrong with the system itself; that abuses like Watergate are the exception, not the rule, and may in fact lead to a welcome renewal of the 'true' American spirit. Thus 'Watergate above all succeeded in imposing the idea that Watergate *was* a scandal – in this sense it was an extraordinary operation of intoxication: the reinjection of a large dose of political morality on a global scale' (p. 173). But one can grasp all this and still misinterpret the signs, as Baudrillard remarks of Pierre Bourdieu, who had analysed Watergate in terms of its ideological effect in dissimulating the *real* power-interests that lay behind the rhetoric of outrage, public morality, democratic values and so forth. Thus Bourdieu sets out to show how these 'relations of force' are both disguised and maintained by a periodic outbreak of moral panic which 'spontaneously furthers the order of capital'. But in adopting this position he unwittingly repeats the very gesture that his argument seeks to expose. For on Baudrillard's reading,

> this is still only the formula of ideology, and when Bourdieu enunciates it, he takes 'relation of force' to mean the *truth* of capitalist domination, and he *denounces* this relation of force as itself a *scandal*; he therefore occupies the same deterministic and moralistic position as the *Washington Post* journalists (p. 173).

And if Baudrillard is right then the same must apply to all versions of *Ideologiekritik* and all attempts to distinguish falsehood from truth on a basis of reasoned argument.

## III

I have offered this lengthy account of Baudrillard's work because I think there is an urgent need both to grasp the sources of its widespread appeal and to put up a resistance to it on principled theoretical grounds. The appeal is, after all, not so hard to understand, given the current political climate in Britain and the United States. The New York *Village Voice* made this connection in a number of articles on the Bush campaign and the 'hyperreality' of US electoral politics. Were Baudrillard's arguments not borne out by the absence of serious debate, the extent of mass-media manipulative influence, and the ease with which the electorate was swung into believing such a mass of ungrounded allegations, half-truths and downright lies? How could one explain Bush's victory except by acknowledging the total obsolescence of ideas like truth, public accountability and the need to answer for past acts and decisions? The *Voice* had done some good work in revealing not only the mendacity of Bush's campaign rhetoric but also the depth of his involvement with Irangate and other such shady (not to say criminal) episodes of the Reagan years. But of course this knowledge had currency only among a small readership, at least as compared with the mass-circulation papers and TV channels where the charges were treated, if at all, as mere distractions from the ongoing media charade. And any comfort in the fact that the Democrats fought a relatively 'clean' campaign was more than outweighed by their having given up on just about every major point of principle. In his televised 'debates' with Bush, one had the impression that Dukakis was reading from a script drawn up by the Republican publicity team and designed to present him as an amiable half-wit who simply hadn't learnt the new rules of the game. By sedulously avoiding any use of the dread word 'liberal' – the Reaganspeak equivalent of 'communist' in McCarthy's era, or 'atheist' in Renaissance drama – Dukakis sacrificed his own best chance of staging an effective comeback. When he *did* start using it, in a last-minute change of strategy, his campaign showed signs of a limited revival. But of course the change came too late and the election was won on what amounted to a wholesale anti-liberal crusade, an Orwellian use of rhetorical tricks and whipped-up populist fervour to which the Democrats more or less surrendered from the outset.

So the *Voice* had some reason for turning to Baudrillard in hopes of understanding just what had gone wrong. One line of argument much canvassed in the run-up was that opinion-polls were perhaps having a harmful influence on the democratic process since voters were unduly swayed by the wording of questions, the 'hidden agenda', or the feedback-effect which told them what to think before they had even started to make their minds up. But Baudrillard rejects such arguments as just another case of the old Enlightenment dream, the craving for a 'truth' behind appearances, in this case a truth that would win out in elections were it not for the polls and their mischievous influence. 'All this would be serious enough', he writes, 'if there were an objective truth of needs, an objective truth of public opinion' (p. 209). But there is no such thing – no *reality* of human needs, desires or interests – and hence no telling whether the polls have an effect on 'public opinion' for better or worse. Thus in Baudrillard's view

> we should agree neither with those who praise the beneficial use of the media nor with those who scream about manipulation, for the simple reason that there is no relationship between a system of meaning and a system of simulation. Publicity and opinion polls would be incapable, even if they wished and claimed to do so, of alienating the will or the opinion of anyone at all, for the reason that they do not act in the time-space of will or of representation where judgment is formed (p. 209).

He does go on to speak of this phenomenon as an 'obscenity', a kind of 'hyperchondriacal madness', persuading the electorate that 'it must at all times know what it wants, know what it thinks, be told about its least needs, its least quivers, *see* itself continually on the videoscreen of statistics' (p. 209). But he also makes it clear that these comments should be taken as a neutral diagnosis of the way things are, and not as an appeal to some saving principle of truth, reality or reason. And, indeed, Baudrillard is in no position to adopt such a critical stance, having argued repeatedly against the idea – the deluded 'Enlightenment' idea – that we could ever think beyond this realm of false appearance to that which it supposedly dissimulates or masks.

But the question remains as to whether this persuasive *diagnosis* of postmodern politics necessarily entails a wholesale abandonment of truth-claims and the reality-principle. That is to say: does the fact that we currently inhabit an unreal world – a realm of mass-media distortion, nuclear deterrence, manipulative opinion-polls and the rest – justify Baudrillard in his further assumption that there is no way out, since reality just *is* (to the best of our knowledge) the world which we thus inhabit? The *Village Voice* was understandably reluctant to draw this conclusion since it had made great efforts, during the run-up period, to uncover some of the facts about Bush's past record and the real power-interests at work behind the Republican campaign. All the same one can understand how the election result might have dented this confidence, suggesting as it did that the line between truth and falsehood had indeed been erased, that the politics of unreality had won out at last, and therefore that no amount of reasoned argument or factual reporting could turn back the tide of mass-media falsification. In fact – as more than one writer suggested – Bush's victory signalled a worse condition in the body politic than Reagan's two terms of office. At least with Reagan there was a sense that this business couldn't be for real; that the B-movie actor had somehow managed to impose his own crazy view of things, but that surely the episode would come to an end when people woke up to the true situation. There were no such comforting thoughts to be had with regard to George Bush and his very different brand of hard-headed cynical opportunism. It looked very much as if Baudrillard had been proved right – whatever that could mean – and the time of false appearances had now given way to a grim new reality-principle, one that no longer had need of Reagan's so-called 'charismatic' appeal.

I think there is good reason to reject this idea, along with the whole postmodernist line of last-ditch sceptical retreat. But it is not enough to say that such thinking has undesirable effects, that it leaves us bereft of argumentative grounds upon which to challenge the current, massively distorted consensus-view. To Baudrillard this would seem just one more instance of the old Enlightenment nostalgia, the failure to perceive how those grounds were always (and are now more than ever) a species of wishful thinking. It would amount to nothing more than a pragmatist case for continuing to believe in truth and reason, since without such beliefs one could muster no defence against the lies and falsehoods put around by unscrupulous opponents. And if this were the bottom line of argument – one that took truth as what is currently 'good in the way of belief' – then Baudrillard would always have the last word in so far as he could point to the various signs that people (or the great majority of people) just don't have any use for such obsolete ideas. There is a parallel here with neo-pragmatists like Richard Rorty and Stanley Fish, those who hold that since all theories, truth-claims, ethical principles etc. *must* be construed in terms of some given consensus or 'interpretive community', then we might as well give up such abstract talk and accept that the best we can ever hope to do is argue persuasively within that existing context of belief.[12] These thinkers would certainly reject the claim that their position has disabling political consequences, or that it leads to an attitude of passively accepting just any kind of current consensus-belief. For if Fish managed to convince us – that is to say, if we lost all faith in the idea that theory has 'consequences', that it is able to affect what we just do believe, one way or another – then it needn't follow from this that we would be stuck for arguments and lose all interest in politics, philosophy, literary theory or whatever. In fact, we would carry on debating these matters in pretty much the same old way, except that we would now be aware (at some level) that there were no ultimate truths to be had, no ground-rules or principles beyond those offered by the range of presently available beliefs.

So theory may have results in so far as it gets us to put things differently by shifting the terms of debate or persuades us to attach importance to some new set of problems and principles. But there is no question of theory having 'consequences' in the stronger sense of that term, i.e., in the sense that one could come up with reasons – purely theoretical reasons – for rejecting what one does in fact believe.[13] There is simply no difference, on Fish's view, between saying 'I believe x to be the case' and claiming to *know* that x is the case on factual, theoretical or other such grounds. More precisely, the difference can only be a matter of rhetorical emphasis or the degree of psychological conviction involved. Knowing just *is* that particular state of mind in which we claim good reason for believing this or that to be the case. And it is wholly inconceivable that anyone could ever arrive at the position of rejecting *in theory* what they took to be true at the level of mere 'ideology' or 'commonsense' belief. For this would entail a contradiction in performative terms, as well as – psychologically speaking – a form of advanced schizophrenic disorder. From this, Fish concludes 1) that truth-claims and beliefs are synonymous for all practical purposes, 2) that theory can never do more than appeal to some existing idea of what counts as a good theoretical argument, and 3) that we should therefore give up the notion that theorising makes any difference, aside from its usefulness in persuading us (and others) to think we have 'grounds' for believing what we do. As for the question whether his own line of argument has 'consequences', Fish can afford to take a relaxed view of the matter. Of course nothing follows in theory from establishing the point that theory is a strictly inconsequential activity. But if everyone were suddenly converted to Fish's persuasion, then this would have the wholly desirable result, as he sees it, of putting an end to such misguided talk and getting us to argue things out on a basis of straightforwardly differing beliefs. Nothing would have changed, bar the realisation that nothing has changed, and that theory had therefore been pointless or redundant all along.

Now Fish would most certainly object to being classified with Baudrillard as a 'postmodern' thinker or exponent of the new irrationalism. In fact, he makes a point of arguing – like Rorty – that his views just reflect what normally goes on in the way of civilized exchange among members of the various 'interpretive communities' (professional, academic and so forth) whose conversation sets the tone of a liberal-democratic culture. If they stopped talking theory, it would scarcely affect this conversation, except to the extent that people found more time for discussing their genuine, substantive differences of view. So there would still be room for all manner of debate on issues of politics, ethics, philosophy, literary interpretation or whatever, just so long as the participants didn't lay claim to any kind of theoretical warrant. If this position might itself seem politically loaded – if it serves (as with Rorty) to endorse the self-image of late twentieth-century North American liberal culture – then Fish can quite happily acknowledge this fact, believing as he does that there is no real option except to keep talking on the terms offered by one's own intellectual community. Like Baudrillard, he flatly rejects the idea that it could ever make sense to look *outside* that community – beyond its currently available range of meanings, values and assumptions – whether in search of legitimising grounds or a basis for radical critique. But, unlike Baudrillard, he clearly thinks that North American culture is healthy enough – or sufficiently in touch with social realities – to warrant an attitude of sturdy pragmatist confidence, a belief that all is well with the current conversation, and therefore with society at large.

I want to suggest that Baudrillard is much nearer the mark in his characterisation of present-day society; that Fish could bring up no arguments against him, since he (Fish) has abandoned the grounds on which such an argument would need to be conducted; and – the main point at issue – that they are both mistaken in rejecting all appeals to anything beyond what is currently 'good in the way of belief'. For Baudrillard, this means that there is just no alternative to the realm of illusory appearances that constitute 'reality' as presently known and experienced. For Fish, less alarmingly, it means that we can carry on believing in the principles of demo-cracy, justice, reason, 'truth at the end of enquiry' and so forth, provided we don't make the further claim of having a *theory* to back up those principles. Thus, according to Fish, it is an obvious fact that we believe what we believe, and that no amount of theorising can change our minds unless we are already – at some level of awareness – either half-way convinced or open to persuasion. His response to Baudrillard would no doubt be in keeping with what Fish has to say about Marxist, deconstructionist and other such challenges to consensual wisdom. That is say, he would argue that postmodernism reduces to manifest nonsense in so far as it thinks to raise questions about truth, meaning, 'common-sense' belief etc. which cannot be raised – at least, not *seriously* –

if one wants to get a hearing and be rightly understood by members of one's own (or any other) 'interpretative community'. But it is far from obvious why Fish should exhibit such a sturdy confidence in the power of this community (roughly speaking: the North American academic, cultural and professional élites, with support from the mainstream of public opinion) to keep the conversation going and preserve the currency of liberal-democratic values. For there is plenty of evidence to the contrary, not only in Baudrillard's extravagant scenario, but everywhere in the mass-media coverage of recent political events. It is hard to see what counter-arguments Fish might offer to anyone who claimed, like Baudrillard, that the conditions of a working consensus (or informed public sphere) had now broken down irretrievably, and that henceforth we had better adjust to living in a world of pervasive hyperreality.

But if Baudrillard is right to this extent – right in diagnosing what is manifestly wrong with the postmodern body politic – we are not, for that reason, necessarily obliged to accept the whole package of irrationalist ideas that he mounts on this gloomy prognosis. That is to say, there is something highly suspect in his habit of constantly jumping from one language-game to another, from descriptive accounts of the way we live now to generalised pronouncements on the postmodern condition, the obsolescence of truth, the non-availability of critical grounds, of rational criteria, and so forth. In fact, it proves impossible for Baudrillard to present his case without falling back into a language that betrays the opposite compulsion at work. Thus he often communicates a sense of sickened loathing for the media, the opinion-polls, the whole apparatus of 'dissimulation', even while insisting that there is just no point in deploring its effects since they constitute 'the real' in so far as we can possibly know it.

This ambivalence comes across most clearly in those passages from his recent text, *The Masses*, where Baudrillard suggests that stupidity or apathy – the sheer indifference to truth – may be the most effective weapon against forms of ideological indoctrination. 'About the media', he writes, 'you can sustain two opposing hypotheses: they are the strategy of power, which finds in them the means of mystifying the masses and of imposing its own truth. Or they are the strategic territory of the ruse of the masses, who exercise in them their concrete power of the refusal of truth, of the denial of reality' (p. 217). The first is yet another form of that old Platonist delusion that would treat the intellectual as a figure apart, a knower of truths ideally exempt from the errors and follies of 'commonsense' belief. The second (absurdly) is Baudrillard's one remaining counsel of hope, his idea that 'the masses' might finally arrive at a stage of such total, unresisting imbecility that they would simply not respond to techniques of mass-persuasion, media hype or whatever. It is only the intellectuals, the heirs of Enlightenment – politicians, television pundits, cultural theorists and their ilk – who deplore the idiocy of everyday life and hold out for the saving power of critical reason. In which case, 'if only for a change, it would be interesting to conceive the mass, the objectmass, as the repository of a finally delusive, illusive, and allusive strategy, the correlative of an ironic, joyful, and seductive unconscious' (p. 217).

This is – to say the least – a pretty desperate line of argument, and one that sits oddly with Baudrillard's attack on 'enlightened' thinkers for their patronising attitude to 'the masses'. But it is also worth noting how his language at this point reproduces the old truth/falsehood distinction in the very act of denouncing its complicity with modern techniques of surveillance and control. Thus

> the media are nothing else than a marvellous instrument for destabilizing the real and the true, all historical or political truth ... And the addiction that we have for the media ... is not a result of a desire for culture, communication, and information, but of this perversion of truth and falsehood, of this destruction of meaning in the operation of the medium (p. 217).

So it would seem that there is (or maybe once was) a 'reality', a 'truth' to be destabilised or perverted, a meaning that was somehow subject to 'destruction', a 'medium' that furthered this bad process by confusing truth and falsehood to the point of an ultimate undecidability ... Baudrillard in effect contrives to have it both ways by playing on these distinctions – without which he couldn't even begin to articulate his case – while rhetorically denying that they possess any kind of operative force. So long as we don't read too carefully he can thus carry off the performative trick of conjuring away with one hand those same criteria (truth, reality, history etc.) which he then summons up with the other for purposes of contrastive definition. This trick is fairly common (maybe universal) among celebrants of the 'postmodern'. For the term has no meaning except in relation to those various, supposedly obsolete notions that make up the discourse of modernity.

But this is not just to score the odd point off Baudrillard by remarking his occasional lapses into a pre-postmodern way of thinking. On the contrary: his work is of value only in so far as it accepts – albeit against the grain of his express belief – that there *is* still a difference between truth and falsehood, reason and unreason, the way things are and the way they are commonly represented as being. Baudrillard is a first-rate diagnostician of the postmodern scene, but thoroughly inconsequent and muddled when it comes to philosophising on the basis of his own observations. For it just doesn't follow from the fact that we are living through an age of widespread illusion and disinformation that *therefore* all questions of truth drop out of the picture and we can't any longer talk in such terms without harking back to some version of Platonist metaphysics. Baudrillard's mistake is to move straight on from a descriptive account of certain prevalent conditions in the late twentieth-century lifeworld to a wholesale anti-realist stance which takes those conditions as a pretext for dismantling every last claim to validity or truth. What this amounts to is, again, a kind of systematically inverted Platonism: a fixed determination to conceive no ideas of what life might be like outside the cave.

## IV

As I have said, it is not enough simply to urge on pragmatist grounds that this makes for bad politics, or leads to a position where no amount of reasoned argument would count against the current 'realities' of public opinion, media influence, manufactured consensus-values and the like. Certainly there is every sign of its having this effect, as witnessed by the scramble of left-wing thinkers (among them contributors to journals like *Marxism Today*) to take on board not only Baudrillard and other postmodernist gurus, but a good deal of Thatcherite ideological baggage besides. What begins as a softening-up of the position on various 'liabilities' in the old marxist line – critique, ideology, class-conflict, forces of production, the labour-theory of value – ends in a more or less total conversion to the postmodernist viewpoint. Thus one finds

Dick Hebdige, in a recent article, expounding Baudrillard's ideas with some enthusiasm and advising his readers (or the old-guard socialists among them) that they had better catch up with these latest rules of the game. 'It is no longer possible', he writes,

> for us to see through the appearance of, for instance, a 'free market' to the structuring 'real relations' beneath (e.g. class conflict and the expropriation by capital of surplus value). Instead, signs begin increasingly to take on a life of their own referring not to a real world outside themselves but to their own 'reality' – the system that produces the signs.[14]

Hebdige goes on to admit a few doubts as to just what this programme might mean in political terms, given its attitude of virtual acquiescence in the 'banal seductions' and 'mindless fascination' of current mass-media psychology. But, in general, the message is clear enough: that if such arguments don't make sense according to the 'orthodox left analysis', then the fault lies more with thinkers on the left – or their old-fashioned Marxist concepts and categories – than with anything intrinsic to the postmodern condition. And this attitude often goes along with a suggestion that Thatcherite consensus-values have now managed to capture the high ground of public opinion, so that any workable strategy for change will have to make terms with this new situation. 'If the generalized scepticism towards mainstream media reportage moves beyond issues of "fact" and interpretation – what happened when, where and why and what does it mean? – to question the line between truth and lies itself, then the whole "economy of truth" collapses'.[15] And it is clear – despite the scattering of queasy quotation-marks – that Hebdige thinks of this as a fair statement of the problems confronting socialist thinkers in an age of post-enlightenment politics.

One's response to such arguments could take a variety of forms. It could begin by pointing out that Baudrillard's strategy of persuasion itself presupposes the truth/falsehood distinction when he offers what purports to be an accurate account – or an informed diagnosis – of the way things stand with us now. In fact he ends up in something very like the classic relativist predicament. That is to say, if he succeeds in undermining all appeals to truth, validity, or rational warrant, then there can be no grounds for counting him right on this or any other question. And if he doesn't thus succeed

– or if his work turns out to be the one exception to its own rule –
then we are equally entitled to reject his case. Philosophers since
Plato have often used this as a knock-down argument against
relativism, scepticism and other such apparently self-refuting
doctrines. But those doctrines have proved remarkably resilient,
reviving periodically in various updated or modified forms, only to
meet with some new counter-argument that reiterates the same
basic line.[16] Thus Baudrillard might say – in fashionable
speech-act parlance – that his claims should be construed as
performatives, not constatives; that they are simply not engaged in
the language-game of giving reasons, theoretical grounds etc., and
therefore cannot be caught off-guard by the old anti-relativist
argument. And the same would apply (as we have seen) to any
pragmatist objection that started out from the supposed existence
of a liberal-democratic consensus, and used this as a pretext for
rejecting Baudrillard's extremist views. For he could then muster
all kinds of evidence that in fact this consensus has more or less
collapsed, and along with it the very possibility of appealing to
'truth' as a matter of agreed-upon language-games or shared
cultural values.

So any adequate response to Baudrillard will need to do more
than denounce postmodernism for its defeatist implications or its
role in promoting what Fredric Jameson calls the 'cultural logic of
late capitalism'.[17] It will have to come up with strong counter-
arguments of precisely the kind that Baudrillard rejects as belonging
to an outworn Enlightenment regime of rationality and truth. I
have addressed these issues at length elsewhere, and now have
room for only a brief indication of the shape such an argument
might take.[18] The most important task would be to point out the
various cogent alternatives to Baudrillard's assumption that truth
is nothing more than a localised product of consensus belief, in
the absence of which it no longer makes sense to invoke truth-
conditions or engage in any form of *Ideologiekritik*. One could
then push back to the origins of postmodernism in that widespread
structuralist 'revolution' across various disciplines – linguistics,
anthropology, political science, literary theory – which took a lead
from Saussure in treating language as the paradigm of all signifying
systems, and moreover in excluding (or bracketing) any consideration of language in its referential aspect. For Saussure, this exclusion
was strictly a matter of methodological convenience, a heuristic

device adopted for the purpose of describing the structural economy of language, i.e., the network of relationships and differences that exist at the level of the signifier and the signified.[19] For his followers, conversely, it became a high point of principle, a belief – as expressed most dogmatically by theorists like Althusser, Barthes and Lacan – that 'the real' was a construct of intra-linguistic processes and structures that allowed no access to a world outside the prison-house of discourse.

In Althusser's case, this belief went along with an attempt to reconstitute Marxist thought by sharpening the distinction between 'science' and 'ideology', identifying the latter with lived experience in its various mystified forms, and reserving the term 'science' for that strictly theoretical discourse whose truth was guaranteed by its own structural logic or system of articulated concepts and categories.[20] It was therefore vital (as Althusser argued) to locate the precise point in Marx's own work where there occurred an 'epistemological break', a transition from the residual humanism of his earlier writings to the truly 'scientific' Marxism that resulted from this labour of conceptual critique. Only then would it be possible to specify exactly what distinguished Marxist 'theoretical practice' from those various misreadings, distortions or perversions that had so far prevented such a science from emerging. And if a model was required – a paradigm instance fo this new-found analytic rigour – then it lay in Saussure's demonstration of the need to separate the study of language in its structural aspect (*la langue*) from the mere multiplicity of individual speech-acts comprised under the term *parole*. In Lacan also, the 'return to Freud' was simultaneously a return to Saussure and Jakobson.[21] It involved not only a studious attention to the detail – the 'letter' – of the Freudian text, but also a reading that took full advantage of these discoveries in the realm of structural linguistics. And indeed, as Althusser noted in his essay on Lacan, this held out the prospect of a certain convergence between Marxism and psychoanalysis, since the Lacanian 'Imaginary' could now be construed in terms of its ideological function, its role in producing effects of specular 'mis-recognition', while the 'Symbolic order' could likewise be treated as an analogue of the pre-given social structures which constitute the field of subjective meaning and desire.[22] In short, the appeal to structural linguistics seemed to promise a degree of theoretical rigour that would utterly transform these and other disciplines.

As this prospect receded – as Marxism went out of fashion among French intellectuals and the structuralist paradigm came under attack from various quarters – so postmodernism emerged as the upshot of a generalised incredulity with regard to all theories, truth-claims or 'scientific' notions of system and method. Thus Foucault offered the lesson that truth was nothing more than a product of the will-to-power within discourse, a value attached to certain privileged ideas thrown up from time to time within the shifting orders of language and representation. Post-structuralists (notably the later Barthes) renounced all versions of the quest for method, invariant narrative structures, a 'grammar' of rhetorical codes etc., and henceforth embraced the idea of an 'intertextuality' that exceeded the grasp of any possible structuralist approach. Lacan was taken up – mainly by literary theorists – with the object of showing how illusory was the notion of psychoanalysis as a 'method' applied to literary texts; how the relation between work and commentary – like that between patient and analyst – was subject to manifold symptoms of transference and counter-transference, such that no line could possibly be drawn between literature and criticism (or language and metalanguage). It then remained for thinkers like Lyotard to declare the whole modernist epoch at an end in so far as we could no longer place any trust in Kantian, Marxist or other such claims for the emancipating power of enlightened critical reason. Baudrillard's position can thus be understood as the furthest stage yet reached in this widespread disenchantment (widespread at least among French intellectuals) with 'theory' in just about every shape and form.

So the case against postmodernism could best make a start by examining the basic assumptions of structuralist method, those same assumptions that later proved vulnerable to various forms of sceptical critique. One direction for this enquiry is to ask whether Saussure's foundational project – more specifically, his treatment of the sign as a two-term relation between signifier and signified, renouncing all concern with its referential aspect – might not itself have been responsible for a good deal of subsequent confusion. For there exists an alternative to this way of thinking in the work of analytical philosophers in the post-Fregean line of descent, a tradition that has been more or less ignored by exponents of recent French ideas. From Frege one could take the argument that 'sense determines reference' *only up to a point*; that although what words refer to is partly established by their role in various sentences, language-games or signifying systems, nevertheless it is the referential aspect of language that fixes truth-conditions and thus serves as a paradigm-case for all linguistic understanding.[23] This position finds support in the work of present-day philosophers like Hilary Putnam and Donald Davidson. What they provide – very briefly – is an argument against the relativist doctrine that every language encodes its own distinctive set of referential or semantic criteria; that truth-values can only be assigned in terms of some particular language (or 'conceptual scheme'); and thus that any act of translation between different languages, discourses or schemes will always be uderdetermined with respect to the various possible ways of construing their semantic or conceptual fit. Davidson comes up with some powerful objections to this line of reasoning, a line that brings together such otherwise diverse thinkers as W. V. Quine (on ontological relativity), B. L. Whorf (on ethno-linguistics) and Paul Feyerabend (on the radically 'incommensurable' character of different scientific paradigms).[24] In each case, Davidson argues, they have created unnecessary problems by supposing that issues of truth only arise in the context of this or that particular language. In fact it makes more sense to start out from the opposite premise: namely, that the *precondition* for our knowing any language – for our ability to produce, recognise or interpret sentences in our own or any other tongue – is the ascription to it of certain basic properties (truth-values, predicative structures, referring expressions etc.) in the absence of which understanding just couldn't make a start. And this argument would also apply to those forms of poststructuralist or postmodernist thinking that likewise fall into error (as Davidson sees it) by relativising truth and reference to the supposed multiplicity of languages, cultures or 'conceptual schemes'. Their mistake is in simply not perceiving that truth is a kind of logical primitive, a starting-point for any genuine attempt to comprehend what is involved in acts of translation, successful or otherwise.

This is just one example of the way that developments in analytical philosophy might challenge some of Baudrillard's rhetorical claims with regard to the obsolescence of truth, the non-availability of rational grounds and the need to break with all forms of 'enlightened' conceptual critique. One could also point to work in the areas of epistemology, philosophy of science, historiography, the analysis of knowledge (or veridical truth-claims) and other such disciplines where a strong case exists for *not* simply adopting the pragmatist stance and equating 'truth' *tout court* with what is currently 'good in the way of belief'. The arguments against this position are too many and complex for any adequate summary here. But they would include (for example) some intensive recent work on the question of what constitutes knowledge, as opposed to justified true belief;[25] various instances from the history of science that presuppose some form of epistemic access (as distinct from making sense only on the terms of an existing consensus or research-programme);[26] and arguments in the analytical philosophy of mind and language that stress – like Kant, though with less in the way of 'metaphysical' baggage – that such issues are posed by every act of self-conscious critical reflection on the powers and limits of rational understanding.[27] In short, the postmodernist 'turn' in recent French thinking begins to look less credible – or more closely tied to its own rather narrow intellectual prehistory – if one takes some account of these alternative views.

The same applies to Baudrillard's more specific critique of Marxist concepts and categories. Here again, it is the Saussurian paradigm – or a form of structural-linguistic *a priori* – that stands behind Baudrillard's wholesale reduction of economic, political and social issues to questions of symbolic exchange and the 'dissimulating' agency of the sign. Thus, 'the crucial thing', he writes,

> is to see that the separation of the sign and the world is a fiction, and leads to a science fiction ... This 'world' that the sign 'evokes' (the better to distance itself from it) is nothing but the effect of the sign, the shadow that it carries about, its 'panto-graphic' extension ... Now the homology between the logic of signification and the logic of political economy begins to emerge. For the latter exploits its reference to needs and the actualiza-tion of use value as an anthropological horizon while precluding their real intervention in its actual functioning and operative structure ... In fact, it is now clear that the system of needs and of use value is thoroughly implicated in the form of political economy as its completion. And likewise for the referent, this 'substance of reality', in that it is entirely bound up with the logic of the sign. Thus, in each field, the dominant form ... provides itself with a referential rationale, a content, an alibi

and, significantly, in each this articulation is made *under the same metaphysical 'sign'*, i.e. need or motivation (pp. 84–5).

I have quoted this passage at length because it brings out very clearly the extent to which Baudrillard transforms Saussure's descriptive–analytical project into a form of wholesale anti-realist doctrine. That is to say, he assumes that 'reality' is structured through and through by the order of signs or symbolic equivalences; that our knowledge of the world can amount to nothing more than our mode of insertion into this all-encompassing economy of signs; and thus that any attempt to distinguish 'real' needs or use-values from their order of 'imaginary' representation is necessarily a vain effort and chimerical delusion.

The response to all this could take various forms, among them the flat rejoinder that there are real and present facts of experience – inequality, deprivation, urban squalor, unemployment, massive and increasing differentials of wealth and power – which make nonsense of Baudrillard's sophistical case that nothing exists outside the endless circulation of ungrounded arbitrary signs. At a more philosophical level, one could cite the work of thinkers such as G. A. Cohen and Jon Elster who analyse cardinal concepts in the Marxian text – concepts like the 'labour-theory of value' and 'forces of production' – but who do so (and herein lies their difference from Althusser) on the assumption that those concepts will or should make logical sense quite apart from any mode of discursive production peculiar to Marxist 'theoretical practice'.[28] This difference is crucial for the reason I suggested above: that the restriction of truth (even 'scientific' truth) to its role within this or that specific order of discourse will always leave room for sceptics like Baudrillard to push yet further and conclude that truth is nothing more than a species of rhetorical imposition. In short, the disenchantment with Marxism among present-day French intellectuals has perhaps as much to do with problems intrinsic to the Althusserian-structuralist paradigm as with anything in the broader context of socio-political events.

It may be said – and pragmatists like Rorty or Fish would certainly take this line – that positions 'in theory' are always adopted on the basis of prior commitments or principles, and that, far from providing 'grounds' for such beliefs, they merely act as a source of heightened conviction or suasive appeal. Any argument would then come down to the choice of some favoured rhetoric – or what Rorty calls a 'final vocabulary' – in which to pursue the conversation. Thus liberal thinkers would opt for a language of rights, first principles, equal opportunity, constitutional guarantees etc., while Marxists would invoke a whole range of alternative notions like alienation, class-conflict, ideology, late-capitalist modes of production and so forth. But there could be no deciding the issue between them on other than rhetorical grounds, since their languages would be wholly incommensurable, and any such decision-procedure could only work by appealing to some alternative rhetoric, some 'final vocabulary' that still carried weight in terms of current consensus-values. If this were the case, then Baudrillard would surely have the last word. For it is impossible to deny much of what he says about the 'hyperreality' of present-day politics, the disappearance of truth as an operative standard and the failure of critical reason – whether liberal, Marxist or whatever – to effect any visible change in this condition. And if validity-claims only have force when understood against a background of agreed-upon values and assumptions, then it would indeed appear that truth is a thing of the past and criticism powerless to make itself heard above the media-babble, the opinion-poll feedback and the endless stream of state-sponsored disinformation.

But this case will appear convincing only to those who are swept along by Baudrillard's relentless hyperboles and his otherwise distinctly familiar 'end of ideology' rhetoric. Against it one needs to reassert the basic claim that issues of truth and right reason are *inescapably* raised by any discourse that presents itself for serious appraisal in the mode of diagnostic commentary. Nor are such arguments confined to the tradition of Anglo-American analytical philosophy. Equally relevant would be Habermas's case for a form of 'transcendental pragmatics', one that adopts a normative standpoint – what he calls the 'ideal speech situation' – from which to criticise existing social arrangements and consensus-beliefs.[29] Thus, according to Habermas, there is a critical dimension built into every act of communicative grasp, each attempt to understand what others are saying or to make our own meaning clear despite the various obstacles of ignorance, prejudice or misinformation that stand in our way. Progress comes about through the shared human interest in overcoming such obstacles by achieving a better, more enlightened consensus or a willingness to engage in reasoned debate with viewpoints other than our own. One can thus conserve what is vital to the Kantian tradition – its commitment to values of rationality, truth and the critique of repressive social institutions – without the appeal to foundationalist arguments which would then be vulnerable to Rorty's line of attack. For Habermas, it is crucial to maintain this distinction between a pragmatist outlook which simply equates 'true' with 'true for all present purposes' (or 'good in the way of belief'), and on the other hand a transcendental pragmatics which allows for critique of existing consensus values. His argument takes in a vast range of evidence from speech-act theory, philosophical hermeneutics, the history of science, the sociology of knowledge and issues in present-day (especially West German) political debate. At every point his aim is to mobilise the resources of critical reason against a levelling consensus-view of meaning and truth, a view that would render criticism powerless to diagnose the signs of a false (i.e. a partial or massively distorted) consensus.

Baudrillard's alternative is stated clearly enough: 'a hyperreal henceforth sheltered from the imaginary, and from any distinction between the real and the imaginary, leaving room only for the orbital recurrence of models and the simulated generation of difference' (p. 167). It is a vision which should bring great comfort to government advisers, PR experts, campaign managers, opinion-pollsters, media watchdogs, Pentagon spokesmen and others with an interest in maintaining this state of affairs. Baudrillard's imagery of 'orbital recurrence' and the 'simulated generation of difference' should commend itself to advocates of a Star Wars programme whose only conceivable purpose is to escalate East–West tensions and divert more funds to the military-industrial complex. There is no denying the extent to which this and similar strategies of disinformation have set the agenda for 'public debate' across a range of crucial policy issues. But the fact remains (and this phrase carries more than just a suasive or rhetorical force) that there is a *difference* between what we are given to believe and what emerges from the process of subjecting such beliefs to an informed critique of their content and modes of propagation.

This process may amount to a straightforward demand that politicians tell the truth and be held to account for their failing to do so. Of course there are cases – like the Irangate–Contra affair or Thatcher's role in events leading up to the Falklands war –

where a correspondence-theory might seem to break down since the facts are buried away in Cabinet papers, the evidence concealed by some piece of high-level chicanery ('Official Secrets', security interests, reasons of state etc.), or the documents conveniently shredded in time to forestall investigation of their content. But there is no reason to think – as with Baudrillard's decidedly Orwellian prognosis – that this puts the truth forever beyond reach, thus heralding an age of out-and-out 'hyperreality'. For one can still apply other criteria of truth and falsehood, among them a fairy basic coherence-theory that would point out the various lapses, inconsistencies, non-sequiturs, downright contradictions and so forth which suffice to undermine the official version of events. (Margaret Thatcher's various statements on the Falklands conflict – especially the sinking of the *General Belgrano* – would provide a good example here.)[30] It may be argued that the truth-conditions will vary from one specific context to another; that such episodes involve very different criteria according to the kinds of evidence available; and therefore that it is no use expecting any form of generalised *theory* to establish the facts of this or that case. But this ignores the extent to which theories (and truth-claims) inform our every act of rational appraisal, from 'commonsense' decisions of a day-to-day, practical kind to the most advanced levels of speculative thought. And it also ignores the main lesson to be learnt from Baudrillard's texts: that any politics which goes along with the current postmodernist drift will end up by effectively endorsing and promoting the work of ideological mystification.

## Notes and References

1. Jean Baudrillard, *Oublier Foucault* (Paris: Edition Galilée, 1977). Trans. Nicole Dufresne, 'Forgetting Foucault', *Humanities In Society*, No. 3 (Winter, 1980), pp. 87–111.
2. See, for instance, Gianni Vattimo, *The End of Modernity*, trans. Jon R. Snyder (Cambridge: Polity Press, 1988).
3. *Jean Baudrillard: selected writings*, ed. Mark Poster (Cambridge: Polity Press, 1988). All further references to this volume given by page-number only in the text.
4. See the essays collected in Richard Rorty, *Consequences of Pragmatism* (Minneapolis: University of Minnesota Press, 1982).
5. Jean-François Lyotard, *The Post-Modern Condition: a report on*

*knowledge,* trans. Geoff Bennington & Brian Massumi (Minneapolis: University of Minnesota Press, 1983).

6. Richard Rorty, *Philosophy and the Mirror of Nature* (Princeton, NJ: Princeton University Press, 1980).

7. See, for instance, Louis Althusser, *For Marx,* trans. Ben Brewster (London: New Left Books, 1977).

8. See especially Friedrich Nietzsche, 'On Truth and Lie in an Extra-Moral Sense', in Walter Kaufmann (trans. & ed.), *The Portable Nietzsche* (New York: Viking, 1954), pp. 42–7.

9. See Baudrillard, *Les Stratégies Fatales* (Paris: Bernard Grasset, 1983). Also Poster (op. cit.), pp. 185–206, for a partial translation of this text.

10. There is a rapidly growing body of work on this question of 'nuclear criticism' and on the possible uses of textual theory (semiotics, post-structuralism, deconstruction etc.) in analysing forms of nuclear-strategic doublethink. Baudrillard's stance of extreme referential agnosticism is just one of the positions adopted by parties to this debate. Others have argued that we can, indeed must, maintain some version of critical realism – some means of addressing a 'nuclear referent' or real-world state of affairs – while acknowledging the extent to which perceptions of the arms-race are constructed in and through the various rhetorics which compete for public acceptance. By far the most ambitious attempt in this vein is J. Fisher Solomon's *Discourse and Reference in the Nuclear Age* (Norman, Okl.: Oklahoma University Press, 1988). Solomon puts the case for a 'potentialist' metaphysics, one that would recognise the strictly unthinkable (aporetic) nature of the nuclear 'real', but not go on to argue – like Baudrillard – against any form of rational critique or resistance on principled grounds. The alternative, as he sees it, is to adopt something more like Aristotle's view of the different criteria applicable to those objects, processes or events that exhibit a certain latent reality, a *Tendenzraum* or capacity for change that is none the less amenable to analysis.

On this topic see also the Cardiff Text Analysis Group, 'Disarming Voices (a nuclear exchange)', *Textual Practice,* Vol. II, No. 3 (Winter, 1988), pp. 381–93; Jacques Derrida, 'No Apocalypse, Not Now: full speed ahead, seven missiles, seven missives', *Diacritics* 14, No. 2 (Summer, 1984), pp. 20–31; Michael Allen Fox and Leo Groarke (eds), *Nuclear War* (New York: Peter Lang, 1985); Robert Mielke, 'Imaging Nuclear Weaponry: an ethical taxonomy of nuclear representation', *Northwest Review,* Vol. XXII, No. 1 (1982), pp. 164–80; Christopher Norris, 'Against Postmodernism: Derrida, Kant and nuclear politics', *Paragraph,* Vol. IX (March, 1987), pp. 1–30; Christopher Norris and Ian Whitehouse, 'The Rhetoric of Deterrence', in Nikolas Coupland (ed.), *Styles Of Discourse* (London: Croom Helm, 1988), pp. 293–322; Daniel L. Zins, 'Teaching English in a Nuclear Age', *College English,* Vol. XLVII, No. 4 (1985), pp. 387–406.

11. See Louis Marin, *Utopiques: jeux d'espace* (Paris: Minuit, 1973).

12. See, for instance, Richard Rorty, *Consequences of Pragmatism* (op.

cit.) and Stanley Fish, *Is There a Text in this Class? The Authority of Interpretive Communities* (Cambridge: Mass.: Harvard University Press, 1980).

13. See the essays by Fish and others collected in W. J. T. Mitchell (ed.), *Against Theory: literary theory and the new pragmatism* (Chicago: University of Chicago Press, 1985).

14. Dick Hebdige, 'After The Masses', *Marxism Today*, January 1989, pp. 48–53; p. 51.

15. Ibid., p. 51.

16. For a useful recent account, see Barry Stroud, *The Significance of Philosophical Scepticism* (London: Oxford University Press, 1984).

17. Fredric Jameson, 'Postmodernism, or, The Cultural Logic of Late Capitalism', *New Left Review*, No. 146 (July/August 1984), pp. 53–92.

18. See the essays collected in Christopher Norris, *Deconstruction and the Interests of Theory* (London: Francis Pinter & Norman, Okl.: University of Oklahoma Press, 1988).

19. Ferdinand de Saussure, *Course in General Linguistics*, trans. Wade Baskin (London: Fontana, 1974).

20. See especially Louis Althusser, *For Marx* (op. cit.) and Louis Althusser & Etienne Balibar, *Reading Capital*, trans. Ben Brewster (London: New Left Books, 1970).

21. See Jacques Lacan, *Écrits: a selection*, trans. Alan Sheridan-Smith (London: Tavistock, 1977).

22. See Louis Althusser, 'Freud and Lacan', in *'Lenin and Philosophy' and other essays*, trans. Ben Brewster (London: New Left Books, 1971), pp. 177–202.

23. See Gottlob Frege, 'On Sense and Reference', in Max Black & P. T. Geach (eds), *Translations from the Philosophical Writings of Gottlob Frege* (Oxford: Basil Blackwell, 1952), pp. 56–78. On this topic, see also Solomon (op. cit.) and Christopher Norris, 'Sense, Reference and Logic: a critique of post-structuralist theory', in *The Contest of Faculties* (London: Methuen, 1985), pp. 47–69.

24. See especially Donald Davidson, 'On the Very Idea of a Conceptual Scheme', in *Inquiries into Truth and Interpretation* (London: Oxford University Press, 1984), pp. 183–98. Also Norris, 'Reading Donald Davidson: truth, meaning and right interpretation', in *Deconstruction and the Interests of Theory* (op. cit.), pp. 59–83.

25. Much of this work has to do with cases (so-called 'Gettier problems') where veridical knowledge involves something more than 1) believing X to be the case, and 2) having good grounds or evidential warrant for holding that belief. See Edmund Gettier', 'Is Justified True Belief Knowledge?', *Analysis*, Vol. XXIII (1963), pp. 121–23. For a useful survey of the subsequent debate, see Robert K. Shope, *The Analysis of Knowing: a decade of research* (Princeton, NJ.: Princeton University Press, 1983).

26. See for instance Karl-Otto Apel, *Towards a Transformation of Philosophy* (London: Routledge & Kegan Paul, 1980).

27. For examples from two rather different traditions of thought, see

P. F. Strawson, *The Bounds of Sense* (London: Methuen, 1958) and Hilary Putnam, *Realism and Reason* (Cambridge: Cambridge University Press, 1983).

28. See especially G. A. Cohen, *Karl Marx's Theory of History* (Oxford: Clarendon Press, 1978) and Jon Elster, *Making Sense of Marx* (Cambridge: Cambridge University Press, 1982). See also Alex Callinicos, *Marxism and Philosophy* (London: Oxford University Press, 1985) and Robert Paul Wolff, *Understanding Marx: a reconstruction and critique of Capital* (Princeton, NJ.: Princeton University Press, 1984).

29. See for instance Jürgen Habermas, *Communication and the Evolution of Society*, trans. Thomas McCarthy (London: Heinemann, 1979).

30. See Arthur Gavshon & Desmond Rice, *The Sinking of the Belgrano* (London: Secker & Warburg, 1984), especially Appendix 7, 'A Catalogue of Inconsistencies', where they establish beyond doubt – on the principle of non-contradiction – that the British government put out more than one item of false propaganda.

# Chapter 6

# Feminism and Postmodernism

Sabina Lovibond

---

## I

The term 'postmodernism' exerts an instant fascination. For it suggests that 'modernity' is, paradoxically, already in the past; and consequently that a new form of consciousness is called for, corresponding to new social conditions. But of course it does not tell us what the distinctive character of these new conditions, or of the accompanying consciousness, is supposed to be.

Expositions of postmodernism in the context of political and cultural theory often take as a negative point of reference the idea of 'Enlightenment'. In this paper, therefore, I propose to look at some recent examples of anti-Enlightenment polemic and to consider their meaning from a feminist point of view. I shall use as source material the writings of three well-known philosophers – Jean-François Lyotard, Alasdair MacIntyre and Richard Rorty.[1]

These writers are among the most forceful exponents of the arguments and values which constitute postmodernism within academic philosophy. Inevitably, then, my response to their work will also be a response to the bigger picture which I shall trace in it. But this does not mean that I believe the whole of postmodernism, even in its philosophical variant, to be wrapped up in the pages I have chosen for study: what follows is, in the first instance, an account of a specific bit of textual exploration.

My chosen texts undoubtedly show certain common preoccupations, of which perhaps the most striking is an aversion to the idea of *universality*. The Enlightenment pictured the human race as engaged in an effort towards universal moral and intellectual self-realisation, and so as the subject of a universal historical experience; it also postulated a universal human *reason* in terms of which social and political tendencies could be assessed as 'progressive' or otherwise (the goal of politics being defined as the realisation of reason in practice).[2] Potmodernism rejects this picture: that is to say, it rejects the doctrine of the unity of reason. It refuses to conceive of humanity as a unitary subject striving towards the goal of perfect coherence (in its common stock of beliefs) or of perfect cohesion and stability (in its political practice).

All of our three philosophers illustrate, in their different ways, the postmodernist advocacy of pluralism in morals, politics and epistemology. All are struck by the thought that justification or 'legitimation' are *practices*, sustained in being by the disposition of particular, historical human communities to recognise this and not that as a good reason for doing or believing something; and all associate 'Englightenment' with a drive to establish communication between these local canons of rationality and to make them answerable to a single standard. But this is just what postmodernists thinkers complain of, for they question the merit of consensus as a regulative ideal of discourse. The policy of working for it seems to them to be objectionable on two counts: firstly as being historically outmoded, and secondly as being misguided or sinister in its own right.

The first claim frequently appears in the shape of triumphalist comments on the defeat of revolutionary socialism in the West. MacIntyre, for example, singles out Marxism for special mention as an 'exhausted' political tradition.[3] In a similar vein, Lyotard argues that 'most people have lost the nostalgia for the lost narrative' (that is, for the idea of humanity as tending towards a condition of universal emancipation, the prospect of which endows the historical progress with meaning;[4] and he connects the declining influence of such 'grand narratives' with 'the redeployment of advanced liberal capitalism [after 1960] . . . a renewal that has elminated the communist alternative and valorized the individual enjoyment of goods and services'.[5]

The second claim, namely that the pursuit of ideal consensus is misguided, finds expression in arguments for a more accepting attitude towards the contingency and particularity of our 'language-games'. It is not that postmodernism subscribes to the view that whatever is, is sacrosanct: quite the reverse, in fact, in the case of Rorty and Lyotard, who prize innovation for its own sake. It does, however, deny that the replacement of one 'game' by another can be evaluated according to any absolute standard (e.g. as being 'progressive' or the reverse, in the sense fixed by a teleological view of history). The thought is that since history has no direction (or: since it is no longer possible to think of it as having a direction), any new configuration of language-games which we may succeed in substituting for the present one will be just as 'contingent' as its predecessor – it will be neither more nor less remote from 'realising (universal) reason in practice'.

It is not surprising, then, to discover in this literature a leaning towards non-teleological descriptions of discursive activity. Rorty wishes to transfer to *conversation* the prestige currently enjoyed by 'enquiry';[6] MacIntyre's reflections on morality lead him to the conclusion that *mythology*, the range of narrative archetypes through which a culture instructs its members in their own identity, is 'at the heart of things'.[7] Neither 'conversation' nor 'mythology' is naturally understood as aiming at a single, stable representation of reality, one which would deserve the name of 'truth' in something more than a contextual or provisional sense. And it is this negative feature which fits the terms in question for their role in expounding a 'postmodernism of the intellect'.

But the divorce of intellectual activity from the pursuit of ideal consensus is too important a theme to be entrusted to one or two happily chosen words. Rorty, as we shall see later, explicitly states that a form of life which no longer aspires towards a more-than-provisional truth will be better, on broad cultural grounds, than one which continues to do so; while Lyotard goes further and equates that aspiration with 'terror',[8] believing as he does that it leads inevitably to the suppression of diversity or 'difference'. He even calls for a 'war on totality' – a reassertion of the familiar liberal teaching that, while it may be a regrettable necessity to place constraints on liberty in the name of social order, one must not actively seek to bind together the multiplicity of thought and practice into a single 'moral organism' or 'significant whole'.[9]

The robust partisanship of these texts entitles us to think of 'postmodernism' as a *movement* defining itself by reference to, and in reaction against, modernity. There is, admittedly, no single way in which our three sources illustrate this reaction.[10] They are united, though, in their opposition to the Enlightenment demand that what exists should justify itself before a timeless 'tribunal of reason'. In their view, justification (or legitimation) is always local and context-relative; and the supersession of one local criterion of legitimacy by another is not to be seen as an approximation towards some ultimate criterion that would transcend all local bias, but at most as the outcome of self-questioning on the part of a particular tradition.

This view of legitimation is sometimes presented as the (more attractive) rival of a view called 'Platonism'. The 'Platonism' in question is defined by reference to just one doctrine taken from the historical Plato: the idea that *truth* goes beyond, or 'transcends', our current *criteria of truth*. A recurrent feature of postmodernist theory is the claim that Platonism in this sense is obsolete – that is, that it is no longer possible to believe in a transcendent truth against which the whole intellectual achievement of the human race to date could be measured and found wanting. And postmodernist scepticism about this conception of truth extends also to the distinctive method of enquiry which Plato envisaged as our means of access to genuine knowledge. It extends, in other words, to the idea of human thought as a *dialectical* process: one which would generate a positive result (a body of beliefs which was perfectly stable, because incapable of further correction) by way of the relentless application of a negative method (the method of hunting down and eliminating internal contradiction).

According to the dialectical view of knowledge, this positive result would mark the *end* of enquiry, the point at which thought would come to rest because there would be no possibility of further progress. But this prospect is no longer viewed with universal enthusiasm; it has become controversial. Thus we are invited to see it as a merit of postmodernist 'conversation' that (in contrast to dialectic) it aims, not at its own closure, but at its own continuation: it offers us the prospect of a limitless future enlivened at one point by episodes of agreement, at another by 'exciting and fruitful disagreement'.[11]

To the postmodern reappraisal of our dealings with the objective world, or with 'reality', there corresponds a striking development on the side of the moral and cognitive *subject*. Here too there is some historical justification for attaching the label 'Platonist' to the view against which postmodernism is in revolt. For in Plato's *Republic* the dialectical progress of theory towards perfect coherence is supposed to go hand in hand with an analogous tendency towards coherence in the mind of the enquirer. As the practice of dialectic strengthens my intellectual grasp of truth and goodness, so I am to picture myself advancing towards perfect mental integration: that is, towards a condition in which no sudden access of emotion, no previously unconsidered aspect of things, is able to disturb the ordering of my beliefs and values.

Ever since its invention, this ideal of integrated or 'centred' subjectivity has been linked with that of *personal freedom*. However, the freedom which it promises is not the merely negative state of exemption from external constraints – the 'liberty of spontaneity' which Hume for example, maintained was the only sort we could intelligibly wish for. It is, rather, a 'positive liberty' arising from the proper internal organisation of the mind. Positive liberty (also known as 'autonomy') results from the achievement of a state of mind in which the decisions or commands issued by the *true* subject (the subject *qua* exemplar of ideal coherence and stability) cannot be overturned by recalcitrant impulses or 'passions'.[12] To be free in this sense is to be emancipated from the influence of beliefs and desires which our critical judgement condemns as irrational.

The logical conclusion of this line of argument is that freedom can be attributed without qualification only to those in whom the potential for reason has been fully realised – that is, only to a perfectly rational being. Others (and that means all of us, though we presumably fall short of the ideal in varying degrees) may enjoy a subjective feeling of freedom in our actions; but if we continue to develop intellectually we are destined, some day, to perceive (with hindsight) the relative unfreedom of our current patterns of behaviour.

We can set down as a further component of the Enlightenment outlook the hope of achieving positive liberty by shaking off all accidental (i.e., non-rational) constraints on the way we think and act. The classical 'centred subject' was free because he was no longer at the mercy of unpredictable bouts of passion or appetite; analogously, the modern one is free in virtue of his or her liberation from the influence of social forces which s/he does not understand, and so cannot resist. Communism, for example, encourages us to work towards freedom in this sense by gaining insight into the capitalist economic order and the ideology that goes with it; feminism, at least some of the time, has invited us (women) to search our behaviour and our inner lives for signs of adjustment to a woman-hating culture, so that we can gradually overcome the *self*-hatred induced by that adjustment. (This was the idea behind 'consciousness-raising').

The long march towards autonomy by way of the conquest of our own stupidity (or more accurately, by making ourselves less susceptible to external determination) can be summed up in the word 'transcendence'. In the moral and political context, as in the epistemological one, to 'transcend' is to go beyond. The pursuit of a fully integrated subjectivity takes the form of an attempt to rise above our present mental limitations.

This related idea of transcendence has also attracted hostile attention in recent years. The hostility comes partly from post-modernist critics of Enlightenment, who have rightly observed its connection with the idea of 'universal reason' (if I'm trying to rise above the limitations of a *local or partial* understanding of things, then presumably what I'm aiming at is a fully-rounded, impartial or *universal* understanding). Thus MacIntyre speaks in positively patronising terms of that last word in Enlightenment-style moral autonomy, the Nietzschean *Uebermensch* or 'man who transcends':[13] isolated, self-absorbed, 'wanting in respect of both relationships and activities', this individual clearly needs help from a psychiatric social worker.

Interestingly for our purposes, though, criticism of transcendence as a moral ideal has also begun to be heard in feminist quarters. It has been argued that, from the outset, Western philosophy has devised one scheme of imagery after another to convey, essentially, a single vision – that of *man*, the normal or complete representative of the species, standing out against a background of mere 'nature'; and that this background has consistently been symbolised by *woman* or femininity. Plato's guardians emerge from the womb-

like Cave of 'common sense' into the daylight of knowledge;
Hegel's citizens attain maturity by leaving the obscure, private
world of the family, of which Woman is the presiding genius. In
short, the passage from nature to freedom, or from 'heteronomy'
to autonomy, has been represented in terms of an escape by the
male from the sheltered, feminine surroundings in which he begins
his life.[14]

We have arrived at a point of apparent convergence between
feminism and postmodernism – a common coolness towards one
of the key elements in the Enlightenment ideal. It is time now to
change tack and to consider, in the light of feminist concerns, how
far these two tendencies might be able to enter into a friendly
relationship.

## II

One of the first thoughts likely to occur in the course of any
historical reflection on feminism is that it is a typically *modern*
movement. The emergence of sexual equality as a practical political
goal can be seen as one element in the complex course of events by
which *tradition* has given way, over a matter of centuries, to a way
of life that is deeply *untraditional* – in fact, to 'modernity' in a
semi-technical sense of the word (the sense in which it denotes a
historical period).

'Modern' conditions are those created by technological progress
and by the ever-expanding commerce of nations. They are the
kind of conditions which uproot people from ancient communities
and force them to negotiate their own survival in a capitalist 'free
market'. A key text in the development of this idea of modernity is
Marx and Engels' famous description of the chaos and anarchy of
life under capitalism – a description offset, however, by their
positive vision of the old economic order as pregnant with a new
one.[15] According to this view, the 'collapse of all fixed, fast-frozen
relations' creates the historic opportunity for humanity, represented in the first instance by the industrial working class, to seize
control over its own collective existence through revolution. In
classical Marxist terms, the urban proletariat has the necessary
qualifications for this role because it is made up of *modern* human
beings – men (and also, though problematically, women[16]) who

have been forcibly emancipated from traditional ways of life, and so from the limited outlook of their peasant ancestors. It is thanks to the formation of such a class that the horror of modernity also contains a promise: *sooner or later, arbitrary authority will cease to exist.*

Anyone who is stirred by this promise is still, to that extent, within the Enlightenment habit of thought. Their response indicates sympathy with the Enlightenment refusal to attach any moral or intellectual force to tradition as such.

Now, it is difficult to see how one could count oneself a feminist and remain indifferent to the modernist promise of social reconstruction. From a female point of view, 'tradition' has (to put it mildly) an unenviable historical record. Yet it is in the area of sexual relations that 'traditional values' (marriage, home ownership, wholesome family life, etc.) are proving hardest to shift. Perhaps no other feature of the pre-modern scene has persisted so stubbornly as male dominance – the class system constructed on the basis of biological sexual difference; certainly the thought of a time when concepts such as 'wife' and 'husband', with all the moral atmosphere they evoke, will be as obsolete as 'villein' or 'lord of the manor' is apt to set off a landslide in the mind. Still, if we assess without prejudice the implications for gender (I mean, for masculinity and femininity as cultural constructs) of the 'modern' repudiation of unearned privilege, we may well conclude that this development is an integral part of the package; and if so, it will follow that feminists have at least as much reason as the rest of the world for regarding the 'project of modernity', at the present time, as incomplete.[17]

What, then, are we to make of suggestions that the project has run out of steam and that the moment has passed for remaking society on rational, egalitarian lines? It would be only natural for anyone placed at the sharp end of one or more of the existing power structures (gender, race, capitalist class . . .) to feel a pang of disappointment at this news. But wouldn't it also be in order to feel *suspicion*? How can anyone ask me to say goodbye to 'emancipatory metanarratives' when my own emancipation is still such a patchy, hit-and-miss affair?

Let us focus again on the idea of 'universal reason', and on the recent questioning of this idea. Among feminists, we noticed, the questions have been prompted by a sense of the historical connection between *rationalist ideals* and the belief in a *hierarchical opposition of 'mind' and 'nature'* – the latter opposition in turn being associated with a contempt for 'immanence', finitude, and the muddle of embodied existence generally (the 'lead weights of becoming', as Plato put it). [18] On this analysis, the Englightenment rhetoric of 'emancipation', 'autonomy' and the like is complicit in a fantasy of escape from the embodied condition; [19] as such, it feeds into one of the most notorious aberrations of European culture, and any philosophy which challenges it is likely to have considerable critical force.

Feminist theory is, in fact, deeply indebted to the efforts of philosophy over the last century and more to 'naturalise' epistemology, or in other words to represent the activity we call 'enquiry' as part of the natural history of human beings. For naturalist or materialist analyses[20] of the institutions of knowledge-production – schools, universities, the wider 'republic of letters' – have made it possible to expose the unequal part played by different social groups in determining standards of judgement. In this way they have revealed the ideological character of value-systems which have previously passed as objective or universally valid (consider, for example, the growth of scepticism about academic canons of 'greatness' in literature). Feminism can benefit as much as any other radical movement from the realisation that our ideas of personal, technical or artistic merit, or of intelligibility and cogency in argument, do not 'drop from the sky' but are mediated by an almost interminable process of social teaching and training.

These achievements seem to demonstrate the critical potential of a local or plural conception of 'reason', and so to underwrite its claim to the confidence of feminists. But before we jump to any conclusions, we had better look more closely at the ways in which postmodernist theory puts that conception to work. In the remainder of this paper, I shall introduce three themes which seem to me to qualify as distinctively postmodern; and in each case I shall suggest grounds for doubting whether postmodernism can be adopted by feminism as a theoretical ally. For ease of reference I shall attach labels to my three postmodernist themes: we can call them respectively 'dynamic pluralism', 'quiet pluralism' and 'pluralism of inclination'.

As we begin our survey, we should bear in mind that there is nothing in the communitarian insight *per se* (I mean, in the idea that standards of judgement are historically and culturally conditioned) which would explain postmodernist hostility to the version of ideal consensus. One might very well be impressed by the perspectival character of knowledge-claims, and yet still see enquiry as necessarily seeking to bring all 'perspectives' on reality into communication – to construct a body of thought, or a system of values, accessible indifferently from any starting-point. This, after all, is the 'cheerful hope' which has animated coherentist theories of knowledge from Plato to C. S. Peirce and beyond,[21] and it is by no means obvious that when such theories take a naturalist turn they are bound to renounce the Kantian postulate of a 'special interest of reason' in picturing reality as a single, unified system.[22] In fact, there is no reason in principle why a naturalist epistemology should not interpret in its own terms – namely, as referring to the regulative idea of a single, unified *human culture* – Kant's metaphor of the 'imaginary point', located beyond the limits of possible experience, upon which all lines of rational activity appear to converge.[23]

To call this point 'imaginary' is simply to record the irrelevance, from an epistemological point of view, of worries about when (if ever) we can actually expect to reach the goal of enquiry. Continuing for a moment in a Kantian vein, we can say that although theory (like morality) would no doubt be impossible if the relevant subjective 'maxims' had *no* general appeal to the mind, still theoretical effort (like moral effort) is essentially non-contractual: that is, you are not genuinely engaged in either if you make your contribution conditional on an assurance that all other contributions required to achieve the goal of the exercise will actually be forthcoming. We are therefore concerned here with the epistemic equivalent of an article of faith, a commitment to persist in the search for common ground with others: in fact, something which could not be relinquished on pain of sinking into 'hatred of reason and of humanity'.[24]

As soon as the rationalist conception of enquiry is represented as a matter of *policy*, however (an idea already implicit in Kant's talk of the 'interests' of reason), it becomes fair game for psychological interpretation: that is, it can be seen as expressive of a certain temperament or cast of mind. And it is on this psychological territory that the tendency I have called 'dynamic pluralism' issues its challenge. Lyotard is an appropriate case-study here, since his historical thesis about the eclipse of 'grand narratives' develops itself into a series of more or less explicit suggestions on the subject of postmodern mental health.

As we saw earlier, Lyotard believes that the Enlightenment ideal of a 'revisable consensus governing the entire corpus of language-games played by a community' [25] has lost its grip on the collective imagination. Nowadays, he thinks, the main motive to intellectual activity is the hope of benefiting from the 'performance capabilities' of a 'complex conceptual and material machinery', whose users, however, 'have at their disposal no metalanguage or metanarrative in which to formulate the final goal and correct use of that machinery'. [26] Under these conditions, the rationalist demand for *legitimation* of a putative bit of 'knowledge' has been superseded by a limitless quest for discursive novelty or 'paralogy'; [27] consequently, any lingering conviction that thought has some overarching *purpose*, some destination where it could rest, must be viewed as a sign of imperfect adaptation to postmodernity. The authentically postmodern consciousness is experimental, combative, 'severe': it 'denies itself the solace of good forms, the consensus of a taste which would make it possible to share collectively the nostalgia for the unattainable'. [28]

Postmodernism then, according to Lyotard, is an extension of modernism in that each seeks to articulate the experience of a disorderly, directionless world – an experience compounded of pleasure and pain, conducted in the glare of high-tech extravagance which, like the Kantian sublime, stuns the imagination. [29] But the two positions differ as to what sort of consciousness would be equal to, or worthy of, such conditions. Modernism remains within the 'Enlightenment project' to the extent that it pictures the cognitive mastery of modernity as a step on the road to *ending* it (by collective reimposition of form on chaos, as in the Marxist theory of revolution;) [30] postmodernism, on the other hand, would have us plunge, romantically, into the maelstrom without making it our goal to emerge on *terra firma*.

How should feminist readers respond to the charge of 'nostalgia' as directed against rationalist ideals? In considering this question, we may find it helpful to draw on historical evidence: that is, to look into the formation of the sensibility expressed in the relevant postmodernist texts. Taking a hint from some respectful comments of Lyotard's [31], we can enter more fully into the anti-Enlightenment spirit by way of the writings of Nietzsche – perhaps the sternest of all critics of 'idealism' in general, in the sense of a disposition to compare the real world with an ideal one and to find it wanting. It is this disposition which, in Nietzschean terms, constitutes 'nihilism' – the tendency which he portrays on a more institutive level as a sickness transmitted to European civilization through the combined impact of Platonism and Christianity. 'Interesting' as humanity may have become by virtue of this sickness,[32] Nietzsche's own thought achieves world-historic signi-ficance (or so he claims) by bringing us to the threshold of recovery, and of a passage into the 'second innoncence' of godless-ness. But the 'godless' condition is not so easily attained as many self-styled free-thinkers imagine. 'They are far from being *free* spirits', Nietzsche comments on the positivists on his own day, '*for they still have faith in truth*'; whereas a more resolute scepticism would rise to the discovery that 'man's truths [are ultimately] only his *irrefutable* errors'.[33]

Nietzsche's critique of truth may seem at first sight to be addressed mainly to adherents of a foundational epistemology on empiricist lines (i.e., to those who believe that knowledge rests on a founda-tion of indubitable, because purely experiential, propositions). Taking a broader view, however, we find that he is at least equally devastating about an alternative way of 'having faith in truth', namely that embodied in the practice of *dialectics* and (by implica-tion) in modern coherentist theories of knowledge. In fact, Nietzsche discerns in the method of argument invented by Socrates and Plato the psychological key to all subsequent manifestations of rationalism. For the Socratic habit of thought is one which assumes the possibility, and desirability, of *eliminating conflict* through the gradual con-vergence of all parties on a single, stable point of view. As such, it has always had a plebeian taint – for the elimination of conflict, Nietsche observes, is a goal apt to appeal, above all, to those who can expect to be worsted in conflict: in other words, to the weak.

> Wherever authority is still part of accepted usage and one does not 'give reasons' but commands, the dialectician is a kind of buffoon ... One chooses dialectics only when one has no other expedient ... Dialectics can be only a last-ditch weapon in the hands of those who have no other weapon left ... That is why the Jews were dialecticians.[34]

Rationalism, in Nietzsche's view, remains true to its origin in the will-to-power of the dispossessed: its lineage is betrayed by its wish to transpose conflict from the arena of blows (or of showmanship) into that of rule-governed argument, where the physical or social underdog has a hope of winning. This wish marks it out as a natural ally of the democratic movements of the modern world. For the aim of these movements is to subvert the social conditions which Nietzsche would regard as necessary to the expression of a 'natural order of rank'; that is, they aim to eliminate various sorts of class relationship, and hence various forms of exploitation or dispossession. (In another idiom: they seek to characterise, ever more rigorously, a social order in which the willing participation of all rational persons can be expected – a 'kingdom of ends' with each traditional impediment to membership, whether in terms of class, religion, race or sex, successively provoking resistance and being swept away). In short, then, truth as a regulative ideal is the creation of a socially inferior type of mind. It is the *ressentiment* of the rabble – their sinister genius for making the 'naturally good' feel bad about themselves – which gives rise to this ideal. For as soon as humanity allows itself to be caught up in the 'pursuit of truth', it slips into the way of defining intellectual *virtue* in terms of contrasting *vice* invented by the rabble as an instrument of psychological warfare against their 'betters': the vice of *contradicting oneself*, or of being committed (unwittingly, no doubt, but this only adds to the intimidatory power of the dialectical method) to the assertion of propositions related as 'P' and 'not-P'. (Notice the daring of Nietzsche's suggestion that self-contradiction is not a fault in any absolute or eternal sense: he insists that it was *human beings*, and a particular category of human beings at that, who hit upon coherence as a criterion of value in assessing thought-processes.)

Nietzsche, too, dreams of overcoming 'modernity' in all its anarchic ugliness. But, in his view, this will be achieved, not through a *realisation* of Enlightenment political ambitions, but through a *recovery* from the 'sickness' of Enlightenment ideals – truth, reason, morality (the modern successors to 'God'). Nietzsche concurs in drawing together under the heading of 'modernity' all the egalitarian tendencies of the last few centuries in Europe – liberalism, socialism and feminism alike. He sees feminism, in other words, as one component of the rationalist political programme. And in fact this is a view which many feminists can probably share.[35] It is a view which can be summed up by saying that feminism, at least in its utopian moods (as opposed to its angry and pugnacious ones, which of course are equally essential to it), aspires to *end the war between men and women* and to replace it with communicative transparency, or truthfulness.

Now, it is well known that any expression of moral revulsion against war is, for Nietzsche, a 'symptom of declining life';[36] but there is, perhaps, no branch of life in which rationalism and pacifism are more offensive to him than in that of sexuality.[37] The force of his conviction on this point suggests to Nietzsche an intimate, even a quasi-conceptual, connection between the idea of an *emancipation from reason*, on one hand, and that of an *end to feminism* on the other. This connection is mediated by his concept of *virility*, the quality supposedly expressed in a love of 'danger, war and adventures' – a refusal 'to compromise, to be captured, reconciled and castrated'.[38]

We must understand this statement not only in its obvious, literal, sense but also in an epistemological one. In a world without truth – a world in which the contrast between 'reality' and 'appearance' has been abolished – the interpretation of experience is itself a field for invention, for *hazarding* one's own expressive gestures or acts without seeking for them the safety of confirmation (i.e., of incorporation into a shared and stable body of theory). The cognitive activity of a future, and better, humanity will involve not the suppression of individuality and sensuality (the 'false private self' of the coherentist regime), but rather their subordination to a commanding will.

> Henceforth, my dear philosophers, let us be on our guard against the dangerous old conceptual fiction that posited a 'pure will-less, painless, timeless knowing subject'; let us guard against the snares of such contradictory concepts as 'pure reason', 'absolute spirituality', 'knowledge in itself': these always demand that we should think of an eye that is completely unthinkable, an eye turned in no particular direction, in which the active and interpreting forces, through which alone seeing becomes seeing *something*, are supposed to be lacking; these always demand of the eye an absurdity and a nonsense. There is *only* a perspective seeing, *only* a perspective knowing; and the *more* affects we

allow to speak about one thing, the *more* eyes, different eyes, we can use to observe one thing, the more complete will our 'concept' of this thing, our 'objectivity', be. But to eliminate the will altogether, to suspend each and every affect, supposing we were capable of this – what would that mean but to *castrate* the intellect?[39]

Consistently with the idea that to attempt an impersonal or 'selfless' view of reality would be to 'castrate' the intellect, Nietzsche elsewhere describes his work in general as 'hostile . . . to the whole of European *feminism* (or idealism, if [we] prefer that word),[40] and speaks of his 'faith that Europe will become more virile'.[41] 'Feminism', then, occurs in Nietzsche's writing not only as the name of a contemporary political movement (though of course he has a good deal to say about women's emancipation on the level of indignant commonplace),[42] but also as a shorthand term for the mental impotence implicit (or so he believes) in the bondage of thought to regulative ideals such as truth, reality and goodness. Thought is *emasculated*, Nietzsche argues, in so far as it consents to be 'drawn aloft' (*à la* Goethe) by the ever-receding goal of a perfectly stable condition in which it could find peace.

My motive in introducing Nietzsche into the discussion has not been purely negative. I have no wish to ridicule his account of the psychological meaning of epistemological and political rationalism – his interpretation of the rationalist enterprise in terms of a desire for the elimination of conflict and of arbitrary relations of command. I wish, simply, to suggest that we take seriously Nietzsche's own understanding of his work as a contribution to the overcoming of 'feminism'; and that we maintain, as feminists, a suitably critical attitude to the reappearance in contemporary philosophy of one of Nietzsche's central themes – that of the supersession of 'modernity' by a *harder*, less wimpish form of subjectivity.[43]

I must stress that to point out the phallic or 'masculine protest' character of Nietzsche's philosophy, and of postmodernist theory in its more overtly Nietzschean moods, is not meant to be a prelude to arguing that the values despised by this tradition deserve to be restored to a position of honour *because* they are 'feminine' and, as such, good. I do not mean to suggest that we should turn to Nietzsche for an understanding of what is 'feminine', any more than to other purveyors of the dominant ideology of gender. Instead, my suggestion is that in reading postmodernist theory we should be on the watch for signs of indulgence in a certain collective *fantasy* of masculine agency or identity. Turning upon the Nietzscheans their own preferred genealogical method, we might ask: *who* thinks it is so humiliating to be caught out in an attitude of 'nostalgia for lost unity', or of longing for a world of human subjects sufficiently 'centred' to speak to and understand one another?[44]

## III

I have been arguing for a sceptical response to the kind of postmodernist position which I labelled 'dynamic pluralism'. This position, I have suggested, is informed by an irrationalism whose historical origin lies in reactionary distaste for modernist social movements, and specifically for the movement towards sexual equality. I turn now to the second of my three postmodernist themes, namely 'quiet pluralism'. Our concern here will be with the postmodern 'rediscovery' of the local and customary – a societal counterpart, perhaps, of the revival of vernacular architecture.

It may appear, at first glance, that there is a world of difference between Nietzsche's own vision of a radical renunciation of the 'Socratic' or truth-orientated way of life, and on the other hand the postmodernist proposal that we scrap the Enlightenment project of *absolute* legitimation (the attempt, for example, to create a society that could not be faulted by any rational being). And with this difference in view, it may be objected that the discovery of Nietzschean echoes in the rhetoric of postmodernist theory is of no more than marginal philosophical interest. For to read that theory as an updated Nietzscheanism (the objection will run) is to miss its central point. Postmodernism does not condemn the pursuit of truth or virtue within *local, self-contained* discursive communities – the quest for 'truth' as distinct from 'Truth', as Rorty might put it, or of 'virtue' as distinct from 'Virtue' (the latter meaning the excellence of a human being simply *qua* human and without reference to any particular social role). It reserves its criticism for the idea that we should evaluate the activity of each of these communities by a universal standard – that we should try to make them all 'commensurable'.

We must recognise that postmodernist theory freely concedes

the ability of local 'language-games' – natural science, moral traditions, etc. – to reflect on themselves and to pass judgements of value on particular 'moves' made or contemplated by participants. (That is to say, they can ask – according to the concession – questions such as 'Is this a valid contribution to scientific theory?' or 'Is this sort of conduct consistent with the received moral ideals of our community?') Thus, for Lyotard, 'the striking feature of postmodern scientific knowledge is that the discourse on the rules that validate it is (explicitly) immanent to it',[45] while MacIntyre, anxious to stress that a revival of virtue-centred ethical theory need not be opposed to debate and innovation, claims that 'a healthy [moral] tradition is sustained by its own internal arguments and conflicts'.[46]

This concession is chiefly interesting, however, for the question it raises: how are we to draw any principled distinction between the *rejection of Enlightenment rationalism* and the *rejection of legitimation as such*? The concession is, after all, a very significant one; for having been told that intellectual traditions incorporate a capacity for critical reflection, we might well suppose that the forces of Enlightenment had captured the high ground in the current argument. If discursive communities are capable of self-criticism in principle, we might ask, then who is to dictate how far they shall take it? Won't there always be room for more, so long as *any* intelligible criticism can be addressed to the moral or cognitive order under which we live? And what is this limitless commitment to the dialectical revision of theory and practice, if not precisely the Enlightenment commitment to haul up everything in life before the tribunal of reason?[47]

The likely reply to this challenge is that, although postmodernism may indeed be at a loss for any formal, *a priori* way of determining how far critical reflection can go, there is no real cause for embarrassment here. For the question is, in any case, best understood in a practical, or existential, sense – that is, as just one among many questions calling for deliberate collective choice, and conspicuous only for its unusual generality. Rorty puts the point succinctly:

The pragmatist [e.g. Rorty himself] is betting that what succeeds the 'scientific', positivist culture that the Enlightenment produced will be *better* ... [This successor culture would be one] in which neither the priests nor the physicists nor the poets nor the Party were thought of as a more 'rational' or more 'scientific' or 'deeper' than one another . . . There would still be hero worship in such a culture, but it would not be worship of heroes as children of the gods, as marked off from the rest of mankind by closeness to the immortal. It would simply be admiration of exceptional men and women who were very good at doing the quite diverse kinds of things they did.[48]

MacIntyre's complaint against what he calls 'liberal individualist modernity', and against the 'modern self' corresponding to it, also rests on cultural considerations. The distinguishing mark of this 'self' is that it stands in a purely external relation to the various roles it may, from time to time, take on; that is, none of the activities in which it may become involved enter so deeply into it that to be severed from them would undermine its integrity.[49] The price paid for this radical emancipation from tradition is illustrated, as we have seen, by the sad fate of the Nietzschean *Uebermensch*, whom MacIntyre uses as a foil to set off the attractions of a revived Aristotelianism. And the practical implication of his own Aristotelian programme is that we should call a halt to the pursuit of moral and political 'transcendence' and 'devote ourselves to the construction of *local* forms of community within which civility and the intellectual and moral life can be sustained'.[50] As for Lyotard, we have already noticed his use of the word 'terror' to characterise the idea of enquiry as a unified dialectical process aiming, ultimately, at its own completion or closure.

But, despite the valuable reminder issued by postmodernism that there is no such thing as a 'pure reason' dissociated from any basis in local custom, I do not think feminists should be unduly impressed by the theory in this modified version either. I think we have reason to be wary, not only of the unqualified Nietzschean vision of an *end* to legitimation, but also of the suggestion that it would somehow be 'better' if legitimation exercises were carried out in a self-consciously parochial spirit. For if feminism aspires to be something more than a reformist movement, then it is bound sooner or later to find itself calling the parish boundaries into question.

To unpack this metaphor a little: feminists need to know, and postmodernist theory fails to explain, how we can achieve a thorough-going revision of the *range* of social scripts, narrative archetypes, ways of life, ways of earning a living, etc. available to individual women and men. Consider, for example, such mind-boggling, yet urgently necessary undertakings as the global redistribution of wealth and resources, the reallocation of work and leisure, the prevention of war and environmental destruction. Well, no doubt we shall be told that there is something *passé* in the very habit of mind which can still frame this kind of classically humanist agenda, given the alleged 'exhaustion' of all our political traditions (MacIntyre) and the extinction of any shared 'nostalgia for the unattainable' (Lyotard). But, on the other hand, if there can be no systematic political approach to questions of wealth, power and labour, how can there be any effective challenge to a social order which distributes its benefits and burdens in a systematically unequal way between the sexes? Thus, although it is courteous of Rorty to include women along with men in the class of 'expert-rulers' who will replace the Platonic philosopher-rulers in his pragmatist utopia, it remains a mystery how we can hope to achieve an equal sexual division of power unless we are 'allowed' (by epistemology and political theory) to address the structural causes of existing sexual *inequality*. But this would mean an assault on every social norm or institution which rests on biologistic assumptions about male and female 'nature' – on everything in our familiar way of life which can be traced to the entrenched functionalist notion that what women are *for* is to reproduce and nurture the species. And this, in turn, is far from being the sort of programme that could coexist with a meek, non-interventionist attitude towards the current inventory of social 'roles' or specialised functions. So postmodernism seems to face a dilemma: either it can concede the necessity, in terms of the aims of feminism,[51] of 'turning the world upside down' in the way just outlined – thereby opening a door once again to the Enlightenment idea of a *total* reconstruction of society on rational lines; or it can dogmatically reaffirm the arguments already marshalled against that idea – thereby licensing the cynical thought that, here as elsewhere, 'who will do what to whom under the new pluralism is depressingly predictable'.[52]

MacIntyre's discussion contains plenty of evidence, at a more intuitive level, for the reactionary implications of the proposed return to customary ethics. It is not that his portrayal of 'mythology' as a source of moral insight and guidance is so very wide of the mark phenomenologically. Who would deny the communal character of the ideas on which we draw when we set about the imaginative construction of our own lives as meaningful and unified chains of events? To be sure, 'myth' in this sense provides us with a more vivid conception of our own experience, it leaves us less bored and more in control. But a closer look at the workings of the process is less than reassuring from the point of view of sexual politics. MacIntyre pictures it as follows:

> I can only answer the question 'What am I to do?' if I can answer the prior question 'Of what story or stories do I find myself a part?' We enter human society ... with one or more imputed characters – roles into which we have been drafted – and we have to learn what they are in order to be able to understand how others respond to us and how our responses to them are apt to be construed. It is through hearing stories about wicked stepmothers, lost children, good but misguided kings, wolves that suckle twin boys, youngest sons who receive no inheritance but must make their own way in the world, and eldest sons who waste their inheritance on riotous living and must go and live with the swine, that children learn or mislearn both what a child and what a parent is, what the cast of characters may be in the drama into which they have been born and what the ways of the world are.[53]

This passage, if seriously intended, conveys the suggestion that the cornerstones of our mythical repertoire are the Bible, Grimm's Fairy Tales, and the Greek and Latin classics; and if that were the case, all good liberals would be bound to ask themselves whether the female half of the population can reasonably be asked to piece itself together out of the semiotic fallout from these sources. (Is it a coincidence that the only female role in MacIntyre's long list, for a human being at any rate, is that of a 'wicked stepmother'?) But, of course, the reality is even harsher. For our *effective* mythology, the one which actually determines the customary ethics of the (post)modern world, invites us to interpret ourselves and our neighbours in terms of a rather more topical range of 'imputed characters': good mothers, bad mothers, ruthless career women, gorgeous (dumb) blondes, ordinary housewives, women who are *no better than they should be*, loony lesbian feminists covered with badges . . . anyone who ever reads a newspaper or watches TV can continue the list.

We might wonder whether it is fair to place such a gloomy construction on the 'narrative' model of personal identity. Why should it not be possible to reclaim some of the available roles and turn them, in a spirit of subversion, towards progressive ends? Aren't most, or at any rate *some*, political cultures of the late twentieth century sufficiently variegated to supply alternative story-lines to people of a critical turn of mind (the tireless activist, etc.)?

But MacIntyre seems to have pre-empted this move. For, although he mentions the 'protestor' as one of the 'stock charac-ter[s] in the modern social drama',[54] he consigns this type (along with the 'aesthete' and the 'bureaucrat') to a kind of limbo inhabited by those who have staked their selfhood on an illusion. These distinctively modern social roles, he suggests, can confer only a pseudo-identity on their bearers, since they all draw in one way or another on moral fictions spawned by the Enlightenment; in regard to the 'protestor' the relevant fiction is that of *natural rights*,[55] the defence of which MacIntyre apparently sees as constitutive of oppositional politics. Any idea that 'protest' might generate a substantive conception of personal virtue, and hence a viable postmodern life-pattern, must therefore be abandoned.

No doubt it is correct to see feminism as standing in a predomin-antly negative relation to the culture from which it springs. To use MacIntyre's idiom, no feminist can be content with the range of 'life-stories' currently on offer to girls and women; on the other hand, if we set our faces against that particular set of mythological suggestions, this does not imply that we ought to look forward with any eagerness to some putative neo-Aristotelian regime of 'morality and civility'.[56] (In fact, the very words kindle an obscure desire to commit social mayhem).

We are not, however, under any obligation to accept the hackneyed characterisation of radical politics in terms of 'protest'. We can point instead to a positive aim which feminism has in common with other movements of liberation – an aim which, paradoxically, qualifies these movements as more genuinely Aris-totelian than MacIntyre himself. For they are all concerned with the specification and construction of a *life worthy of human beings*:

the very question under which Aristotle himself takes that of the individual 'good life' to be subsumed.[57] Interestingly, this is the question at which MacIntyre baulks; or rather, his moral epistemology reverses the direction of Aristotle's by treating the individual enterprise as a source of insight into the collective one:

> In what does the unity of an individual life consist? The answer is that its unity is the unity of a narrative embodied in a single life. To ask 'What is the good for me?' is to ask how best I might live out that unity and bring it to completion. To ask 'What is the good for man?' is to ask what all answers to the former question must have in common.[58]

The effect of this reversal is to bar the way to political *theory* and to force the aspiring theorist back into the ideologically saturated field of 'mythology' – i.e., back to a choice between the various narrative archetypes furnished by existing society. Ironically, then, it turns out that despite his use of Nietzsche as an object lesson in the perils of rampant individualism, MacIntyre's motives are not so very different from Nietzsche's own – at any rate, in those relatively unmetaphysical moments when the latter is pondering the 'immense stupidity of modern ideas'.[59]

## IV

Finally, it remains to consider the third of my postmodernist themes, the 'pluralism of inclination'. I offer this (admittedly rather makeshift) term as a means of conferring some positive character on a development which has already been mentioned under its negative aspect – namely, the reaction against rationalist ideals of positive liberty and of the fully integrated human subject.

It would be beyond the scope of this paper to review the arguments for picturing subjectivity in general as 'decentred' or 'in process': these arguments have, in any case, been clearly expounded for the benefit of Anglophone readers by linguistic, literary and cultural theorists.[60] Nor can I offer any general appraisal of the 'philosophy of desire' as a possible successor to the historical-materialist tradition (I mean, in inspiring resistance to agencies of political and social control). We can, however, take advantage of the fact that these strains of anti-Enlightenment thinking have already begun to make their mark on the kind of cultural commentary produced by British feminists and socialists.[61]

Feminism has always given a central importance to the politics of personal choice and taste, and it is therefore significant that over the last few years the movement has made large concessions, in its treatment of these matters, to the anti-rationalist mood of the times. Perhaps the most important trend has been a loss of confidence in the idea of *false consciousness*: in other words, in the thought that our spontaneous aesthetic and emotional responses might require criticism in the light of a feminist analysis of sexual relationships.

To reject 'false consciousness' is to take a large step towards abandoning the politics of Enlightenment modernism. For it means rejecting the view that personal autonomy is to be reached by way of a progressive transcendence of earlier, less adequate cognitive structures: in our case, the transcendence of less adequate levels of insight into the operation of male power.

Many feminist writers now seem to hold that we shall be better equipped to think about the politics of personal life if we put the Enlightenment behind us. Influential in this respect has been Elizabeth Wilson's book *Adorned in Dreams: Fashion and Modernity* (1985), which deplores the 'rational dress' tendency within feminism and affirms 'fashion' as a (potentially) oppositional medium of expression:

> Socially determined we may be [writes Wilson], but we consistently search for crevices in culture that open to us moments of freedom. Precisely because fashion is at one level a game ... it can be played for pleasure.[62]

The same theme has been taken up by journalist Suzanne Moore, who has written in defence of women's glossy magazines:

> We are waking up to the importance of fantasy, pleasure and style, and to awareness that a politics that excludes them will never be truly popular ... We cannot just pull pleasure into the correct ideological space through political intention alone. The idea that we ever could results from an air of moral élitism prevalent on the left and unwittingly absorbed by feminism.[63]

And more recently, Brenda Polan of *The Guardian* has mounted the following attack on feminists who reject standard notions of how women ought to look:

The puritans whose criticism disturbs me most are women who are self-righteous in their espousal of the belief that lack of artifice equals virtue. Aggressive lack of artifice ... declares a refusal to please, to charm, to be easy on the eye. It is an awesome arrogance; a declaration that no improvement is necessary, that the aesthetic consensus is mistaken and those subscribe to it fools (25th August 1988).

In all these texts the idea of *pleasure* is prominent – either our own, or, in Polan's cruder version of the argument, the pleasure we give others (thereby justifying our own existence and, presumably, gaining something of the narcissistic satisfaction traditionally allowed to women). The word 'pleasure', at all events, is apt to be brought out with a flourish, as if it clinched the case for seeing progressive or creative possibilities in something previously viewed with suspicion. The suggestion is that feminists have harmed their cause, they have *put people off*, by their gratuitous asceticism about make-up, frilly knickers and the like. But this invites the objection: whoever wants to claim that conventional femininity, even at its most abject, cannot be *pleasurable* for women?[64] Not long ago, it would have been widely accepted as self-evident that if for example I find that buying new clothes helps me to stave off boredom or sadness, that is not an argument in favour of shopping but a starting-point for reflection on my otherwise unsatisfied needs. If this is no longer common ground among feminists, it's arguable that the change is indicative not so much of an advance in wisdom or humanity as of a recourse to the consolations of the powerless – or rather, the consolations of those who have more purchasing power than power to influence the course of their common life.

There is, of course, something right in postmodernist warnings against insisting too much on 'ideological soundness', whether from oneself or – still worse – from others. No doubt there are pitfalls here; arrogance and self-deception are the most obvious. It would be sensible, therefore, to concede that there is no future in trying to conform on theoretical grounds to a definition of pleasure which is hopelessly remote from our current capacities for actually enjoying life. But if we accept that changes in these capacities can be emancipating – that they hold out a prospect of repairing some of the damage done to us in turning us out as women – then we are already committed to the idea that how things stand with a person in respect of her powers of enjoyment is a matter for political evaluation. And in that case, the occasional moralism or 'moral élitism' of radical movements will have to be understood as a vice of excess, rather than as a symptom of fundamental wrong-headedness: the danger lies, in other words, not in wishing to bring our (felt, empirical) desires into line with our rational understanding, but in tackling the job in a ham-fisted way that is doomed to provoke disgust and reaction.

Again, the postmodernist celebration of pleasure sometimes wins a trick by appealing to the role of immediate feeling in subverting psychic order.[65] The idea of subjectivity as socially (or discursively) constructed, and thus as inherently fluid and provisional, opens up a world of possibilities here.[66] But if feminism disowns altogether the impulse to 'enlighten', it will be at a loss to speak the wish to make these possibilities real. Subjectivity can be as fluid as you please, but this insight – once decoupled from the feminist ambition to *reconstruct* sensibility in the interest of women – will no longer be of any specifically political interest. Its political significance lies in the implication that contrary to appearances (to the nightmarish uniformity, give or take routine variations in 'style', of the cultural representation of gender), we can remake ourselves as better – more autonomous, less pathetic – people: 'better' by our own present lights, of course, but that is simply a condition of engagement in cognitive activity. Did anyone expect feminist theory to wipe out overnight every trace of the mythology which is, sexually speaking, at the heart of things? And if not, isn't the present surge of enthusiasm for 'pleasure' really the sign of a terrible pessimism?[67]

The alternative to this kind of pessimism, I suggest, is that feminists should continue to think of their efforts as directed not simply towards various local political programmes, but ultimately towards a global one – the abolition of the sex class system, and of the forms of inner life that belong with it. This programme is 'global' not just in the sense that it addresses itself to every corner of the planet, but also in the sense that its aims eventually converge with those of all other egalitarian or liberationist movements. (It would be arbitrary to work for *sexual* equality unless one believed that human society was disfigured by inequality *as such*).

If this is a convincing overall characterisation of feminism, it follows that the movement should persist in seeing itself as a component or offshoot of Enlightenment modernism, rather than as one more 'exciting' feature (or cluster of features) in a postmodern social landscape. What does *not* follow is that it would be desirable for the women's movement – either world-wide, or in any one country – to be kept in order by some central authority (the 'totalitarian' spectre which postmodernists, in common with old-fashioned Cold Warriors, are fond of invoking). If, for example, European and/or North American feminism is alleged by black women to share in the racism of the surrounding culture, then their complaint rightly creates a new political agenda – a new set of pointers towards the goal of a genuinely 'heterogeneous public life';[68] and this sort of development certainly makes the movement (empirically speaking) less unified than before. But it does not prejudice the *ideal* unity of feminism.[69] Instead, it calls attention to a certain respect in which feminism has fallen short of its own idealised self-image as an occupant of the 'universal standpoint' (in contrast, say, to the traditional – male-dominated – Left). It is not 'liberal guilt', or conscientiousness in the abstract, which gives accusations of racism their urgency: it is the background commitment of feminism to the elimination of (self-interested) cognitive distortion.

## Notes and References

1. Specifically, I shall draw on Lyotard, *The Postmodern Condition: A Report on Knowledge*, trs. Geoff Bennington and Brian Massumi (1984). Manchester, Manchester UP (hereafter *PMC*); MacIntyre, *After Virtue: A Study in Moral Theory* (1981), London, Duckworth (hereafter *AV*); Rorty, *Philosophy and the Mirror of Nature* (1980), Oxford, Blackwell (hereafter *PhMN*) and 'Pragmatism and Philosophy' in his *Consequences of Pragmatism* (1982), Brighton, Harvester – reprinted in Kenneth Baynes, James Bohman and Thomas McCarthy (eds) *After Philosophy: End or Transformation?* (1987), Cambridge, Mass., MIT Press.

Obviously the attempt to capture any complex argument in a brief survey is liable to lead to some oversimplification, and in particular it should be noticed that Rorty in *PhMN* refers to the Enlightenment separation of science from theology and politics as 'our most precious cultural heritage' (p. 333). The main motive of his book, however, is to voice a 'hope that the cultural space left by the demise of epistemology [i.e., of the commitment to rendering all discourse commensurable] will not be filled' (p. 315), and this identifies him for our purposes as an anti-Enlightenment theorist.

The themes of *After Virtue* are developed further in MacIntyre's more recent book, *Whose Justice? Which Rationality?* (1988), Notre Dame, Indiana, University of Notre Dame Press.

2. For an expression of this kind of intellectual monism, cf. Kant, Preface to *The Metaphysical Principles of Right* (in *The Metaphysical Principles of Virtue*, trs. James Ellington, 1964, p. 5): '... inasmuch as there can be only one human reason, so likewise there cannot be many philosophies; that is, only one true system of philosophy based on principles is possible, however variously and often contradictorily men may have philosophized over one and the same proposition'.

3. *AV*, p. 244.

4. *PMC*, p. 41.

5. *PMC*, p. 38.

6. *PhMN*, p. 318.

7. *AV*, p. 201.

8. *PMC*, p. 82.

9. For 'moral organism', cf. F. H. Bradley, *Ethical Studies*, Oxford, Oxford UP, 1962, p. 177; and for 'significant whole', cf. H. H. Joachim, *The Nature of Truth* (1906, republ. 1969), Westport, Conn., Greenwood Press, pp. 68 ff.

10. Lyotard, for example, sees in the postmodern experience the 'truth' of the modern one (the former, he says, is *part* of the latter and inherits from it the maxim that 'all that has been received ... must be suspected' (*PMC*, p. 79); MacIntyre's position by contrast seems more akin to that of postmodernists in the field of art and design, where the distinguishing mark of the school has been found in a certain relation to the past – a reappropriation of traditional forms of expression, combined, however, with a historical knowingness acquired in the passage through modernity (cf. Charles Jencks, *What is Postmodernism?*, 1986, London, Academy Editions, p. 18).

11. *PhMN*, p. 318.

12. For this characterisation of 'positive' and 'negative' liberty, cf. Isaiah Berlin, 'Two Concepts of Liberty' in his *Four Essays on Liberty* (1969), Oxford, Oxford U.P.

13. *AV*, p. 239.

14. For this reading of *Republic* VII, cf. Luce Irigaray, *Speculum of the Other Woman*, trs. Gillian C. Gill (1985), Ithaca, Cornell University Press, pp. 243 ff.; and for a fuller reconstruction of the idea of masculinity as transcendence, cf. Genevieve Lloyd, *The Man of Reason: 'Male' and 'Female' in Western Philosophy* (1984), Minneapolis, Unversity of Minnesota Press.

15. Marx and Engels, 'Manifesto of the Communist Party' in Karl Marx, *The Revolutions of 1848: Political Writings*, Vol. I, ed. David Fernbach (1973), Harmondsworth, Penguin/NLB p. 70: 'Constant revolutionizing of the means of production, uninterrupted disturbance of all

social conditions, everlasting uncertainty and agitation distinguish the bourgeois epoch from all earlier ones. All fixed, fast-frozen relations, with their train of ancient and venerable prejudices and opinions, are swept away, all new-formed ones become antiquated before they can ossify. All that is solid melts into air, all that is holy is profaned ...'

Marshall Berman pursues this analysis in depth in *All That Is Solid Melts Into Air: The Experience of Modernity* (1982), New York, Simon and Schuster, ch. II.

16. For a review of the problems here, cf. Alison M. Jaggar, *Feminist Politics and Human Nature* (1983), Lanham, Maryland, Rowman and Allanheld ch. 4. More polemical discussions of the shortcomings of orthodox Marxist approaches to the 'woman question' can be found in Christine Delphy, 'The Main Enemy' in her *Close to Home: A Materialist Analysis of Women's Oppression* (trs. and ed. Diana Leonard, London, Hutchinson, 1984) and in Heidi Hartmann, 'The Unhappy Marriage of Marxism and Feminism: Towards a More Progressive Union' in Lydia Sargent (ed.) *The Unhappy Marriage of Marxism and Feminism: A Debate on Class and Patriarchy* (1981), London, Pluto Press.

17. Cf. Jürgen Habermas, 'Modernity – An Incomplete Project' in Hal Foster (ed.) *Postmodern Culture* (1985), London, Pluto Press.

18. *Republic* VII, 519ab.

19. The exposure of this fantasy has been one of the concerns of feminist writing on pornography: cf. Susan Griffin, *Pornography and Silence: Culture's Revenge Against Nature* (1981), New York, Harper and Row.

20. 'Naturalist or materialist': there exists in the theory of knowledge a spectrum of positions prompted by the failure of the Cartesian quest for certainty. At one end of the spectrum – the 'positivist' end, so to speak – we have for example, W. V. Quine's vision of 'epistemology, or something like it, simply fall[ing] into place as a chapter of psychology and hence of natural science', and his programmatic statement that 'We are after an understanding of science as an institution or process in the world' (cf. 'Epistemology Naturalized' in his *Ontological Relativity and Other Essays,* 1969, New York, Columbia U.P., pp. 82, 84); at the other, 'critical', end we have a variety of views which take the latter programme in a political sense and search out the hidden power-relations underlying not only (natural) science, but everything else to which the honorific title of 'knowledge' is assigned. 'Epistemic naturalism' can function as an umbrella term covering this whole spectrum of positions; 'epistemic materialism' is probably best reserved for a subset of them, namely those which seek to apply the Marxist method of historical materialism to the processes in question. (But Marxism does not exhaust the subversive options, which indeed can no longer be summed up without residue under the heading of 'critique' – witness the work of Nietzsche and Foucault).

21. For Peirce's position, cf. 'How to Make Our Ideas Clear' in his *Collected Papers*, Vol. V, Harvard, Mass, Harvard U.P. 1934, p. 268: '... all the followers of science are animated by a cheerful hope that the process of investigation, if only pushed far enough, will give one certain

solution to each question to which they apply it ... This great hope is embodied in the conception of truth and reality'.

22. *Critique of Pure Reason*, A648/B676.
23. Ibid., A644/B672.
24. Plato, *Phaedo* 89d.
25. *PMC*, p. 65.
26. *PMC*, p. 52.
27. *PMC*, pp. 65–6. This theme is echoed by Rorty's account of the motive forces of post-epistemological discourse, which includes a reference to 'individual men of genius who think of something new' (*PhMN*, p. 264).
28. *PMC*, p. 81.
29. *PMC*, p. 77; cf. Kant, *Critique of Aesthetic Judgement*, §23.
30. Cf. Perry Anderson, 'Modernity and Revolution' in *New Left Review* 144, p. 113 – a passage which, incidentally, contains a useful corrective to the tendency to confuse *eliminating contradiction* with *suppressing difference*. (For a more extended reply to the charge that discourse aiming at (universal) truth necessarily seeks to 'unify coercively a multiplicity of standpoints', cf. Peter Dews, *Logics of Disintegration: Poststructuralist Thought and the Claims of Critical Theory* (1987), London, verso, pp. 220 ff.; the words quoted appear on p. 222).
31. *PMC*, p. 39. For reasons of space I have omitted any discussion of Lyotard's conspicuous *divergence* from Nietzsche in claiming that 'justice as a value is neither outmoded nor suspect' (p. 66). I do not think this need prevent us from getting to grips with his overall argument, since the idea that justice ought to be salvaged receives very perfunctory attention in *PMC* in comparison with the idea that universality ought to be jettisoned.
32. Cf. Nietzsche, *The Genealogy of Morals*, New York, Random House, 1969 (hereafter *GM*), Essay II, §16.
33. *GM*, Essay III, §25 (trs. Walter Kauffmann, 1969); *The Gay Science*, New York, Random House, 1974, (hereafter *GS*), §265 (trs. Kauffmann, 1974).
34. *Twilight of the Idols*, 'The Problem of Socrates', §6 (trs. R. J. Hollingdale, 1968), Harmondsworth, Penguin.
35. 'Many', not all: obviously this conception rides roughshod over the claims of a 'feminism of difference'. I believe that reflection on sexual difference can be both intellectually and politically enabling, but incline ultimately towards the view that 'Glorification of the feminine character implies the humiliation of all who bear it' (Theodor Adorno, *Minima Moralia*, trs. E. F. N. Jephcott, 1974, London, NLB, p. 96). However, I cannot argue the point here.
36. Cf. *GM*, *loc. cit.* (Kauffmann, p. 154): 'A predominance of mandarins always means something is wrong; so do the advent of democracy, international courts in place of war, equal rights for women, the religion of pity, and whatever other symptoms of declining life there are'.

This feature of his thought should be kept clearly in view over against reminders – however valid – that Nietzsche is not a crude prophet of aggression, nor his 'will to power' equivalent to bloodlust (cf. Gillian

Rose, *Dialectic of Nihilism: Poststructuralism and Law* Oxford, Blackwell 1984, pp. 200 ff). No doubt it was vulgar of the Italian Futurists to babble about 'war, the sole hygiene . . .', but the fact remains that for Nietzsche it is, in the end, a sign of spiritual poverty to regard war, injury and exploitation as detracting from the perfection of the world.

37. F. Nietzsche, *Ecce Homo*, New York, Random House, 1969 'Why I write such good books', §5, trs. Kauffmann: 'Has my definition of love been heard? It is the only one worthy of a philosophy. Love – in its means, war; at bottom, the deadly hatred of the sexes'.

38. *GS*, §377 (trs. Kauffmann).

39. *GM*, Essay III, §12 (trs. Kauffmann).

40. F. Nietzsche, *Daybreak*, Cambridge, Cambridge U.P., Preface, §4 (trs. Hollingdale, 1982).

41. *GS*, §362; and cf. *GM, Essay III ad fin.*, where the statement that 'morality will gradually perish now' refers to the same historical prospect.

42. Cf. F. Nietzsche, *Beyond Good and Evil*, 1973, Harmondsworth, Penguin §§231–9.

43. In the neo-Nietzschean discourse of the present day, the theme of 'hostility to feminism' is, not surprisingly, repressed. But this repressed material has a way of returning in contexts where the Enlightenment project of legitimation is up for criticism. An example is supplied by Vincent Descombes, expounding the views of Lyotard in *Modern French Philosophy*, trs. L. Scott-Fox and J. M. Harding (1980) Cambridge, Cambridge U.P., p. 182: '. . . in more general terms, no sooner do we become aware that truth is only the expression of a will to truth than we must face the fact that this "truth" betrays a timid rejection of the world in as much as it is not a "true world" (stable, ordered and just)'. Notice the taunt: a *timid* rejection! This is the same rhetoric by means of which Nietzsche seeks to put the Enlightenment on the defensive – a rhetoric which associates the truth-orientated habit of thought with 'castration' (in the psychoanalytic sense).

44. Certainly, the idea of the outsider or 'nomad' (the individual who gets by, morally speaking, without any home base) has its own pathos, and even – in a rationalist context – its own justification (we have to deny ourselves *false* comforts in order not to be diverted from the quest for *true* ones, i.e., for a better world). But as the badge of a self-constituting élite – a Nietzschean 'aristocracy of the spirit' – it is merely the flip side of the bourgeois order. The nomad is the 'other' of the reliable paterfamilias; he is the 'untamed' male who has escaped from the trap of domesticity (cf. Gilles Deleuze's 'terrible mothers, terrible sisters and wives': *Nietzsche and Philosophy*, London, Athlone Press, trs. Hugh Tomlinson, 1983, p. 187). This cultural cliché is beginning to attract some well-deserved feminist criticism: cf. Deborah Cameron and Elizabeth Frazer, *The Lust to Kill: A Feminist Investigation of Sexual Murder* (1987), Oxford, Polity Press, esp. pp. 52–69; 155–62. (Barbara Ehrenreich's *The Hearts of Men: American Dreams and the Flight from Commitment* (1983), New York, Doubleday, also contains relevant material).

44. *PMC*, p. 54.

46. *AV*, p. 242.

47. It is sometimes suggested that this kind of 'legitimation from within' could not serve to keep the Enlightenment project in being, since its internality to the discourse on which it operates prevents it from being a *genuine* legitimation at all. This seems to be the reasoning of Lyotard, who also says of (postmodern) science that it is '*incapable* of legitimating itself, as speculation assumed that it [science] could' (*PMC*, p. 40, emphasis added). But this comment would be entirely out of place, were it not for an (unexamined) assumption that any 'legitimation' worthy of the name requires access to an *absolutely* transcendent standard of validity, i.e., to something exempt from the finite and provisional character attaching to all human discourse. (A related assumption can be seen at work in the attempt to discredit Enlightenment modernism by attaching fetishistic capital letters to the regulative ideas it invokes: 'Reason', 'Truth', etc.).

48. 'Pragmatism and Philosophy' in Baynes, Bohman and McCarthy, *After Philosophy*, pp. 55–6.

49. Cf. *AV*, p. 30.

50. *AV*, p. 245, emph. added.

51. And of course those of socialism too, though it seems desirable to streamline the argument here.

52. Cf. Cameron and Frazer, *The Lust to Kill*, p. 175. (In its original context this remark refers to a 'pluralism' of sexual practice.)

53. *AV*, p. 201.

54. *AV*, p. 238.

55. *AV*, pp. 68–9.

56. *AV*, p. 244.

57. Aristotle, *Nicomachean Ethics*, I, 2 (ethics is a branch of politics).

58. *AV*, p. 203.

59. Cf. *Beyond Good and Evil*, §239; other relevant passages are *GS*, §356 and *Twilight of the Idols*, 'Expeditions...', §39. MacIntyre is of course aware of the contentiousness of his all-things-considered portrayal of Nietzsche as an *Aufklärer*, but decides to brazen it out (*AV*, p. 241); however, in view of Nietzsche's clear perception of his own work as a logical development of the Kantian 'critique of reason', I am unconvinced that MacIntyre succeeds in locating any flaw in the self-consciousness of his (Nietzsche's) texts.

As a postscript to the foregoing discussion, I can warmly endorse these words of Seyla Benhabib and Drucilla Cornell in their Introduction to Benhabib and Cornell (eds) *Feminism as Critique* (1987), pp. 12–13: 'Despite many common elements in their critique of the liberal concept of the self, feminist and communitarian perspectives differ: whereas communitarians emphasize the situatedness of the disembedded self in a network of relations and narratives, feminists also begin with the situated self but view the *renegotiation* of our psychosexual identities, and their *autonomous reconstitution* by individuals as essential to women's and human liberation'.

60. Cf. for example Deborah Cameron, *Feminism and Linguistic*

*Theory* (1985), London, Macmillan, Ch. 7; Toril Moi, *Sexual/Textual Politics: Feminist Literary Theory* (1985), pp. 99 ff.; Jacqueline Rose, *Sexuality in the Field of Vision* (1986), London, Verso, esp. Introduction; Chris Weedon, *Feminist Practice and Poststructuralist Theory* (1987), Oxford, Blackwell, Chs 4, 5.

61. For a non-feminist statement of the case against 'political correctness' in the sphere of taste, cf. Robert Elms in *New Socialist,* May 1986. Curiously, some of Elms' 'designer socialist' claims in this article have a very Platonist ring ('. . . there is no divide between form and content, they are both a reflection of each other. Good things look good . . .'); but in his mouth these claims are far from bearing a rationalist meaning, since Elms assumes, in defiance of any 'Platonist' tradition, that what *looks good* is more knowable than what *is good* – that, in fact, appearances outweigh theory in the making of political value-judgements.

62. Elizabeth Wilson, *Adorned in Dreams*, London, Virago, 1985, p. 244. Notice that in her chapter on 'Feminism and Fashion' Wilson does not limit herself to a simple critique of puritanism, but closes with a strong prescriptive message: 'The progressive project is not to search for some aesthetically pleasing form of utilitarian dress, for that would be to abandon the medium; rather we *should* use dress to express and explore our more daring aspirations' (p. 247, emphasis added).

63. 'Permitted Pleasures' in *Women's Review*, August 1986 (order of excerpts reversed).

64. Cf. Catharine A. MacKinnon's description of sexism as 'a political inequality that is sexually enjoyed, if unequally so' (in her *Feminism Unmodified: Discourses on Life and Law*, Harvard, Mass, Harvard U.P. 1987, p. 7).

65 Moore (*op. cit.*) tells us that 'Femininity is not indelibly stamped onto us, but continually in a process of recreating itself.' But this does not deter her from writing of 'the early seventies, [when] some women were desperately trying to have the right kind of sexual fantasy that didn't actually involve any of the things that make sex exciting'. Despite the playful tone, these words clearly imply that we *know what it is* that 'makes sex exciting'. Well, *do* we know? It is too easy to say that if you are interested in 'sex' then you can't help knowing. On one level that is no doubt true; but strategically, a more fruitful principle for feminists (and other opponents of patriarchy) would be to assume that we still have everything to learn.

66. These are the possibilities I once tried to capture in terms of Quine's notion of a 'pull toward objectivity': what this phrase suggests is that we can pull the other way, i.e., that there can be a conscious, politically-motivated resistance to the processes of socialisation (cf. Sabina Lovibond, *Realism and Imagination in Ethics*, Oxford, Blackwell, 1983, pp. 58 ff., 194).

67. Terry Eagleton's words about the 'characteristic post-structuralist blend of pessimism and euphoria' ('Capitalism, Modernism and Postmodernism', *New Left Review* 152, p. 64) seems very much to the point as a comment on the politics of 'crevices' and 'moments'.

186 *Feminism and Postmodernism*

68. Cf. §4 of Iris Marion Young, 'Impartiality and the Civil Public: Some Implications of Feminist Critiques of Moral and Political Theory' in S. Benhabib and D. Cornell, Eds *Feminism as Critique* Oxford, Polity, 1987. As should be clear by now, I am unpersuaded by the view of 'Enlightenment' which prompts Young's statement that 'we cannot envision such a renewal of public life as a recovery of Enlightenment ideals' (p. 73).

69. That is, it does not constitute an argument against conceiving of feminism as essentially a single movement (because constituted by a single aim – the aim of ending sexual oppression).

# Chapter 7

# Postmodern Theory and Feminist Art Practice

Janet Wolff

Postmodernism has been welcomed enthusiastically by many feminist artists and critics, frustrated by their continuing exclusion from the dominant modernist tradition in the visual arts. The particular strategies of postmodernist art practice are seen as potentially critical and radical interventions into what is still predominantly a patriarchal culture. Craig Owens, in one of the first of the now numerous collections of essays on postmodern theory, suggested the close affinity of feminism and postmodernism: 'the kind of simultaneous activity on multiple fronts that characterizes many feminist practices is a postmodern phenomenon.' (Owens, 1985, p. 63) This claim on behalf of recent developments in the visual arts has also been made with regard to so-called postmodernism in other media: for example, dance, music television and popular culture. In this essay I shall review the arguments about the feminist potential of postmodern art, and consider some of the difficulties with this particular alliance.

## The Failure of Modernism

Disillusion with modernism lies behind the optimism about postmodern cultural practices. Modernism was never, of course, a uniformly radical project. As Perry Anderson has pointed out, it was as diverse in its political affiliations as it was in its media, styles and manifestos (Anderson, 1984). But a central part of the modernist project was always avant-garde, in the sense of being both aesthetically and politically radical. (See Lunn, 1985.) This project, however, in common with every movement in the history of art in the West, marginalised women and barred any possible feminist dimension, whether in painting and sculpture or in criticism.

Feminist art historians in the past fifteen years have achieved tremendous success in retrieving the work and lives of women artists from a history which managed to obliterate them from the record. Modernism is no exception to the general tendency of the art world to exclude women from production, and to refuse to acknowledge their work (in criticism, in art history) when they do paint. The women artists among the early modernists are better known than they once were, thanks to the efforts of feminist historians: they include Berthe Morisot, Mary Cassatt, Suzanne Valadon, Rosa Bonheur. More recently, the Surrealist movement has been reassessed, to rediscover the work of artists like Leonor Fini, Leonora Carrington, Lee Miller, Meret Oppenheim and Frida Kahlo. The invisibility of women artists in the history of modernism reproduces that process whereby work by men (often the husbands or lovers of women artists) is taken seriously and that by women ignored: Lee Krasner and Jackson Pollock are an example of this tendency to partial blindness on the part of art historians, and there are numerous others.

Part of the problem with modernism, then, has been the systematic exclusion of women from its institutions and its self-conception. (It has been shown, in two recent books, that literary modernism operated an identical process of exclusion. Benstock, 1987; Hanscombe and Smyers, 1987). It has been suggested that the very conception of modernism depends on an identification of the artist as male. Griselda Pollock, for example, argues that the notion of 'creativity', so central to late nineteenth-century and twentieth-century art, is essentially a notion of *male* creativity (Pollock, 1982, p. 4). Andreas Huyssen has demonstrated that modernism, as any form of high culture, is gendered as male, in opposition to mass culture which is gendered as female or feminine (Huyssen, 1988). The male mystique, he maintains, is central to modernism, and particularly to painting (p. 50).

There is little doubt that women are marginal to modernist art practice, which has become the dominant aesthetic institution in this century. The Tate Gallery in London, the Museum of Modern Art in New York and the other major institutions of modernism in the visual arts produce and sustain a history of art which is mainly a history of the achievements of men. Women artists and feminist artists have recognised the closure of this arena, and turned elsewhere in order to engage critically with this establishment.

But it is not only feminists who have exposed the myth of the radical pretensions of modernism. There have always been those who have criticised the élitism of high modernism, and its denigration of all forms of mass or popular culture. The bureaucratisation and institutionalisation of modernism since the Second World War has been seen to coincide with its atrophying as a potentially critical movement (Gablik, 1984). The availability of Abstract Expressionism for use in American propaganda in the Cold War has been cited as further evidence of the total collapse of the original project of modernism (Cockcroft, 1974; Guilbaut, 1983). And it is clear that the most vehement defenders of modernism against both postmodernism and mass culture are critics of the right, for example those associated with the journal *New Criterion*.

**The Promise of Postmodernism**

If modernism no longer holds the promise of aesthetic and political transformation, postmodernism is often perceived as the new standard-bearer of the avant-garde. (The relationship between the two is complex, and depends both on the political evaluation of each category, and on whether postmodernism is seen as a continuation of modernism, or as a diametrically opposed phenomenon. The various possible permutations have been mapped out by Fredric Jameson [1984b].) Here I shall consider the claims to the radical and critical perspective of postmodern culture in general, and specifically with regard to feminist art practice.

Postmodernism is seen as progressive because it operates outside the dominant, and moribund, academies of high modernism, and evades the bureaucratisation and incorporation many have criticised in modernist work. Further, it blurs the boundaries between high art and popular culture, and enthusiastically takes advantage of the most up-to-date developments in technology, thus producing an anti-élitist and potentially democratic and accessible cultural form. Most importantly, postmodernism effects a 'critical deconstruction of tradition' (Foster, 1985, p. xii). Here postmodern cultural practice meets postmodern theory. The writings of Lyotard, Baudrillard and Derrida, diverse though these are, definitively establish the impossibility of universalism in theory and the errors of any commitment to a notion of a transcendent (or at least accessible) Truth.

Given this critique, the radical task of postmodernism is to deconstruct apparent truths, to dismantle dominant ideas and cultural forms and to engage in the guerrilla tactics of undermining closed and hegemonic systems of thought. This, more than anything else, is the promise of postmodernism for feminist politics. For the dominant discourses in our culture are invariably patriarchal, and it is the aim of postmodern feminist strategies to expose and discredit these. Craig Owens' suggestion of the close link between feminism and postmodernism, quoted at the beginning of this essay, is founded on this recognition.

It is not only in the arts that the potential of postmodernism for feminism has been recognised. American feminists who have been developing a critique of the natural sciences as partial and patriarchal practices have come to similar conclusions. The so-called 'objectivity' of science has been shown by several writers to be a partial view, based on a projection of men's experience of the world (Rose, 1983, 1986; Harding and Hintikka, 1983; Harding, 1986a, 1986b). This is explained by some of these writers in terms of a psychoanalytic account of the construction of masculinity in our culture, and in particular the need for males to develop autonomy and detachment in the early relationship with the mother (Hartsock, 1983; Keller, 1983; Flax 1983). The critique of 'androcentric' knowledge leads to a debate about whether or not feminist approaches would entirely reject such notions of objectivity and attempts to develop theory. Opinions about the ensuing 'successor sciences' differ. Sandra Harding, an important and influential contributor to this debate, takes the view that 'feminist standpoint epistemologies' must not repeat the mistake of existing science, namely to propose a uniform and totalising theory. Rather, she argues, 'we must embrace instead the permanent partiality of feminist inquiry' (Harding, 1986b: 194). (An additional and important reason for this is the fact there is no single category of 'woman'; class, national, ethnic and other differences have to be acknowledged).

Harding's conclusion is that feminist postmodernism, as an essentially deconstructive strategy, is an invaluable tool for the critique and reconstitution of science and epistemology. The inherently critical and destabilising effects of postmodern theory make possible the direct engagement with androcentric systems of thought, without necessarily attempting to replace these with new, women-centred, theories. The parallel with work in cultural studies and the arts is clear, for here, too, feminists have been arguing that deconstructive strategies are the most profitable (McRobbie, 1986; Kaplan, 1987; Weedon, 1987). Postmodern interventions, apart from anything else, achieve what a more separatist, alternative, woman-centred culture could not: namely engagement with the dominant culture itself. By employing the much-cited postmodern tactics of pastiche, irony, quotation and juxtaposition, this kind of cultural politics engages directly with current images, forms and ideas, subverting their intent and (re)appropriating their meanings, rather than abandoning them for alternative forms but thereby leaving them both untouched and still dominant.

**Problems of Postmodernism**

There are a number of serious difficulties with this conception of postmodern theory and practice, and before going on to discuss postmodernism in the visual arts I want to consider two of these. The first, which is already apparent in the discussion of feminist science, is the problem of *theory*. For fundamental to the post-modern critique of metanarratives, dominant discourses and so on is the view that theories can no longer be seen as anything other than partial and provisional. Indeed, the development of structuralist and post-structuralist theory, hermeneutics, and the sociology of knowledge in recent decades has rendered impossible the retention of the view of science and knowledge which has lasted from the Enlightenment to Modernism, and which is founded on a faith in the uniformity of science and the possibility of a transcendent objectivity. In the late twentieth century, we know that all knowledge is socially and historically located (and therefore partial), and that any theory is a product of (and limited by) language and discourse.

However, as several people have now pointed out, there is a certain inconsistency in this position. It has been argued that Lyotard's critique of theory is itself (necessarily) founded on theory (Honneth, 1985; Kellner, 1988). Feminist postmodernism faces the same dilemma. For the deconstructive strategies of postmodern cultural practice, or of epistemological critique, depend on the theory of feminism – the articulated argument that society is structured around sexual inequality. Acknowledging this, Sandra Harding proposes replacing a confidently universal theory with a limited, provisional 'successor science' (Harding, 1986b). Nancy Fraser and Linda Nicholson have recently argued for the retention of 'large narratives', and for a postmodern-feminist theory which would be 'pragmatic and fallibilistic' (Fraser and Nicholson, 1988, pp. 380, 391). But it has to be said that resolutions to this dilemma to date *are* mainly pragmatic. The epistemological paradox remains, and it may be that the justifica-tion of new critical theories can only be made on other, non-epistemological, grounds, including those of usefulness (one theory explains more of the world than another), politics (acknow-ledged commitment to a point of view) or self-reflexive provision-ality (admission that this theory, though valuably deconstructive of dominant discourses, is itself open to such deconstruction) (see Wolff, 1988).

The second difficulty concerns the definition and identification of postmodernism itself. Although the history of the concept has been traced back at least to the 1950s, the introduction to a recent collection of essays on the topic can still conclude that 'there is, as yet, no agreed meaning to the term postmodern' (Featherstone 1988, p. 207). The term has had particular currency in the 1980s, when the debates have ranged confusingly over a variety of media: literature, architecture, dance, painting, film, television, pop music video, dress and fashion. It is often difficult to see how the concept transfers from one medium to another. The supposedly essential characteristics of postmodern art necessarily vary be-tween media, leaving us more with an extremely elastic notion – a family of resemblances – than with a clearly identifiable category. To take one example of this: the demise of the unitary subject, central to postmodern film and literature, makes little sense in relation to architectural design.

The list of characteristics of postmodern culture is in any case a constantly shifting one. It includes pastiche, parody, historical quotation, depthlessness, loss of affect, decentring of the subject (but also, in the case of some so-called postmodern visual art, the resurrection of figurative art), eclecticism, self-reflexivity of the medium itself, and so on. The postmodern is also perceived by different writers as essentially aligned with quite varied, and sometimes opposed, political positions. Postmodern architecture has generally been seen as in some senses reactionary; postmodern dance, on the other hand, is associated with developments which are progressive (aesthetically and politically). This diversity within a category recalls Perry Anderson's warning about the complexities of modernism (Anderson, 1984). More, it suggests very strongly that the term, rather than describing and encapsulating a clearly visible phenomenon, is a construct of cultural critics, invented more for their own professional and ideological reasons than for its immediate usefulness. (A critical essay by Fred Orton and Griselda Pollock on the term 'Post-Impressionism' analyses a different historical moment and mercilessly deconstructs a similar catch-all but uncritical concept. For, as they argue, '"Post-Impressionism" has no foundation in history and no pertinence to, or explanatory value for, that historical moment it is used to possess... The use of the designation "Post-Impressionism" is part of a strategy to classify and contain diverse and complex practices and to blanket over difficulties and differences' [Orton and Pollock, 1980, p. 314]).

In addition, the term 'postmodernism' blurs important questions of periodisation. The postmodern has variously been said to date from the Second World War, the 1950s, 1968, the late 1970s and the 1980s. So far, few cultural critics have attempted to locate this cultural phenomenon within the particular social, economic and historical transformations which have produced it. Jameson's now classic essay on postmodernism made a preliminary, though far too simplistic, attempt to do this in terms of broad periods of socio-economic development (Jameson, 1984a). One or two more recent contributions have started to take this further (Tagg, 1985/ 6; Bauman, 1988; Cooke, 1988; Zukin, 1988). In general, though, the debate about the postmodern employs the quintessentially postmodern practice of detaching representation from reality. It is as if its critique of naive conceptions of 'the real' justifies a blanket rejection of any further efforts in social and cultural history.

Lastly, the promiscuous use of the term 'postmodern' moves uneasily between the philosophical and the cultural. The debate about the 'postmodern condition' and about postmodernity, in which Lyotard's work has been central, concerns the epistemological question of the failure of the project of modernity – the recognition of the ultimate impossibility of grand narratives and of universal theories. The debate about postmodern*ism* as cultural practice, however, concerns the failure of modern*ism*, and the commitment to critical, fragmentary, democratic cultural politics. Of course there are links between the two discourses (postmodern cultural politics often relies on the advances of post-structuralist theory which underlie postmodern philosophy), but it is a mistake to assume any straightforward identity of the two. Many so-called postmodern art forms (for example, neo-classicism in painting and architecture) are far removed from, and indeed hostile to, the philosophically radical project of postmodern philosophy.

Given the complexities of the current debates about postmodernism, in what follows I shall concentrate on a relatively narrow area: postmodernism in painting. It will become clear that even here there is no easy definition of the postmodern. I shall begin by outlining the issues involved in the field of the visual arts, and go on to consider the potential for feminist art practice in postmodern painting.

## Postmodernism and the Visual Arts

What is postmodern painting? In general in this area we find assumption rather than analysis, description rather than definition. As a result, there is no agreement on what constitutes postmodern painting. Fredric Jameson's influential article on postmodernism discusses Andy Warhol's painting *Diamond Dust Shoes* as a key example of a postmodern work, contrasting this with the modernist Van Gogh painting *Peasant Shoes* (Jameson, 1984a, pp. 58–60). Waldemar Januszczak, in an overview of contemporary postmodernism in the visual arts, refers to neo-expressionist and neo-classical painters of the 1980s, including Kiefer, McKenna,

Baselitz, Clemente and Schnabel (Januszczak, 1986). He does not define postmodern art, but refers to its characteristics of 'sensationalism, titillation, frilliness, pastiche, dumbness and narcissism' (which he compares with those same characteristics in Rococo painting). The sole ambition of postmodernism, he says, is to please. It has no moral ambition and no educational or creative purpose.

Charles Jencks, the main critic and defender of postmodern architecture, defines postmodernism as *double coding*, which he sees as at the same time the continuation and transcendence of modernism (Jencks, 1986, pp. 14–15). Postmodern art, he argues, started in about 1960 with Pop Art, Hyperrealism and other departures from modernism (p. 23). He pays particular attention to three Italian 'postmodern' painters: Carlo Maria Mariani, Sandro Chia and Mimmo Paladino. He includes, in passing, David Hockney, Malcolm Morley, Eric Fischl, Lennart Anderson, Paul Georges and Ron Kitaj and a few others who 'make use of the classical tradition in portraying our current cultural situation' (Jencks, 1986: 30). For Jencks, many of the painters described as 'postmodern' by other critics (including Jameson, Foster and Owens, already mentioned in this essay) are not postmodern but rather 'late modern'. Missing in the work of such artists is the 'return to tradition' and to the 'classical' which is central to the double coding.

This conception of the postmodern is totally at variance with that of writers like Craig Owens. Owens' definition of postmodern art, unlike Jencks', is work which undermines representation, and which operates a deconstructive action within art (Owens, 1985). Artists he discusses include Martha Rosler, Mary Kelly, Barbara Kruger, Sherrie Levine, and Cindy Sherman. What these have in common, as well as a radical and feminist intention, is a theoretically informed interrogation of representation, including, in the case of the first three, the use of text and caption together with image. This is to return to a view of postmodern cultural practice which connects with poststructuralist and postmodern theory, and whose radical project is the destabilising of the image.

Just as 'post-Impressionism' operates as an eclectic category, covering an enormous variety of styles and movements which have in common only the fact that they are 'after Impressionism', so 'postmodernism' in art appears to be a moveable category whose only commitment is to identify what comes after modernism. For this reason, figurative painting has been called 'postmodern', since it reverses and challenges the orthodoxy of modernism (as established and maintained by the Museum of Modern Art in New York and, to some extent, the Tate Gallery in London). It is clear, though, that like postmodern architecture, this could equally be a retrograde rather than progressive step. But whether painting is abstract or representational does not alone determine its political orientation. The rejection of modernism can be the rejection (from the right) of its original radical project, or the attempt (on the left) to revive that project in terms appropriate to the late twentieth century.

Given the confusion and lack of clarity of the debate in the field of painting, it is not surprising that one solution has been to suggest that there is more than one postmodernism. Hal Foster differentiates between a postmodernism of reaction and a postmodernism of resistance (Foster, 1985). The debate between Habermas and his critics, too, seems to me to depend on opposite notions of the postmodern, Habermas' critique being of Foster's 'postmodernism of reaction' (Habermas, 1981; Bernstein, 1985). Of course, as is always the case when confronted with different uses of the same concept, the point is not to legislate for a 'correct' usage. The word means what people use it to mean. My own strategy, for the rest of this essay, will be to adopt a particular usage, and to assess postmodernism thus defined.

I would argue that the most useful definition of the postmodern, in painting as in other media, is that work which self-consciously deconstructs tradition, by a variety of formal and other techniques (parody, juxtaposition, re-appropriation of images, irony, repetition, and so on). Such an interrogation is informed by theoretical and critical consciousness. This definition excludes those other playful practices which fragment and disrupt narrative and tradition, and which refuse any grounding or closure in favour of a free play of signifiers. The critique of metanarratives notwithstanding, this disavowal of theory is unacceptable, for two reasons. In the first place, cultural intervention as political critique is necessarily grounded in a particular analysis of social inequalities (as well as in a theoretical grasp *of* culture and the possibilities of its subversion). And in the second place there is always something disingenuous about the insistence on a free-floating critical consciousness, engaging in the guerrilla tactics of local disruption but uncontaminated by theory. There is always a point of view (theory), implicit if not explicit, which motivates and organises such a critique.

In a recent review of the 'postmodern' television series, *State of the Art*, John Roberts (1987) has exposed this well. The series abandoned the traditional documentary style of voice-over narrative and contextualisation of interviews and work. Roberts points out that the consequence of this was that those viewers without the relevant knowledge would not only find it difficult or impossible to grasp the 'relentless flow of uncontextualised information' (p. 124), but that important differences were glossed over – facts about race, class, different economic positions of the artists, and so on. His suggestion that links between economic and critical success can be extrapolated, though they are not made explicit by the programmes, indicates that, despite the commitment to anti-narrative (postmodern) film strategies, the makers of the programmes had a clear analysis, and the apparently random interviews, quotations and shots of paintings were in fact far from random.

This conception of postmodern art abandons the broad inclusive category of all painting which is after (or anti) modernism. It excludes neo-Expressionism and neo-Classicism, for even historical quotation (or double coding) is not postmodern if it is merely aimless play. The notion of the postmodern as informed, critical cultural practices which engage with tradition in order to subvert it brings us back to the consideration of postmodernism in feminist art practice.

## Feminism and the Visual Arts

Deconstructive strategies are not the only kind of feminist artistic practice. Some feminist artists, most famously Judy Chicago, have chosen to make work which foregounds women's history, women's lives, and women's traditional art and craft activities. In feminist art criticism, there has been a good deal of debate about the virtues, limits and dangers of such cultural politics – marginalisation, essentialism, uncritical and undifferentiated notions of the (female) subject, and so on. (See, for example, Barry and Flitter-

*Figure 7.1*   Judy Chicago, *The Dinner Party*

Chicago's best known work, *The Dinner Party*, is a life-size triangular table with 39 settings, each with an embroidered runner and painted china plate representing a particular woman in history. The tiled floor inside the triangle bears the names of 999 other women.

man, 1980.) This essay, which focuses on postmodern cultural practices, should be seen in the context of a far wider range of feminist strategies. Some of the reservations which have been expressed about deconstructive practices, which I shall discuss below, register an unwillingness to rule out other, less confrontational kinds of work.

---

Barbara Kruger has been quoted as saying 'I see my work as a series of attempts to ruin certain representation, to displace the subject and to welcome a female spectator into the audience of men' (Kruger, 1984). Her work combines image and text, superimposing accusatory texts onto black and white photographs (Kruger, 1983). The message, often addressed to the male viewer, confronts society's construction of women. 'We won't play nature to your culture', placed in large irregular letters over an image of a woman's face, her eyes covered by two leaves, both speaks of and challenges the traditional association of women with nature (and her exclusion from culture). The intertextuality of her work subverts the patriarchal ideology of our society by engaging directly with its representation, and subverting this in ways which are inescapable.

Mary Kelly's monumental project, *Post-Partum Document*, explored the mother–child relationship through text, diary, image and exhibited objects (Kelly, 1983b). It is informed by Lacanian analysis of that relationship, and, as Griselda Pollock has pointed out, rather than producing 'a fixed coherent autobiographical work with an integrated woman as its subject', it operates with fissure, fragment, absence. For Pollock, this work epitomises feminist art practices, which are political 'because of the relations they do, or do not, sustain to dominant discourses and modes of representation' (Pollock, 1987: 98) Like all work which is here being labelled 'postmodern', these practices engage with representation in order to deconstruct the given categories of gender and to reposition the spectator in relation to the hitherto unquestioned images and ideologies of contemporary culture. Mary Kelly's latest work, *Interim*, interrogates the discourse of ageing in patriarchal culture, again using text, image, object (Kelly, 1986).

An exhibition of 1985, entitled *Difference: On Representation and Sexuality*, included the work of Kruger and Kelly among that of twenty British and American artists. The exhibition was shown in New York and London (Smith, 1985; *Difference*, 1984). It included the work of a few men involved in the exploration of masculinity as part of the project of the critique of the subject in culture and of the representation of gender in contemporary society. Most of the work shown investigated the relationship between text and image; all of it was committed to an exploration of language and representation in the construction of gendered

*Figure 7.2*   Barbara Kruger, *Untitled*

*Your gaze hits the side of my face* confronts the implied, active, male viewer with a female passivity and indifference far removed from the engaged response of women as traditionally depicted by and for men.

subjects. Like an earlier show, curated by Mary Kelly (*Beyond the Purloined Image*, at the Riverside Studios, London, 1983), the exhibition was organised around the postmodern principle of deconstructing contemporary culture *through* art and representation (Kelly, 1983a). The radical potential of an art practice which not only poses alternative images and ideologies, but refuses pre-existent and unitary categories of 'woman' and 'feminine', is clear.

However, some feminist art critics have taken issue with the apparent centrality of postmodernism, particularly in the context of British feminist art. Unlike the United States, where there is a more liberal pluralism of art practices among feminists, postmodern, deconstructive art has become something of an orthodoxy, which is resented as both intimidating and exclusive by artists working in humanist and other traditions. A frequent objection to feminist deconstructionism is its relative inaccessibility; a knowledge of Freud, Lacan and post-structuralist theory often seems a prerequisite to understanding the work. Angela Partington has argued against the notion of a 'correct' textual strategy in feminist art, partly on these grounds (Partington, 1987; n.d.). Her article is a plea for an audience-centred art practice, which stresses *extra*-textual strategies (taking into account the actual relations of artistic production and consumption). Deconstruction prioritises the producer–text relationship at the expense of the consumer–text relationship. Humanist or celebratory strategies (Nancy Spero, Judy Chicago, Sylvia Sleigh, Susan Hiller, Miriam Schapiro are mentioned, among others) enable a shared experience of 'the feminine' in a way which, she claims, need not be essentialist (that is, illegitimately ahistorical and non-social). Deconstructive strategies, on the other hand, as a primarily textual strategy, ignore audiences and viewers, and opt for formal critique instead of engagement with women's actual social position and viewing practices.

Katy Deepwell documents and criticises the dominance of deconstructive work (which she terms 'scripto-visual') (Deepwell, n.d.). Characteristic of this work, she says, is a rejection of painting in favour of photography, film, video, performance. She writes in favour of continuing to allow those other feminist practices, mainly based on painting, by artists 'who believe in a coherent humanist subject 'woman' and embrace woman-centred, and *sometimes* essentialist, views about a separate female culture in their work' (p. 11). Artists she mentions include Judy Chicago, Rose Garrard, Nancy Spero and Therese Oulton. In passing, she also makes the point that black women's practices are ignored by the scripto-visual ascendancy, and it has indeed emerged in a number of recent debates among feminists that black women artists in Britain show few signs of allegiance to deconstructive practices.

Rosa Lee makes a different case against deconstruction as feminist art (Lee, 1987). Against the representational strategies of postmodern art, she counterposes the possibility of non-representational art as potentially radical. (Her main example is the work of Therese Oulton – large landscape-like abstract canvases.) Like Katy Deepwell, she stresses the importance of working with (or returning to) oil paint and the gestural mark. Engagement with the material language of the medium itself is central, in which the subversive act consists in the use of traditional conventions without the representational (and perhaps compromised) content which might be expected. Her objection to deconstructive postmodernism seems to be mainly to its hegemony within the women's art movement, to its marginalisation of painting, and to the fact that it therefore does not allow the possibility of a radical reconstruction of artistic language.

A final objection to postmodernism as feminist art practice is that it might not, after all, be achieving its radical cultural and political aims. Barbara Creed, in a discussion of postmodernism and film, suggests that the crisis of the master narratives may not necessarily benefit women (Creed, 1987, p. 66). Rosa Lee argues that 'the choices and "options" supposedly up for grabs within postmodernism are available only for the male of the species' (Lee, 1987, p. 8). And Griselda Pollock warns against the temptation for feminist artists to abandon modernist strategies in favour of postmodernism (Pollock, 1987, p. 104). I shall conclude by assessing the prospects of deconstructive postmodernism as feminist art practice in the late twentieth century.

## Postmodernism as Modified Modernism

Tactically, celebratory feminist art may well connect with viewers' experience and mobilise a certain critical consciousness. To that

*Figure 7.3* Nancy Spero, *Re-birth of Venus*

extent, Partington and Deepwell are right to object to the more authoritarian rejection of such humanist work by deconstructionists. They are also right to insist that cultural political strategies cannot be purely textual ones; that any such intervention must be judged in terms of the specific circumstances of viewers, contemporary meanings, potential (mis)interpretations (including by critics) and so on. However, the major difference between postmodernism, as I have been using the term, and other kinds of feminist art practice is the commitment of the former to engage critically with contemporary culture and with the very categories of gender themselves. To that extent, there is no question of a liberal plurality of feminist strategies, since such work is clearly fundamentally radical in a way that other work is not. It is arguable, too, that since it does engage in this way with dominant cultural forms, re-appropriating and subverting imagery, it may be less likely to be marginalised and ignored in the way that woman-centred art generally is.

It is true that the majority of the works I have been discussing under the heading of deconstructive postmodernism have abandoned painting in favour of photography and other visual forms. Unlike Lee, I do not think it has to be a central project of feminist art to reconstruct the traditional language of art (namely oil paint), though there is no real reason why postmodern art cannot employ paint as well as photography (except for the obvious one that mechanically reproduced images lend themselves more to fragmentation, re-arrangement, superimposition, and other deconstructive strategies). The medium itself is not essentially compromised in a way which excludes feminist appropriation, as the work of artists like Alexis Hunter, Susan Hiller and Sutapa Biswas shows.

As for the warning that postmodernism may be co-opted by men, the immediate and pragmatic answer must be that feminists should nevertheless employ those strategies as long as they are available and as long as they seem effective. It has been true throughout the history of Western art that all major art movements have been dominated by men (and also that the part played in them by women has been written out of the historical account). This does not seem to be a good reason for abdicating in advance. The deconstructive strategies of postmodern cultural practice are invaluable for feminists, and a realistic politics for artists is one which judges the availability and effectivity of particular strategies in the moment.

I return finally to the question of theory. It has often occurred to me that the characteristics of so-called postmodernism appear to duplicate many of those adduced more than half a century ago in relation to modernism: self-relexivity, de-centring of the subject, alienation-effect, consciousness of, and attention to, the medium itself, montage, use of new media, and so on. If anything, the key difference was the reliance of modernism on theory, whether this was Marxism (in the case of Brecht and some of the Russian Futurists) or other theories of industrial society and social change. Since the development of structuralist, semiotic and discourse theories, postmodernism has claimed to be based on a rejection of grand theory. But as I have already argued, this rejection of theory is inconsistent and ultimately indefensible. Although we may now have a less naive view of objectivity, recognising the inevitably perspectival nature of any theory, postmodernism cannot be atheoretical any more than modernism.

It is for this reason that I want to conclude by suggesting that the best kind of postmodern theory and practice is in fact a kind of modified modernism. To understand this we have to detach the project of modernism from its fate in terms of particular institutions of art and culture. The so-called 'failure' of modernism is, of course, the impasse it reached as a result of certain processes of bureaucratisation, institutionalisation and commercialisation. As Griselda Pollock has argued recently, we must separate modernism-as-institution from modernism-as-practice (Pollock, 1987, p. 106). The latter is by no means a monolithic entity, and it is thus still available for radical initiatives. She doubts that postmodernism is a real aesthetic break from modernism, and in another essay she argues strongly in favour of Brechtian modernism, whose 'theoretical and practical contributions for a political art practice remain a valid and necessary component of the contemporary women's art movement' (Pollock, 1988, p. 199).

Postmodern theory and postmodern cultural practices have a good deal to offer feminist artists and critics. As I have argued, however, the radical relativism and scepticism of much postmodern thought is misplaced, unjustified, and incompatible with feminist (and indeed any radical) politics. The project of postmodernism as cultural politics is more usefully seen as a renewal and continuation of the project of modernism, and the specific strategies, techniques and technologies of the late twentieth century enable the energetic and constantly innovatory pursuit of a feminist art practice.

## Bibliography

ANDERSON, PERRY (1984), 'Modernity and Revolution', *New Left Review*, 144.
BARRY, JUDITH AND FLITTERMAN, SANDY (1980), 'Textual Strategies: The Politics of Art-Making', *Screen*, Vol. 21 No. 2.
BAUMAN, ZYGMUNT (1988), 'Is there a Postmodern Sociology?', *Theory, culture & Society*, Vol. 5 Nos. 2–3. Special issue on *Postmodernism*.

BENSTOCK, SHARI (1987), *Women of the Left Bank. Paris, 1900–1940*, London, Virago.

BERNSTEIN, RICHARD J. (ed.) (1985), *Habermas and Modernity*, Cambridge, Polity Press.

COCKCROFT, EVA (1974), 'Abstract Expressionism: Weapon of the Cold War', *Artforum*, XII No. 10.

COOKE, PHILIP (1988), 'Modernity, Postmodernity and the City', *Theory, Culture & Society*, Vol. 5 Nos. 2–3. Special issue on *Postmodernism*.

CREED, BARBARA (1987), 'From Here to Modernity – Feminism and Postmodernism', *Screen*, Vol. 28 No. 2.

DEEPWELL, KATY (n.d.), 'In Defence of the Indefensible: Feminism, Painting and Post-Modernism', *Feminist Arts News*, Vol 2 No 4.

*Difference: On Representation and Sexuality* (1984), New York, The New Museum of Contemporary Art.

FEATHERSTONE, MIKE (1988), 'In Pursuit of the Postmodern: An Introduction', *Theory, Culture & Society*, Vol. 5, Nos. 2–3. Special issue on *Postmodernism*.

FLAX, JANE (1983), 'Political Philosophy and the Patriarchal Unconscious: A Psychoanalytic Perspective on Epistemology and Metaphysics' in Harding and Hintikka (eds), op.cit.

FOSTER, HAL (1985), 'Postmodernism: A Preface' in *Postmodern Culture*, London, Pluto Press.

FRASER, NANCY AND NICHOLSON, LINDA (1988), 'Social Criticism without Philosophy: An Encounter between Feminism and Postmodernism', *Theory, Culture & Society*, Vol. 5, Nos 2–3. Special issue on *Postmodernism*.

GABLIK, SUZI (1984), *Has Modernism Failed?*, London, Thames and Hudson.

GUILBAUT, SERGE (1983), *How New York Stole the Idea of Modern Art. Abstract Expressionism, Freedom, and the Cold War*, London, University of Chicago.

HABERMAS, JÜRGEN (1981), 'Modernity versus Postmodernity', *New German Critique*, No. 22. Special issue on *Modernism*.

HANSCOMBE, GILLIAN AND SMYERS, VIRGINIA L. (1987), *Writing for their Lives. The Modernist Woman 1910–1940*, London, The Women's Press.

HARDING, SANDRA (1986a), 'The Instability of the Analytical Categories of Feminist Theory', *Signs*, Vol. 11 No. 4.

HARDING, SANDRA (1986b), *The Science Question in Feminism*, London, Cornell University Press.

HARDING, SANDRA AND HINTIKKA, MERRILL B. (eds), (1983) *Discovering Reality. Feminist Perspectives on Epistemology, Metaphysics, Methodology, and Philosophy of Science*, London, D. Reidel.

HARTSOCK, NANCY C. M. (1983), 'The Feminist Standpoint: Developing the Ground for a Specifically Feminist Historical Materialism' in Harding and Hintikka (eds), op. cit.

HONNETH, AXEL (1985), 'An Aversion Against the Universal: A

Commentary on Lyotard's *Postmodern Condition'*, *Theory, Culture & Society*, Vol. 2, No. 3. Special issue on *The Fate of Modernity*.

HUYSSEN, ANDREAS (1988), 'Mass Culture as Woman: Modernism's Other' in *After the Great Divide. Modernism, Mass Culture and Postmodernism*, London, Macmillan.

JAMESON, FREDRIC (1984a), 'Postmodernism, or the cultural Logic of Late Capitalism', *New Left Review*, 146.

JAMESON, FREDRIC (1984b), 'The Politics of Theory: Ideological Positions in the Postmodernism Debate', *New German Critique*, No. 33. Special issue on *Modernity and Postmodernity*.

JANUSZCZAK, WALDEMAR (1986), 'Decline and Fall of Modern Art', *The Guardian*, December 2.

JENCKS, CHARLES (1986), *What is Post-Modernism?*, London, Academy Editions.

KAPLAN, E. ANN (1987), *Rocking Around the Clock. Music Television, Postmodernism, and Consumer Culture*, London, Methuen.

KELLER, EVELYN FOX (1983), 'Gender and Science' in Harding and Hintikka (eds), op. cit.

KELLNER, DOUGLAS (1988), 'Postmodernism as Social Theory: Some Challenges and Problems', *Theory, Culture & Society*, Vol. 5, Nos. 2–3. Special issue on *Postmodernism*.

KELLY, MARY (1983a), 'Beyond the Purloined Image', *Block*, 9.

KELLY, MARY (1983b), *Post-Partum Document*, London, Routledge & Kegan Paul.

KELLY, MARY (1986), *Interim*, Edinburgh, The Fruitmarket Gallery.

KRUGER, BARBARA (1983), *We Won't Play Nature to Your Culture*, London, Institute of Contemporary Arts.

KRUGER, BARBARA (1984), Press Release, New York, Annina Nosei Gallery.

LEE, ROSA (1987), 'Resisting Amnesia: Feminism, Painting and Postmodernism', *Feminist Review*, No. 26.

LUNN, EUGENE (1985), *Marxism and Modernism*, London, Verso.

McROBBIE, ANGELA (1986), 'Postmodernism and Popular Culture' in Lisa Appignanesi (ed.) *Postmodernism*, I.C.A. Documents 4, London, Institute of Contemporary Arts.

ORTON, FRED AND POLLOCK, GRISELDA (1980), 'Les Données Bretonnantes: la Prairie de Répresentation', *Art History*, Vol. 3. No. 3.

OWENS, CRAIG (1985), 'The Discourse of Others: Feminism and Postmodernism' in Hal Foster (ed.), *Postmodern Culture*, London, Pluto.

PARTINGTON, ANGELA (1987), 'Feminist Art and Avant-Gardism' in Hilary Robinson (ed.), *Visibly Female. Feminism and Art Today*, London, Camden Press.

PARTINGTON, ANGELA (n.d.), 'Conditions of a Feminist Art Practice', *Feminist Arts News*, Vol. 2 No. 4.

POLLOCK, GRISELDA (1982), 'Vision, Voice and Power. Feminist Art History and Marxism', *Block*, 6.

POLLOCK, GRISELDA (1987), 'Feminism and Modernism' in Rozsika

Parker and Griselda Pollock (eds), *Framing Feminism. Art and the Women's Movement 1970–1985*, London, Pandora.

POLLOCK, GRISELDA (1988), 'Screening the Seventies: Sexuality and Representation in Feminist Practice – a Brechtian Perspective' in *Vision and Difference. Feminity, Feminism and Histories of Art*, London, Routledge.

ROBERTS, JOHN (1987), 'Postmodern Television and the Visual Arts', *Screen*, Vol. 28, No. 2.

ROSE, HILARY (1983), 'Hand, Brain, and Heart: a Feminist Epistemology for the Natural Sciences', *Signs*, Vol. 9 No. 1. Also in Sandra Harding and Jean O'Barr (eds) 1987), *Sex and Scientific Inquiry*, Chicago, University of Chicago.

ROSE, HILARY (1986), 'Women's Work: Women's Knowledge' in Juliet Mitchell and Ann Oakley (eds), *What is Feminism?*, Oxford, Blackwell.

SMITH, PAUL (1985), 'Difference in America', *Art in America*, April.

TAGG, JOHN (1985/6), 'Postmodernism and the Born-Again Avant-Garde', *Block*, 11.

WEEDON, CHRIS (1987), *Feminist Practice and Poststructuralist Theory*, Oxford, Blackwell.

WOLFF, JANET (1988), 'The Critique of Reason and the Destruction of Reason' in Roy Landau (ed.), *The Relative and the Rational in the Architecture and Culture of the Present*, London, Architectural Association (forthcoming).

ZUKIN, SHARON (1988), 'The Postmodern Debate over Urban Form', *Theory Culture & Society*, Vol. 5. Nos. 2–3. Special issue on *Postmodernism*.

# Chapter 8

# These New Components of the Spectacle: Fashion and Postmodernism*

Elizabeth Wilson

Postmodernism, or the Postmodern,[1] is often brought forward as a challenge to 'totalising' explanations of the world, and as the chance for various 'Others' to find a voice.[2] It is presented, too, as the opportunity to re-evaluate popular, kitsch and 'low' aesthetic and cultural forms, and to break down the distinction between high art and popular culture.

This would seem to offer a superb opportunity for the rehabilitation of fashion. For, on the one hand, fashion is, rightly or wrongly, primarily associated with Woman, one of the most important of the Others for whom postmodernism claims to find a space; and, on the other, in Western capitalist societies fashions in dress have always borne a clear relationship to aesthetic movements and practices, albeit that fashion is the degraded or unacceptable face of art. Its blatant consumerism shocks the culture whose heart it yet speaks so well, and this produces an intense cultural ambivalence about dress, and links it to moral behaviour and ultimately to politics.[3] In the postmodern world, designer mass fashion and style seem more important than ever, and for this reason also we would expect it to be welcomed, as a form of popular art, into the discussion of postmodernism as a further manifestation of pluralism, pleasure and the demotic. Not so: the cultural critics who investigate the postmodern continue to ignore or denounce it.

Fashion as we understand it arose in Europe in the thirteenth century, with early cloth trading and the very earliest manifestations of consumption orientated society.[4] It was particularly the preserve of a courtly aristocracy, yet there is evidence that the early bourgeoisie and even the peasantry aspired to be fashionable from the beginning. Sumptuary laws which were passed in many European countries, for example, could never be enforced and were abruptly dropped in the early seventeenth century.[5]

With the coming of the industrial period, dress underwent profound modifications. This was at two levels, which are connected, although not in any obvious or simple way. First, the production of cloth and clothing was revolutionised by technology. Initially only those garments were mass-produced that were intended for the lowest ranks in society – uniforms were the first clothes to be made in bulk, and they were sold, along with working clothes, in the 'slop shops' of ports and slums (although, in fact, the majority of poor men and women wore secondhand clothes for much of the time). But gradually throughout the nineteenth century, and to an even greater extent in the twentieth century, mass production was extended to more and more different kinds of garments, until today it is almost universal.

Technology therefore – the cotton mills, the sewing machine (marketed in 1851), man-made fibres, the chain store – transformed dress. These, however, taken on their own need not have led to mass fashion as we have it today; we might just as easily have ended up in that 'nightmare' of the *Brave New World*[6] and *1984*[7] dystopias: uniforms. Instead, mass production *began* with uniforms, but it has led to the mass dissemination of greater and greater varieties of fashionable styles.

This means more than just the ready availability of clothes that are 'in fashion' at relatively low cost; it means the proliferation of fashion as an essential component of life. Western societies (and increasingly the whole globe) have become saturated with (Western) fashion and images of fashion. Industrialisation and urbanisation were the transformative processes that enabled the longstanding aspirations of the middle and working classes to 'fashionability' to be fulfilled.

So, secondly, nineteenth century urban life assigned fashion a central and indispensable place in the spectacle that was the city. Fashion served to underline the elaborate rituals of bourgeois life – there was an appropriate costume for every activity and every hour of the day or evening – and, perhaps even more importantly, fashion in the city served to signal to the other strangers in the crowded streets and public places the class and status of the individual, thus countering to some extent the social disorientation threatened by urban life.[8]

In the twentieth century, when mass fashion really takes over, it is used to designate not just class and status (and always, of course, gender) but an expansion of elaborate self-definitions and group affiliations – individual and collective identities. Also, with the coming of a society that is more and more orientated towards the mass media, the performance becomes more knowing. Indeed, parody and performance to some extent replace the former deadly earnest signalling of class. As recently as thirty years ago it was still possible (just) for my grandmother to announce that 'a lady always wears gloves' (in the street, that is), or for the father of a friend to insist that 'you can tell a gentleman by his shoes'. Today, such deadpan and unselfconscious snobbery is hardly possible, indeed the very concept of 'vulgarity' has almost disappeared, and in any case is no longer associated only with the *nouveaux riches* or with 'common' persons. The mingling of show-biz and the Royals has made it permissible for the aristocracy to be 'vulgar' too. Perhaps, really, they always were. And when Sir Roy Strong, former director of the Victoria and Albert Museum (and a sharp dresser himself in the 1970s), recently bewailed[9] the way in which Princess Diana and the Duchess of York have become associated with 'fashion victim' dressing – since in his view this entailed a loss of dignity for the Crown – he was really appealing to notions of status and correct dress that have, to a large extent, ceased to have currency.

For the costuming of well-bred understatement has become just another style, another status symbol. The Japanese, American and European bourgeoisie flock to Burberrys to buy what was once the practical country wear of the gentry and, as such, far removed from fashionable dressing. Today, however, the style is in the label, to wear a Burberry raincoat almost a parody of styleless style.

James Laver maintains, in fact, that modern male wear evolved out of eighteenth century country clothes for men,[10] and, a hundred years later, Chanel brought about the same transformation for women.[11] However, although the 'birth' of the modern woman is popularly associated with the styles of the 1920s, the revolution in women's appearance was well under way before the First World War. The dress designer Paul Poiret simplified the female silhouette; the first decade of the twentieth century saw the end of the fashion for tight-lacing and constricting corsets, and the introduction of looser clothing for women, short hair and rising hems. Chanel was then beginning to design, using knitting and jersey material, masculine suitings and styles adapted from riding wear. She and Jean Patou popularised neutral colours after the war – black, navy, grey, and, above all, that twenties creation, beige. They presided over the evolution of the female silhouette into the sleek minimalist, pinheaded, boyish 1920s woman.

This new woman is drawn and photographed with other images of modernity, and above all as a traveller – in trains, ocean-going liners, sometimes aeroplanes, and particularly motor-cars. At times, the association of woman and automobile seems almost to create a mechanical feminine centaur, and becomes the very representation of modernity. The streamlined silhouette is modelled after Bauhaus modernism and Futurism with its associations of speed, movement and function.

These fashions, because they renounced obvious luxury, seemed classless – little nothing clothes, a uniform for the girl in the street, the office typist, shop assistant fashions for the international jet set. This was a representation of democracy, and to that extent the appearance of the fashionable woman of the 1920s was a representation of 'the modern'. We might see this as an example of the way in which the female form is used to represent the unrepresentable (a very postmodern idea), in the same way that, Marina Warner tells us,[12] the female form in public sculpture is used to represent abstract virtues such as 'Justice'. According to this interpretation, the passive female form is deployed by others (the state, or male artists, presumably) and there is no sense of women's active appropriation of or involvement in the creation of their own image. So, while the fashionable woman of the 1920s may represent modernity, this use of her follows a well-established tradition.

Yet the new fashions *were* more functional than the old, and the new streamlined woman relevant to the 'woman in the street'. Jerry White, in *Campbell Bunk: the Worst Street in North London*,[13] a social and oral history of one Islington street between the Wars, is in no doubt that dress was one means whereby women even of the slums were better able to escape the worst aspects of their environment than the men. He argues that:

> If clothes were important for young men, they were a public (and sometimes private) obsession for young women. Underpinned by an adaptable mass production industry absorbing technological advances from America and the continent, and by a universal system of credit selling, women's fashions were one of the absorbing interests of the age. They embodied postwar newness as much as any of the growth industries or suburbs or architecture, and were as much a consciously radical transformation of what had gone before: in the changing body shape, for instance, the very reverse of the Edwardian fullness of bust and hips, now replaced by tubular lines, 'the cult of the slim figure' and boyish shape; in the frequent allusions to men's fashions . . . and in the tendencies to reveal more of women's bodies . . . Clothes were clearly indicative of a dramatic redefinition of feminity at this time.[14]

New industries offered expanding opportunities – if they could dress at all presentably – to the women of Campbell Bunk and the surrounding districts, opportunities that simply did not exist for their fathers, brothers and husbands: 'the factory was becoming a structural element in a new "feminine" culture,' Jerry White tells us, quoting from a local Islington newspaper of the period to illustrate how working class girls were beginning to be perceived as fashionably dressed:

> A queue of over 1,000 women and girls was to be seen outside the Tottenham Employment Exchange on Friday morning. They were waiting to receive their 25s [£1.25] out-of-work bonus. It was a well dressed queue; the musquash and seal coat, eloquent of the former munition worker, was not absent . . .[15]

The relationship of modernism to fashion did not end with the

1920s: Punk, for example, as we shall see, may be interpreted as modernist, as postmodernist, *and* as an avant garde manifestation. In the 1930s, however, women's fashions did move away from the Bauhaus ideal, although continuing to be influenced by contemporary artistic movements, particularly surrealism. One of the foremost designers of the period, for example, Elsa Schiaparelli, used surrealist motifs – a hat like a shoe, or a jumper printed with a trompe l'oeil design of a chest of drawers. But romanticism in dress was perhaps the dominant vogue both before and after the Second World War, despite the wartime influence of uniforms and workdress.

In the 1950s, on the other hand – often misperceived as a period of total conservatism, at least so far as women are concerned – Chanel made a hugely successful comeback. She now aimed explicitly to cater for the woman in the street: 'I am no longer interested in dressing a few hundred women, private clients; I shall dress thousands of women. But a widely repeated fashion, seen everywhere, cheaply produced, must start from luxury'.[16] The 'luxury' lay in the simplicity of style and perfection of cut. And her models were enthusiastically taken up and mass-produced by American ready-to-wear. This created a world-wide image of the modern, up-to-date and above all *young* woman.

Because of its intimate relation to the body, fashionable dress can never be wholly 'modernist' in the sense of modernism as the creation of a hermetic work of art concerned with the conditions of its own creation, or as an artefact to be judged solely in terms of its own dynamic: abstract art. Some of the Paris designers did, however, unlike Chanel, move in this direction after the Second World War; notably Cristobal Balenciaga, whose austere creations in the late 1950s, together with those of his disciple, Givenchy, might be seen as attempts in that direction; indeed Balenciaga's creations were discussed in abstract terms of perfection of seams, cut, moulding and semi-abstract ovoid shapes. These designs *did*, perhaps, reflect the conservative artistic modernism of that period.

In the 1960s this abstraction took off into space age and science fiction styles in which women's clothes, particularly the new trouser suits designed by Courrèges, were completed with space bootees and helmet-type hats, the general effect being of a moon mission outfit. Man-made materials were popular – in PVC macs, for example; while one Paris designer, Paco Rabanne, made his name from using plastic disks to create skimpy clothes that could have come out of a Dr Who programme.

These were representations – again through the means of the female form – of a scientific utopia as mediated through popular culture. (In reality, there was only one woman in space throughout the whole period, and she was a Soviet astronaut). Alternatively, 1960s fashion created an infantile waif. As in the 1920s, women's greater freedom was interpreted sartorially as being not only a state of childlessness, but as a state of childishness as well. This fashion imagery – of gawky, pre-pubertal Lolita, or of woman as space pilot – cut across the traditional association of woman and nature, so deeply bound up with motherhood and reproduction in the dominant Western imagery of womanhood. Indeed, as if in reaction, in the later sixties a riot of hippy and ethnic styles with Pre-Raphaelite or Art Nouveau motifs reintroduced the earth Mother, and these styles in turn paved the way for an eclectic appropriation in the 1970s of various exotic modes and forms of decoration.

The fashions of the 1960s were also, however, and perhaps more significantly, consistent with the rise of Pop Art, performance art 'happenings' and psychedelic and Op Art imagery and motifs. Andy Warhol[17] wrote of the fashions of the period as an essential component of the New York avant-garde scene. Now art came down onto the street; became both 'pop' and avant-garde, while fashion strove to incorporate body painting, nudity and 'unnatural' materials such as the plastic and PVC referred to above.

Pop Art attempted to dissolve the distinction between high and low art. The further expansion of a mass fashion industry directed at the young dissolved the distinction between high class fashion and the vulgar; self presentation and performance were substituted for any lingering notion of the sartorial as good manners; 'understated chic' was on the wane.

This iconoclastic atmosphere brought high fashion and counter-cultural fashions close together in the sixties. For, if the young pop fashions represented one way of breaking out from the conservatism of 1950s Parisian haute couture (designed for a rich, conservative, upper-middle and upper class clientele), another way of dispelling the conformity of correct dress was the development of dissident youth modes of dress, (counter-cultural fashions), associated with rock music, radicalism and alternative lifestyles.

And the apotheosis of counter-cultural fashion was the initially, and perhaps, in the end, predominantly British phenomenon of Punk. There is a sense in which Punk could be said to be modernist in an entirely new way, for it is not simply a representation of 'the modern', but *does* question the terms of its own existence, challenging the very notion of fashion as somehow conforming to 'nature'. Punk denaturalises the body, and questions every canon of good taste. It is also one of the few counter-cultural fashions to have raised questions about the nature of femininity. Although long-haired male hippies were perceived as – threateningly – crossing a gender boundary, in practice, their long hair was offset by their long and highly patriarchal beards, their robelike garments by their often traditionalist values where women were concerned, while the female hippy was an earth mother who could modulate without too much difficulty into Laura Ashley cretonnes and home counties cottagey style. But with punk, *women* transgress norms of feminine beauty; when a young woman shaves her head and draws red lines round her eyes the very notion of make up and hairstyles as an enhancement of what 'nature' has provided is gone and the body is treated more radically than ever before as an aspect of performance.

Punk was avant-garde in the way in which it collapsed the boundaries between life and art.[18] The extreme Punk was a walking art object and performance, and punk had many points of contact with the pop art and happenings of the sixties, which themselves seem, in retrospect, to prefigure the postmodern manifestations of the eighties.

More often, however, what was termed the 'confusion' of fashion in the 1970s was interpreted as a response to feminism, the oscillation between romantic nostalgia and heavily masculine and punk modes signalling – it was said – this confusion. These interpretations followed the traditional path of treating fashion as a social and/or psychological manifestation. So, for example, Alison Lurie[19] interpreted punk amusingly in social psychological terms as a symptom of collective maternal deprivation, but this is the sort of interpretation from outside fashion which, on the one hand, reduces fashion to a symptom, and on the other assumes an always questionable 'mass psychology' or 'collective neurosis'.

(Why were British teenagers suddenly maternally deprived in 1976? Unemployed – yes; but are we to argue that their political protest via clothing and art was *simply* a displacement of psychological trauma? This surely is to depoliticise, and is therefore a very conservative explanation). Dick Hebdige's way of relating political protest, sartorially expressed, to aesthetic preoccupations – especially the tradition of the avant-garde – seems much more insightful and apt.[20]

This brings us to the theorisation of fashion. In this first, capsule-history-of-fashion section, of my essay I have implied that fashion is related to artistic movements contemporary with it. This is not, however, the position traditionally taken by fashion theory, which has more often fallen back on over-simplified forms of social history and sociology. So, for example, the fashions of the 1970s and early 1980s are interpreted as a kind of representation of society's reaction to feminism. This, at best, is an over-simplification. But it reflects the under-development of theories of fashion, and in turn this underdevelopment is partly due to the embeddedness of costume history within the wider discipline of art history, with its conservative emphasis on empirical details of dating, provenance, 'great art' and so on. Where theories of fashion have developed, therefore, they have tended to come from outside fashion, and to have relied on one – usually functionalist – framework.

The single most influential work remains Thorstein Veblen's *The Theory of the Leisure Class*.[21] Veblen perceived fashionable dress as simply and solely an aspect of conspicuous consumption, functional for capitalism, for the status of the bourgeoisie, and for the enslavement of women. He did not relate fashion to aesthetic practices nor to its own history. Another influential theorist was J C Flugel, a psychoanalyst, and he remains popular today because he took cognisance of gender. Kaja Silverman,[22] for example, refers to Flugel's *The Psychology of Clothes*[23] as the 'classic' psychoanalytic text on the subject, and both she and Peter Wollen[24] appear to accept Flugel's theory of 'the great masculine renunciation'. This theory, to which James Laver also subscribed, asserts that with the coming of industrial society men 'renounced' fashion, both in the sense of display and in the sense of changing

styles, and opted instead for the sober bourgeois suit, which they
see as an unchanging, un-self-displaying form of uniform.

Dress had indeed become increasingly gendered during the
eighteenth century. The dandies[25] adapted the modes of the shires
(navy woollen coat, tight buff breeches, long leather boots and
snowy linen and cravat) for day wear, and were among the first to
abandon the wig in favour of short, natural (that is, unpowdered)
hair, yet in certain crucial respects dandyism represented an even
more marked form of display than the silks and satins of eighteenth century court dress. Woollen cloth could be shaped more
closely to the body than silk, and breeches became extremely tight
and revealing. The abandonment of cosmetics, too, was hardly a
renunciation of male beauty and/or exhibitionism, rather it inau-
gurated a new and *different* style of male beauty: more gendered,
more 'masculine'.

Male fashions did continue to change throughout the nineteenth
and twentieth centuries, although more slowly and less showily
than women's. And at the same time, the industrial period saw a
development and elaboration of uniforms and ritualised forms of
public dress:

> Your clothes ... make us gape with astonishment. How many,
> how splendid, how extremely ornate they are – the clothes worn
> by the educated man in his public capacity! Now you dress in
> violet; a jewelled crucifix swings on your breast; now your
> shoulders are covered with lace; now furred with ermine; now
> slung with many linked chains set with precious stones. Now you
> wear wigs on your heads; rows of graduated curls descend to
> your necks. Now your hats are boat-shaped or cocked; now they
> mount in cones of black fur; now they are made of brass and
> scuttle shaped; now plumes of red, now of blue hair surmount
> them. Sometimes gowns cover your legs; sometimes gaiters.
> Tabards embroidered with lions and unicorns swing from your
> shoulders; metal objects cut in star shapes or in circles glitter
> and twinkle on your breasts. Ribbons of all colours – blue,
> purple, crimson – cross from shoulder to shoulder. After the
> comparative simplicity of your dress at home, the splendour of
> your public attire is dazzling.
>
> But far stranger ... every button, rosette and stripe seems to
> have symbolical meaning. Some have the right to wear plain

buttons only; others rosettes... Rules again regulate the gold
wire on the shoulders...[26]

Such rule-bound rigidity is the very opposite of fashion in one way,
but Virginia Woolf, in poking fun at male ceremonial attire, alerts
us to the intensity of the display and exhibitionism it involves. The
attempt to 'fix' male attire was, anyway, never complete, nor was
self display ever renounced, even if it was displaced onto the
collectivity of public apparel.

Flugel's account is therefore empirically unsatisfactory. Also,
far from being a 'classic text', the book's eugenicist preoccupations
betray its epoch. Flugel was a member of the Men's Dress Reform
Society in the 1920s and 1930s, the aim of which was to assimilate
male attire to the more 'rational' dress of women at that period.
The Society argued that men should wear shorts and lighter
materials, to free them from the fusty three piece suits, stiff
collars, spats and so on in which at that time they were still
imprisoned. Male dress, it was felt, was now lagging behind the
healthy minimalism of female fashions. (At an earlier period,
dress reformers, including feminists, were much more likely to
object to women's fashion, both on health grounds and because its
stereotyping of women was held to constitute an obstacle to their
advancement, fixing them so irrevocably in a feminity that both
caricatured womanhood and stood in the way of their freedom).

Flugel also, like other scientific writers at that time, held an
evolutionist view of human progress, and expected that the human
race would eventually be able to give up the 'neurosis' of clothing
altogether. His views were not too far removed from those of J. D.
Bernal, the leftwing scientist, or of H. G. Wells, both of whom
imagined and wrote of utopias in which not only clothing but even
the body itself would have atrophied with the increasing development and dominance of the human mind.

Flugel then, like Veblen, conceptualised fashion as a problem,
an aberration in a civilised society, the explanation and the
solution for which were to be found outside fashion. His
psychoanalytic explanation is a functionalist one: fashion is a
neurotic symptom, a compromise formed to reconcile the conflicting demands of exhibitionism and modesty. Fashion, therefore, is irrational, and is to be analysed away.

If Veblen and Flugel are amongst the most influential writers on fashion theory from the past, there are writers today who are often cited in debates on postmodernism, and who also address the question of fashion. Jean Baudrillard is one of these. He denounces fashion with all the ferocity of a fifteenth-century divine.[27] Like Veblen, he defines fashion as ugly, and perceives it as the artificial irritant which encourages ever higher levels of consumption, while ideologically it is there to mask the unchanging nature of domination under capitalism. His rejection of consumer society incorporates the Situationist repulsion for contemporary bourgeois society – its boredom, conformism and alienation. But this draws him into crude functionalism: it is the 'needs' of capitalism that cause fashion to arise, for in reality we do not 'need' all these changing styles in dress, interior decoration and so on. This compulsion towards change is part of the irrationality of fashion. Baudrillard implies that change and variety in style are somehow intrinsically wrong, indeed he takes this as read, and offers no defence for such a view, merely bringing forward an undefined ideal of 'beauty' to set against the 'ugliness' of fashionable ephemera. Beauty is assumed to reside in function, and therefore there must be ideal types of object – whether a cup or a coat, a saucepan or a hat – which function well and are therefore the most 'beautiful'. A Burberry must therefore be more 'beautiful' than a 'showerproof' coat made of, say, pale pink satin; but there is still a problem, for how are we to determine whether or not it is more useful, and therefore more 'beautiful' than a see-through, fold-up plastic mac? Consumption is posed against 'use' by Baudrillard and its wastefulness is emphasised. From there it is only a small step to the condemnation of objects themselves as 'ugly' and non-functional, and there is implicit recourse to aesthetic standards that are not adequately examined. For it does not necessarily follow that everything 'useless' is also 'ugly'. Nor do change and waste *necessarily* go together. Nor is it necessarily less 'bourgeois' to nurture old and prized possessions (eighteenth century furniture, a valuable painting, a fur coat, even) than to throw things away before they are worn out. Nor is it clear who is to determine what in this style utopia shall be judged 'useful' and what 'useless', or what styles are to be allowed as functional. Computers, buses, saucepans and cups, perhaps will be sanctioned, art-deco dressing tables and men's ties banned. But even then, *which* cups will pass the censor's eagle eye – do we 'need' patterns on the outside of our cups, or curly handles?

Secondly, Baudrillard's argument, like Veblen's, is reductionist – in the capitalist order *everything* expresses capitalist values, and there is therefore no room for contradiction or escape. Nor, certainly, is there any room for the idea that the most civilised form of life resides in the cultivation of beauty for its own sake – as Freud put it: 'as though seeking to repudiate these utilitarian achievements' (the achievements, that is, of an over-rationalistic Enlightenment order), 'we welcome it as a sign of civilisation . . . if we see people directing their care to what has no practical value whatever, to what is useless . . . to reverence [of] beauty'.[28]

Roland Barthes, too, in his acute analysis of the language of fashion magazines in the 1950s,[29] sees the function of the 'fashion system' as being to 'naturalise the arbitrary', but, like Baudrillard, he never thinks to relate fashion to other aesthetic practices, nor does he see the evolution of style as meaningful in its own terms. Style degree zero is required – but then minimalism itself, like naturalism, has turned out to be – just another style. Embedded in these texts is a set of moral assumptions based on a pessimistic world view and a rejection of consumerism.

We need to acknowledge, though, that fashion is difficult to theorise because it pertains to more than one set of practices, and cannot, therefore, be quite encompassed within a single discourse or academic 'discipline'. Costume as art is incomplete without the body it is destined to adorn. A cup is a cup, whether filled with coffee or standing empty in a cabinet; not so a garment, although one might modify this statement to argue that the ideal marriage of garment and body is not the daily trudge along the high street, or to the office, or even to the office party; it is a stylised presentation which may achieve its apotheosis in frozen form in the photographic still or with a glorious moment of 'entrance' or 'appearance'. It is the costuming of the daily theatrics of social life. Fashion, bringing together as it does art and the body, is a field upon which a whole variety of arts and discourses meet. We cannot reduce it to mere false consciousness (as Baudrillard and so many others seek to do); what is needed, perhaps, for its analysis is what Georges Devereux called a 'double discourse',[30] that is, any single form of explanation of fashion will inevitably be reductionist, and we must not only, in Devereux's terms, allow that there may be more than one possible explanation, but go further and say that only a multiple (interdisciplinary) explanation will be adequate to the fashion phenomenon. At the same time, we should be aware that its association with the body and with behaviour makes it particularly vulnerable to moralistic interpretations.

Of theorists of fashion, I have singled out those who are hostile and negative to the whole phenomenon: the pessimists. These argue that its influence is baneful on a number of grounds: 1) on economic grounds, because it encourages unnecessary consumption and props up capitalism; 2) on ideological grounds, because it legitimates the bourgeois order and, incidentally, oppresses women, feeding snobbery, class envy and status; and 3) on aesthetic grounds, in that it is ugly, and we should therefore devise some form of 'natural' and unchanging dress.

Such views tend to be aligned with the political right or left, while it tends to be more among liberals that we find greater tolerance, or even wholesale enthusiasm for fashion. These, the optimists, argue that it is to be welcomed because: 1) on economic grounds, it creates a higher standard of living and is part of a more comfortable, more hygienic and more attractive environment; 2) on social grounds – it is a necessary aspect of social life, giving us valuable clues about one another and giving rise to a rich symbolic culture, or at least contributing to it; and 3) on ideological grounds, it is democratic (in its contemporary form, at least) and enhances social and erotic life.

I turn now to look at what light fashion and postmodernism shed on each other. Today, there is a blurring between mainstream and countercultural fashions: all fashion has become 'stagey', self-conscious about its own status as a discourse, about its irrationality, about its message. The work of Jean Paul Gaultier, a Parisian designer who draws inspiration from punk and street clothes, is relevant here, for when the 'subversive' questionings of punk appear on the Paris catwalk itself, who is to say what is for real and what is parody? Gaultier's own pronouncements on his work add to this uncertainty, since he appears to mount an attack on what we think of as fashion: 'People who make mistakes or dress badly are the real stylists. My "You feel as though you've eaten too much" collection [clothes deliberately designed to look "too tight"] is taken from exactly those moments when you are mistaken or embarrassed[31], while Carl Lagerfeld at Chanel has produced outfits that parody the original styles, and 'pudding' hats that parody the surrealist motifs of the 1930s. This cuts the ground from under our feet and decentres our perception of fashion. This is one aspect of the compulsory confusion of contemporary modes. Its eclecticism and oscillation is part of its 'postmodern-ness'. Its irony and cynical self-parody also seem very postmodern, its knowingness about its own performance. Thus the 'confusion' that so puzzled fashion writers in the 1970s, the apparent ending of the orderly evolution of one style out of another, is explicable once it is seen as part of postmodernism.

On the other hand, if we examine, from the point of view of fashion, some of the critiques of postmodernism, we may begin to have reservations about the arguments that are deployed. Frederic Jameson, for example, in his brilliant article 'Postmodernism, or the Cultural Logic of Late Capitalism', attempts to relate postmodernism to the economic and ideological developments of late capitalism, and treats postmodernism as a general contemporary sensibility. It is rather surprising, therefore, that he does not include fashion explicitly in his denunciation, which could certainly be applied very directly to it:

> modernist styles ... become postmodernist codes: and that the stupendous proliferation of social codes today into professional and disciplinary jargons, but also into the badges of affirmation of ethnic, gender, race, religious and class-fraction adhesion, is also a political phenomenon, the problem of micropolitics sufficiently demonstrates. If the ideas of a ruling class were once the dominant (or hegemonic) ideology of bourgeois society, the advanced capitalist countries today are now a field of stylistic and discursive heterogeneity without a norm.[32]

For as we saw, it has become a cliché of fashion journalism that the tyranny of fashion crumbled in the 1970s. No longer did Paris dictate a line every season, compelling women to lower and raise their hemlines and transform their silhouettes in obedience to some haute couture guru. From Jameson's perspective, this pluralism – or anarchy – would surely represent simply another instance of the *compulsory* confusion of styles, which, for him, exemplifies the postmodern, a sensibility in which all sense of development and history are lost, so that the jumble of stylistic mannerisms becomes as 'schizophrenic' as the consumer culture that spawns them. The era of haute couture dominance *would* then appear, retrospectively as 'modernist': the great designers saw themselves as unique artists, and the evolution of fashion has its own internal aesthetic dynamic. This has now been lost – so the argument might go – and the promiscuity of contemporary modes is just part of the fragmentation and depersonalisation of postmodern times. In so far as fashion has relied heavily on 'retro chic' in recent years, this too fits into Jameson's description of the postmodern, since pastiche – 'parody without laughter', 'statue with blind eyeballs' – is, for him, a significant aspect of postmodern culture, or even its typical moment.

But although fashion fits so well into Jameson's postmodern dystopia, we are forced, when we investigate the use of pastiche and retro in fashion, to question whether Jameson is correct in placing 'nostalgia mode' and pastiche as so central not simply to contemporary art, film and architecture, but to a generalised postmodern panorama. Is retro so exclusively *de nos jours*? Fashion, in fact, has relied on pastiche and the recycling of styles throughout the industrial period. Christian Dior[33] believed that until designers such as Madame Vionnet introduced revolutionary techniques of cutting into fashion design in the early twentieth century, the shapes of garments changed only very slowly, and that the impression of change was created by the use of superficial decoration, stylistic motifs often rifled from the past. The Victorians incorporated all sorts of historical styles – the classical Greek and the medieval, for example – into their fashions. The Pre-Raphaelites, also in love with the medieval, harnessed the fashions of that remote period to their particular version of dress reform, but dress designers, too, looked to the past for inspiration. And in the Edwardian period Liberty catalogues advertised evening gowns in a variety of 'historical' styles: Egyptian, medieval, Elizabethan, Madame de Pompadour.

Even in the 1950s, which have now been invested with a seamlessly perfect style and ambience, the then reality was more complex. Fashion in the 1950s flirted more than once with – of all periods – the 1920s: Dior's sack dress of 1958, and Sandy Wilson's 1955 musical, *The Boyfriend*, are two examples of how

the 1950s' interest in the modern and forward-looking turned quite
naturally to the 1920s for images of emancipation and leisure. The
enormous popularity of Nancy Mitford's novels about the 1920s,
*The Pursuit of Love* and *Love in a Cold Climate*, is another
example of 1950s' nostalgia. (In the late 1960s, *The Boyfriend* was
made into a film that was very much of *that* period, and which
starred Twiggy, the most famous fashion model of the 1960s.)
Again, the 1954 Diaghilev exhibition took London by storm; and it
was in 1956 that Liberty relaunched their original Morris designs
for fashion and furnishing fabrics – all these events anticipating
recycled motifs we now think of as more characteristic of the
1970s. 'Our' fifties is already not 'the' fifties. Jameson finds a
specific quality in contemporary re-creations of the past:

> [Nostalgia mode] was never a matter of some old-fashioned
> 'representation' of historical content, but approached the 'past'
> through stylistic connotation, conveying 'pastness' by the glossy
> qualities of the image, and '1930s-ness' or '1950s-ness' by the
> attributes of fashion (therein following the Barthes of *Mythol-
> ogies*, who saw connotation as the purveying of imaginary and
> stereotypical idealities. 'Sinité', for example, as some Disney–
> EPCOT 'concept' of China).[34]

Jameson does not, however, make clear just what is the difference
between an 'old-fashioned "representation" of historical content'
and 'stylistic connotation'. We might enquire when one ceases to
be and the other comes into existence. Are the operas of Verdi,
for example, straightforward 'representations of historical content'? Walter Scott's novels would be another possible example.
Indeed, Walter Scott appears to have invented a whole mythology
of 'Scottishness' for the Royal Family, for whose benefit, on a visit
to Scotland, tartans were reintroduced. The Lairds had forgotten
the colours of their clan tartans, which had to be rediscovered, or
indeed invented for the occasion. To take a more recent example,
is the superficial pastiche of contemporary architecture *the same
thing* as the loving re-creation of the early 1960s in *American
Graffiti*, or the careful (if self-indulgent) evocations of the British
Raj in *The Jewel in the Crown* and *Passage to India*?

Jameson uses the example of contemporary film to develop his
argument against pastiche and retro style, arguing that recent
'nostalgia films' attempt the re-creation of that 'lost object of

desire', the fifties, (a kind of kitsch utopia). Yet he also questions
whether the 'cannibalising historicism' of postmodern architecture
*is* nostalgic, for it is, he argues, too affectless, too flat.

In fact, the re-creation of a sentimentalised past evoked through
stereotype has been a pervasive feature of cinema for years. What
of a whole string of French films from the 1940s: *Les Enfants du
Paradis, Madame de, The Golden Marie* and many others; while
Anne Hollander,[35] in her discussion of Hollywood costume films
of the 1920s and 1930s, argues that despite an at times obsessive
preoccupation with accuracy of period detail, the results were
distinctively 'twenties' or 'thirties'. She tells us that although
Oliver Messel, a specialist in sixteenth-century costume, was
invited to California to advise on the designs for *Romeo and Juliet*,
the star, Norma Shearer, preferred those of Adrian, the resident
MGM designer. 'Flavour' and 'suggestion' were more important
than historical accuracy, film and stage costume being primarily a
series of signals whereby 'powdered hair' equals the eighteenth
century, 'a ruff' the Elizabethan period, and a 'Juliet cap' Renaissance Italy (even though this cap was invented for Theda Bara in
1916 and did not even exist in the *Quattrocento*). This evidence
from the past that pastiche and nostalgia have been pervasive in
popular culture throughout the twentieth century and indeed
earlier appears to contradict Jameson's belief that 'nostalgia mode'
is peculiarly a feature of his postmodern epoch.

Hal Foster argues that in the nineteenth century use of styles
from the past there was at least some sense of protest:

> What . . . does this 'return' imply if not a flight from the present?
> Clearly, this was the thrust of eclectic historicism in nineteenth
> century art and architecture (especially British): a flight from
> the modern – in its romantic form, from the industrial present
> into a preindustrial past; in its neoclassical (academic) form,
> from lived class conflict to the ideal realm of myth. But then this
> flight expressed a social protest, however dreamy; now it seems
> symptomatic of sheer *post histoire* escapism.[36]

But I would find it difficult to argue that there is any sense of
'social protest, however dreamy' in the majority of historical
Hollywood confections of the 1930s.

During the years between the death of the tight-laced corset and
the short skirts and boyish modes of the 1920s, the influence of the

designer Paul Poiret was at its height. Then, as now, exotic motifs were 'in', and shapeless clothes, which often seemed exaggerated and eclectic, sent forth no clear message. Marcel Proust, walking in the Bois de Boulogne, longed for the elegant women of his youth, and could see no meaning in the fashions of 1912. Where once there had been the splendour of horse-drawn carriages, was now nothing 'but motor cars driven each by a moustached mechanic'. And:

> I wished to hold before my bodily eyes . . . little women's hats so low crowned as to seem no more than garlands. All the hats now were immense, covered with all manner of fruits and flowers and birds. In place of the beautiful dresses in which Madame Swann walked like a queen, Graeco-Saxon tunics, pleated à la Tanagra, or sometimes in the Directoire style, accentuated Liberty chiffons sprinkled with flowers like wallpaper... And seeing all these new components of the spectacle, I had no longer a belief to infuse into them to give them consistency, unity and life; they passed before me in a desultory, haphazard, meaningless fashion, containing in themselves no beauty which my eye might have tried, in the old days, to recreate. They were just women, in whose elegance I had no faith, and whose clothes seemed to me unimportant. But when a belief vanishes, there survives it – more and more vigorously so as to cloak the absence of the power, now lost to us, of imparting reality to new things – a fetishistic attachment to the old things which it did once animate, as if it was in them and not in ourselves that the divine spark resided, and as if our present incredulity had a contingent cause – the death of the gods.[37]

So a sense of the loss of meaning is already present in the high modernist *À La Recherche des Temps Perdus*, and, set against Proust's insightful comments on the subjective quality of our aesthetic judgments, Jameson's lament for the loss of norms is revealed as a romantic longing for some past that is never made explicit. Is it modernism? Is it realism? Is it the orderliness of bourgeois society or the unrealised collective purpose of a socialism infused with functional aesthetic values? We do not know.

In the 1970s, Kennedy Fraser, then fashion correspondent to the *New York Times*, saw retro chic as merely another twist in the fashion cycle. In her awareness of the 'irony' of retro dressing she touches on Jameson's themes:

Clothes came to be worn and seen as an assemblage of thought –
our paradoxes, as irony, whimsy, or deliberate disguise. Thrift
shop dressing carried it all to its ultimate. We took to clothes for
which we had spent little money, which didn't necessarily fit us,
and which had belonged in the past to some dead stranger's life.
Behind the bravado of what came to be known as 'style', there
may have lurked a fear of being part of our time, of being locked
into our own personalities, and of revealing too much about our
own lives.

Above all, what ultimately characterised the fashion of the
past decade was detachment.[38]

But Kaja Silverman takes issue with this view. For her, retro is a
counter cultural mode, a 'sartorial strategy which works to denatur-
alise its wearer's specular identity, and one which is fundamentally
irreconcilable with fashion'. Far from destroying the past, 'it
inserts its wearer into a complex network of cultural and historical
references'.[39] She agrees with Kennedy Fraser that there is a
'masquerade' quality about it, but for her this has radical potential. Roland Barthes argued that fashion journalism strove to
'naturalise the arbitrary': each successive fashion was, for him,
actually meaningless, the 'fashion system' alone giving it (spu-
rious) meaning; whereas, for Kaja Silverman, counter cultural
dressing, at least, draws attention to its own work of representation, and it could be argued that it is therefore 'modernist' rather
than 'postmodernist'.

Jameson castigates the nostalgia of postmodernism while Hal
Foster notes the absence of utopian vision in postmodern art. Yet
Western dress reveals how close together utopianism and nostalgia
lie. Utopianism has always been nostalgic and in a curious way
backward looking – a search for the lost happiness of a romanti-
cised infancy in which contradiction and conflict did not exist. This
utopian nostalgia is expressive of the wish to recall the lost –
narcissistic – object of desire, the idealised image of Lacan's
mirror stage,[40] in which the unstable infant body is magically
'fixed' in a never-to-be-realised perfection. The self you see in the
mirror is a self made permanent, divested of its fragmentary,
fleeting, changing quality.

The dress reform project was utopian in a different sense: the
transcendence of the 'ugliness' and above all the *change* that is

central to fashionable styles.[41] Literary utopias, such as the first, Thomas More's *Utopia*,[42] and that of William Morris in *News From Nowhere*,[43] have often been fashion-free – Thomas More's was written specifically as a critique of Tudor courtly consumerism in the period of early mercantile capitalism. Yet, paradoxically, fashion itself is also utopian in its attempt to fix the fleeting moment as final, always to present its every new manifestation as the final solution to the problem of what to wear.[44] Fashion tries to hold back, or rather to deny, change, decay and death. In this sense, fashion is consolatory, as Foucault argues that utopias also are.[45] (Julia Emberley[46] suggests that in contemporary fashion this utopian consolation is produced in a 'heterotopic' or 'heterogenous' way – another way of accounting for or, rather, alluding to its eclecticism).

Dress is like a 'mirror phase'. Denounced as narcissistic in the lay sense of self-regard, it places a line around the shifting, vulnerable and indeterminate contours of the body, acts as armour, as carapace. Dress, in this sense, is less Kennedy Fraser's 'masquerade', which puts an 'ironic distance' between the self and the costume/uniform/camouflage which it sports as mask or disguise, than the form in which the body actually manifests itself. The language in which we habitually speak of dress alludes to this notion of manifestation: we take a pride in our 'appearance'; we are seen by others as 'visions' of loveliness' we look like 'a dream'. As Kaja Silverman puts it so well:

> Clothing and other kinds of ornamentation make the human body culturally visible . . . clothing draws the body so that it can be culturally seen, and articulates it in a meaningful form . . . Clothing is a necessary condition of subjectivity . . . in articulating the body it simultaneously articulates the psyche.[47]

It is a 'vestimentary envelope' that holds body and ego together. Our finished 'appearance', therefore, is the end result (yet itself alterable and altering) of an often elaborate construction, both bodily and mental, of identity itself. The very concept of 'appearance' (after all, ghosts and visions 'appear' to the blessed and the cursed) suggests the ghostly aspect of apparel without a wearer, it's 'uncanniness', and the ambiguity of the relationship between 'ourselves' and our clothes. Many attempts to theorise fashion have foundered on this ambiguity between 'appearance' and an assumed 'reality' behind it, dress reform being one of the most radical attempts to justify this separation of the two.

Within postmodernism, discourse theory seems to offer the possibility of an interpretation of fashion within the proliferation of discursive and social practices that centre on the human body. Here, the work of Michel Foucault, especially *Discipline and Punish*,[48] and *The History of Sexuality*[49] is important. For Foucault, modernity inaugurates a multitude of practices which act upon the body – to discipline it, to make it more apt, in a 'positive' sense to alter and adapt it to the modern world. This discursive universe does not repress, but, on the contrary, actively produces the body: drilling, eurythmics, aerobics – and of course fashion and beauty culture – may all be seen as part of this disciplinary mode, and, like dieting, exercise and dance they have become integral to twentieth century life. For Foucault, the very inescapability of this discursive and regimentary universe appears as one aspect of the 'carceral' nature of modern society.

Fredric Jameson objects to this proliferation of practices for the opposite reason to Foucault. For Jameson, the hysteric overflow of possibilities, the hypertrophy of styles destroys meaning.

What these and many writers on postmodernism do is themselves create an imprisoning universe. Although some writers, Angela McRobbie[50] and Andreas Huyssen[51] for example, emphasise the optimistic possibilities of the postmodern, it is the dystopic vision of the postmodern world that usually wins out:

> In a postmodern culture typified by the disappearance of the Real and by the suffocation of natural contexts, fashion provides *aesthetic holograms* as moveable texts for the general economy of excess . . . An entire postmodern scene . . . brought under the double sign of culture where, as Baudrillard has hinted, the secret of fashion is to introduce the *appearance* of radical novelty, while maintaining the *reality* of no substantial change. Or is it the opposite? Not fashion as a referent of the third (simulational) order of the real, but as itself the spectacular sign of a parasitical culture which, always anyway excessive, disaccumulative, and sacrificial, is drawn inexorably towards the ecstasy of catastrophe.[52]

This overblown passage is rather typical of writing about the postmodern, which, whatever the overt ethical or political position of the writer, often seems to exude a fascinated horror or gleeful immersion in the most decadent and even in the grimmest aspects of the 'postmodern' world. A feature, indeed, of the explosion of writing on postmodernism is its peculiarly hyperbolic tone. At one moment, postmodernism is seen as a totalising *Zeitgeist* in which we inhabit a seamless dystopia, Foucault's carceral society spread across the globe; at another, the disintegration of the postmodern is what is emphasised, and welcomed as offering cracks and fissures in a terroristic totality – and thereby the means of escape (although into what is not clear). And yet, behind this embrace of the new and what sometimes seems like an aesthetic idealisation of the ugly, lie some very old moral assumptions about hedonism, consumption and worldly enjoyment: that they are unworthy. Both those who denounce and those who claim to welcome the postmodern implicitly portray a world of selfishness, greed and narcissism, whether they rejoice in or denounce the consumerism at the heart of it all. If some writers reject Marx for his refusal of the utopian vision, they themselves seem to wallow in a *dystopia* of negation, while relying on a never explicitly stated set of conservative and often utilitarian assumptions. They inhabit a new zone of romanticism, in which there is a curious simultaneous denunciation and idealisation of pollution, consumerism, novelty, media bombardment, an aestheticisation of the excesses of the post-industrial landscape, 'B Movie' cities and junk in all its forms.

I have tried to show that, if we look at fashion, we find that some of the themes and hallmarks of what is today termed postmodernism have been around for a long, long time, so that it is doubtful whether a postmodern *Zeitgeist* or ethos does exist in the way in which writers such as Jameson and Baudrillard would have us believe. Their generalisations begin to seem to have more to do with the creation of a cultural myth about 'our times' which flattens out the contradictory, refractory reality nature of contemporary existence and seeks to create a stereotype of the present in the present. It has been a feature of post-war culture to create stereotypes of past decades – 'the twenties', 'the thirties', 'the fifties', 'the sixties' – but now this is extended into the fabric of the very moment in which the critic is living and writing. Perhaps this in itself simply demonstrates how 'postmodern' the present has become, involved even as it unfolds in a simulacrum of itself, in a collapse of 'reality' into 'image'.

Yet to examine the discourse of the cultural critics themselves is to become aware of their conservatism, not in any directly political sense, necessarily, (although there is that too), but rather in the sense in which they remain anchored in the *project* of defining a *Zeitgeist* – a surely unpostmodern concept. Furthermore, there is the tendency to accept what amounts to a reflexionist notion of ideology – another Marxist sin. Both John Urry and Scott Lash, for example, in their detailed work on 'disorganised capitalism', assume that there is a general cultural parallel to economic transformations: that postmodernism is, as it were, the ideology of 'disorganised capitalism'; and they even assume a collective psyche typical of a given period. Fredric Jameson, perhaps metaphorically, speaks of schizophrenia, but Lash and Urry cite the supposed empirical decline of neuroses, typically conversion hysteria, which are said to have been replaced by personality disorders. They refer also to the work of Heinz Kohut on narcissism and to the sweeping generalisations of Christopher Lasch on the same subject, and to Bryan Turner's assertion of 'a shift in dominant psychopathologies from hysteria to narcissism and anorexia'.[53] But not only are the shifts determined in part by fashions in diagnosis (anorexia may be more common today simply because it is more recognised), it is also questionable whether there is any such thing as a periodised collective psyche. The attempt to align mental disorder, all cultural phenomena and the economy seems inescapably reductionist in writers some of whom have precisely rejected what they see as the reductionism of Marx.

In a balanced overview, Andreas Huyssen suggests that post-modernism:

> operates in a field of tension between tradition and innovation, conservation and renewal, mass culture and high art . . . a field of tension which can no longer be grasped in categories such as progress vs. reaction, Left vs. Right, present vs. past, modern-ism vs. realism, abstraction vs. representation, avant garde vs. Kitsch.[54]

For him, it is the fact that such categories have broken down which creates a crisis – of representation, among other things. And postmodernism is the representation of the crisis. He saves post-modernism from its own ambiguity by making it the site from which the Others – as opposed to the Western modernist male

intellectual who believed he stood at the cutting edge of history –
may find a site from which to speak: women, the non-Western
world, the ecology movement. These movements can create a
'postmodernism of resistance' as opposed to '"anything goes"
postmodernism'. Translated to the field of fashion, this would
seem to support alternative, counter cultural fashions. Yet some
would argue that postmodern eclecticism destroys any perspective
from which a fashion could truly be defined as counter-cultural,
precisely *because* 'anything goes'.

So far as women are concerned[55] – and fashion is still primarily
associated with women – contemporary fashions arguably have
liberatory potential (whether or not this is realised). For in
'denaturalising the wearer's specular identity' contemporary
fashion refuses the dichotomy, nature/culture. Fashion in our
epoch denaturalises the body and thus divests itself of all essentialism. This must be good news for women, since essentialist
ideologies have been oppressive to them. Fashion often plays with,
and playfully transgresses, gender boundaries, inverting stereotypes
and making us aware of the masquerade of femininity. Hal Foster
takes a different view of essentialism, arguing that it may now be
more important to struggle against the notion of 'woman as
artifice' than that of 'woman as Nature'.[56] But it would be more
subversive to extend the notion of artifice to masculinity.

The postmodern disturbance of accepted meanings does not
inevitably involve Jameson's 'schizophrenia'. The expression of
dissidence, whether in artworks or in fashion, is obviously open to
recuperation and does often represent a displacement of overtly
political protest. Yet, as fashion increasingly extends its ambiguous sway over both sexes, it acts not to reinforce a Veblenesque
set of meanings organised around 'woman as cultural display', nor
does it necessarily contribute to the carceral society – also implicit
in Veblen's picture of the capitalist world – in which everything is
imposed from without. Rather it creates a space in which the
normative nature of social practices, always so intensely encoded
in dress, may be questioned.

Fashion, as the most popular aesthetic practice of all, extends
art into life and offers a medium across the social spectrum with
which to experiment. In our anxiety about the environment and
our new found sensitivity to the destruction of nature, it is
tempting to forget that urban life has always offered advantages

that cannot be matched by rural existence. And fashion is an inescapable part of the urban scene. We are in danger, too, of creating a one-dimensional, oversimplified account of postmodernism that both loses its ambiguity and exaggerates its grip. Better than envisaging it as a total system, a nightmare of the mind, would be to use it as an intuitive interpretative tool, one possible way of many in which we may investigate 'these new components of the spectacle'.

## Notes and References

\* For the elaboration of the discussion on fashion in this article see Wilson, Elizabeth (1985), *Adorned in Dreams: Fashion and modernity*, London, Virago.

1. Foster, Hal (1985), *Recodings: Art, Spectacle, Cultural Politics*, Port Townsend, Washington: Bay Press, differentiates between the postmodern, which 'plays with literal and pastiched references to art history and pop culture alike', and postmodernism and postmodernist art, which is 'posed theoretically against modernist paradigms', and 'question[s] the truth-value of representation'. p. 214, note 13. I have not distinguished the two words in this precise way.

2. Huyssen, Andreas (1984), 'Mapping the Postmodern' in *New German Critique*, Number 33, Fall; and Owens, Craig (1983), 'The Discourse of Others: Feminists and postmodernism' in Foster, Hal, (ed.) (1985), *The Anti-Aesthetic: Essays on Postmodern Culture*, Port Townsend, Washington, Bay Press.

3. Bell, Quentin (1947), *On Human Finery*, London, The Hogarth Press, discusses the way in which sartorial behaviour gets conflated with moral worth.

4. Mukerji, Chandra (1983), *From Graven Images: Patterns of Modern Materialism*, New York, Columbia University Press.

5. Baldwin, Frances Elizabeth (1926), *Sumptuary Legislation and Personal Regulation in England* Baltimore, Johns Hopkins Press.

6. Huxley, Aldous (1955), *Brave New World*, Harmondsworth, Penguin.

7. Orwell, George (1948), *1984*, Harmondsworth, Penguin.

8. Sennett, Richard (1974), *The Fall of Public Man*, Cambridge, Cambridge University Press.

9. Strong, Roy (1987), in *The Independent*, 'Revive the Royal Rule of Taste', 21 August 1987.

10. Laver, James (1969), *A Concise History of Costume*, London, Weidenfeld and Nicolson.

11. Charles-Roux, Edmonde (1975), *Chanel*, London, Jonathan Cape.

12. Warner, Marina (1985), *Monuments and Maidens: The Allegory of The Female Form*, London, Weidenfeld and Nicolson.

13. White, Jerry (1986), *Campbell Bunk: The Worst Street in North London*, London, Routledge & Kegan Paul.

14. Ibid., pp. 191–2.

15. Ibid.

16. Quoted in Wilson, Elizabeth, op. cit., p. 89.

17. Warhol, Andy and Hackett, Pat (1980), *POPism: The Warhol '60s*, New York, Harcourt Brace Jovanovich.

18. Burger, Peter (1984), *Theory of the Avant Garde*, Minneapolis, University of Minnesota Press, sees this collapse as a hallmark of the avant garde.

19. Lurie, Alison (1981), *The Language of Clothes*, London, Heinemann.

20. Hebdige, Dick (1979), *Subculture: The Meaning of Style*, London, Methuen.

21. Veblen, Thorstein (1899), *The Theory of the Leisure Class*, London, Allen and Unwin.

22. Silverman, Kaja (1986), 'Fragments of a Fashionable Discourse', in Modleski, Tania, (ed.) (1986) *Studies in Entertainment: Critical Approaches to Mass Culture*, Bloomington and Indianapolis, Indiana University Press.

23. Flugel, J. C. (1930), *The Psychology of Clothes*, London, The Hogarth Press; and see also Burman, Barbara and Leventon, Melissa (1987), 'the Men's Dress Reform Society', *Costume*, No. 21.

24. Wollen, Peter (1987), 'Fashion/Orientalism/The Body', in *New Formations*, No. 1, Spring.

25. Moers, Ellen (1986), *The Dandy: Brummell to Beerbohm*, London, Secker and Warburg; and Laver, James (1968), *Dandies*, London, Weidenfeld and Nicolson.

26. Woolf, Virgina (1938), *Three Guineas*, Harmondsworth, Penguin, p. 23.

27. Baudrillard, Jean (1981), *For a Critique of the Political Economy of the Sign*, St Louis, Mo., Telos Press.

28. Freud, Sigmund (1949), *Civilisation and Its Discontents*, London, The Hogarth Press, p. 54.

29. Barthes, Roland (1957), *Système de la Mode*, Paris, Éditions du Seuil.

30. Devereux, Georges (1978), *Ethnopsychoanalysis*, Berkeley, University of California Press.

31. quoted in Wilson, Elizabeth, op. cit., p. 10.

32. Jameson, Fredric (1984), 'Postmodernism, or the Cultural Logic of Late Capitalism', *New Left Review*, number 146, July/August, p. 65.

33. Dior, Christian (1957), *Dior by Dior*, London, Weidenfeld and Nicolson.

34. Jameson, Fredric, op. cit., p. 67.

35. Hollander, Anne (1975), *Seeing Through Clothes*, New York, Avon Books.

36. Foster, Hal, op. cit., (1985), pp. 122–3.

37. Proust, Marcel (1981), *Rememberance of Things Past*, Volume I, London, Chatto and Windus, p. 460.

38. Fraser, Kennedy (1985), *The Fashionable Mind: Reflections on Fashion, 1970–1982*, Boston, David R Godine, p. 238.

39. Silverman, Kaja, op. cit., p. 150.

40. Lacan, Jacques (1949), 'The Mirror Stage as Formative of the Function of the I', in Lacan, Jacques (1981), *Écrits: A Selection*, London, Tavistock.

41. Newton, Stella Mary (1974), *Health, Art and Reason: Dress Reformers of the Nineteenth Century*, London, John Murray.

42. More, Thomas (1965), *Complete Works*, Volume IV, New Haven/ London, Yale University Press.

43. Morris, William (1980), *News From Nowhere and Selected Writings and Designs*, Harmondsworth, Penguin.

44. König, René (1973), *The Restless Image*, London, Allen & Unwin.

45. Foucault, Michel (1970), *The Order of Things*, London, Tavistock, p. xxiii.

46. Emberley, Julia (1988), 'The Fashion Apparatus and the Deconstruction of Postmodern Subjectivity' in Kroker, Arthur and Kroker, Marilouise (eds) (1988), *Body Invaders: Sexuality and the Postmodern Condition*, London, Macmillan.

47. Silverman, Kaja, op. cit.

48. Foucault, Michel (1977), *Discipline and Punish*, Harmondsworth, Penguin.

49. Foucault, Michel (1979), *the History of Sexuality: An Introduction*, Harmondsworth, Penguin.

50. McRobbie, Angela (1986), 'Postmodernism and Popular Culture', in Appignanesi, Lisa, (ed.) (1986), *ICA Documents 4* London, ICA.

51. Huyssen, Andreas, op. cit.

52. Kroker, Arthur and Kroker, Marilouise, op. cit., p. 45.

53. Lash, Scott and Urry, John (1987), *The End of Organised Capitalism*, Cambridge, Polity Press, Ch. 9.

54. Huyssen, Andreas, op. cit., p. 48.

55. for a further discussion on women and postmodernism, see Wilson, Elizabeth (1988), 'Rewinding the Video', in Wilson, Elizabeth (1988), *Hallucinations*, London, Radius/Century Hutchinson.

56. Foster, Hal, op. cit. (1985), p. 213, note 27, where he cites a feminist writer, Jane Weinstock in defence of this view, which he qualifies by adding: 'I take this not as a call to any essentialism as such but as the need, in "the post-natural world of late capitalism" (Jameson) in which patriarchal structures are continually recoded, to move beyond the opposition nature/culture to a genuine order of difference'. This argument is unclear to me, since I do not understand what is meant by a 'genuine order of difference'. How is the genuine to be distinguished from the essential? It seems merely to substitute some sort of ethical in place of the biologically based definition.

# Chapter 9

# Postmodernism in the Visual Arts: A Question of Ends

Paul Crowther

## Introduction

The question of postmodernism in the visual arts has been dominated by a number of themes, notably the idea that art, its history, and its theory, have come to an end; and that postmodernism is largely the product of a force external to art – namely, the market. It might be argued that, for the most part, these themes have been set forth and received with rather more enthusiasm than understanding (the works of Victor Burgin are perhaps a case in point here). However, in the writings of the philosopher and art critic Arthur Danto, the themes are linked in a more coherent and incisive way as part of an interesting discourse concerning the end of modernity in the visual arts. In this chapter, therefore, I shall use a critique of Danto's theory as a means of answering the question of postmodernism in the visual arts. Specifically, in Part I, I will outline Danto's theory at length, and will argue that it is not philosophically decisive. In Parts II and III, I will go on to offer a more plausible alternative reading of modernity and postmodernity; and in Part IV, will offer a final refutation of

Danto's claim that, (through being rendered posthistorical in the postmodern era) art has come to an end.


# I

The premise of Danto's argument concerning the end of art is that the advent of cinematography precipitated a traumatic crisis in the art world. This crisis consisted in the fact that, whilst art had always taken itself to be essentially bound with imitating the world, it was now recognised that cinematography could achieve this in a more total way. Twentieth-century modernist art, therefore, turned towards a kind of self-interrogation. As Danto puts it,

> In its great philosophical phase, from about 1905 to about 1964, modern art undertook a massive investigation into its own nature and essence. It set out to seek a form of itself so pure as art that nothing like what caused it to undertake this investigation in the first place could ever happen to it again (Danto, 1987, p. 217).

This interpretation is, according to Danto, confirmed by the fact that modernist movements seem to be in perpetual conflict with each other. Again, in his words,

> There have been more projected definitions of art, each identified with a different movement in art, in the six or seven decades of this modern era, than in the six or seven centuries that preceded it. Each definition was accompanied by a severe condemnation of everything else, as *not* art (Danto, 1987, p. 217).

On these terms, then, the discontinuity and conflict between modern movements should be taken as signifying the fact that all were involved in a search for art's essence, and that all were offering different, mutually exclusive, answers.

Now for Danto, this search ends at a quite specific point – namely in Warhol's Pop Art, and, in particular the exhibition at the Stable Gallery in 1964 where the infamous *Brillo Boxes* were shown for the first time. Since Warhol's Boxes were ostensibly indistinguishable from real Brillo cartons, the question of what differentiates artworks from real things was posed in the most naked and unambiguous fashion, or, as Danto has it, 'its true philosophical form'. And the answer emerged as follows. It is only an atmosphere of theory which differentiates artworks from other things. The essence of art does not consist in some perceptible property or set of properties, but rather in art's institutional setting. Broadly speaking, the artwork is what the artist designates as such, on the basis of some theory about art.

Now, this answer – and its reiteration in minimal and (one presumes) conceptual art – effectively brought the internal logic of modernist art's quasi-philosophical questioning to fulfilment. But this created a hiatus. As Danto puts it, '. . . the institutions of the art world continued to believe in – indeed to expect – break-throughs, and the galleries, the collectors, the art magazines, the museums and finally the corporations that had become the major patrons of the age were also awaiting prophets and revelations' (Danto, 1987, p. 205). Danto's point, then, is that the radical improvements of modernist work had by the late 1960s and 1970s found a market, and thence created a *demand* for art that was innovative and new. But what came next was a mere pluralism – a repetition or refinement of proceeding styles (be they representa-tional or abstract) and a willingness to accept these on their own terms, rather than on a partisan basis of mutual exclusivity. Indeed, in the terms of Danto's argument this is an entirely logical development, in so far as once modernist art has worked through to and declared art's essence, there is nothing new for art to do. It can only rework old ground. The advent and triumph of neo-expressionism in the 1980s is simply a special case of this. According to Danto, 'Neo-Expressionism raised, as art, no philo-sophical question at all, and indeed it could raise none that would not be some variant on the one raised in its perfected form by Warhol' (Danto, 1987, p. 209).

Neo-Expressionism, then, is to be seen as an exaggerated and empty response to the art market's demand for innovation. It provides, as it were, a show of newness, but in terms of strict artistic criteria, can only be an inflated repetition of what has gone before.

The central substantive claims of Danto's position, then, are these. In response to the usurping of its mimetic functions by cinematography, modernist art became energised by an internal 'logic' necessarily progressing towards the revelation of art's real essence – an essence that would not be assimilable in terms of other forms of communication. In Warhol's Pop Art, this progression issues in its logical culmination. The essence of art is, in effect, declared as institutional. This self-congruence of art with its own essence is the culmination of art history. After it there can be nothing new in a distinctively artistic sense. On these terms, in other words, postmodern art is essentially *posthistorical*. Art, in effect, has come to an end.

Having outlined Danto's theory, I shall now make some observations concerning its strengths, and some philosophical points concerning its weaknesses. Its strength lies in two basic achievements. First, Danto has pinpointed a crucial fact – namely that in the modern epoch, art practice has been taken to its *logical* limit. For once what counts as art is determined by artistic intention alone – rather than by possession of specifiable phenomenal characteristics – then we have reached a point beyond which there can be no *new kinds* of artwork. Anything and everything is admissible in the context of artistic theory and intention. The second strength of Danto's theory is that this first point enables him to explain exactly why postmodern art is fundamentally empty and a product of market forces. Rather than simply declaring it as regressive or the result of a general cultural 'slackening' (Lyotard), he provides a model wherein the origins of the slackening can be traced to art's progression towards logical exhaustion at the end of the modernist era. Postmodern art is empty because it is post-historical. However, whilst Danto thence offers a superficially plausible explanation of the origins and nature of postmodernism, it is not, I think, an ultimately satisfying one. For even if we allow Danto's claim that twentieth-century modernism consists fundamentally in a necessary progression towards the logical limit of art, there is no reason why the attainment of this limit should be regarded – as Danto clearly does – as a restriction upon the creativity and historical development of art. What is lacking here is an argument to establish that creativity and artistic advancement are necessarily connected to the having of new ideas about what counts as the essence of art. For example, we might not count something as creative and quality art unless it does embody some new and novel feature, but this feature does not *have* to take the form of an embodiment of new ideas about what kind of item should be counted as art. It could, rather, take the form of a new style of handling, or the refinement of an existing style to an optimum degree. Indeed, it is the pattern and structure of just these sorts of developments which are the key elements in the history of art. The fact that, on Danto's reading, modernist art fixes on a particular sort of innovation bound up with quasi-philosophical questioning, could simply be regarded as the kind of extended detour from the standard preoccupations of art. Indeed the fact that this detour leads to the logical limits of art acts only as a restriction on the scope of art which is explicitly orientated towards the question of what counts as art. On these terms, in other words, the logical limit reached by modernist art does not exhaust the possibilities of artistic creativity and advancement as such. Hence, we do not *have* on philosophical grounds to regard postmodern art as essentially posthistorical.

The second major area of difficulty raised by Danto's approach concerns his very reading of twentieth-century modernism as a kind of quasi-philosophical endeavour. For one must ask whether there is anything which *compels* such a reading? As I interpret him, Danto might offer us two putatively compelling reasons. First, the fact that modernist movements offer, in effect, different and mutually exclusive definitions of what counts as art – and hence embody rival philosophical viewpoints. Now in relation to this, whilst it is true that the twentieth century has seen more conflicting philosophical theories of art than any other, these have generally been put forward by philosophers rather than artists. Indeed, whilst many modernist artists have rejected the *worth* of traditional art in relation to modern experience, very few have claimed that it – or the work of rival modern movements – should not be regarded as art at all. What we find, rather, is a willingness to expand the field of art, rather than to restrict it to one style or one kind of artefact. Danto, in other words, wholly ignores the crucial bonds of practical and theoretical *continuity* which link modern movements. Now, the second reason which Danto might argue as justifying his reading of modernism concerns the traditional supposed function of art. He claims that because the advent of cinematography finally vanquished art's mimetic function, art was led to a necessary progression towards the discovery of its essence. This, however, makes some pretty simplistic assumptions about the life which art traditionally plays in our culture. It is certainly true – as Aristotle noted – that mimesis seems to have an intrinsic fascination for human beings, but one might argue that the fascination with mimesis for its own sake has rarely been regarded as art's *definitive* function. Mimesis, has, rather, been seen as a means to the end of various salutary effects – such as moral improvement, or the expression of feeling. Hence, one might see the impact of photography and cinema not as precipitating a crisis of philosophical questioning, but rather as a liberation. Artists were now free to orientate their work towards salutary effects that eluded more conventional techniques of representation.

I am arguing, then, that Danto's approach to the question of twentieth-century modernism and postmodernism is not philosophically decisive. In particular, he overlooks possible dimensions of practical and theoretical continuity and salutary effects which might link modernist and, indeed, postmodern movements together. In the following section of this chapter, therefore, I shall continue my critique of Danto by constructing an alternative historical interpretation which takes full account of the dimension of continuity.

## II

Modernist art in the twentieth century has moved in two dominant directions. On the one hand in, say, Fauvism, Futurism, Expressionism and Surrealism, we find a *revisionary* approach towards representation which seeks to reappropriate it for the needs of modern experience. On the other hand, in, say, Suprematism, Neo-Plasticism, and Abstract Expressionism, we find a *tendency* towards purely abstract form. Now, these two tendencies are linked in two crucial respects. First, virtually all of them embody to greater or lesser degree a debt to Cézannesque and Cubist form or space. That is to say, they employ a formal vocabulary which tends to reduce form to more basic geometric shape, and/or which distributes such forms in a hyper-pictorial space i.e. one which accentuates the two-dimensionality of the picture plane, and diminishes the sense of three-dimensional illusion. Hence, whilst modernist movements tend in different stylistic directions, they do so on the basis of a root vocabulary derived from Cézanne and Cubism. Now although this vocabulary is one that departs from, and to some degree, subverts, conventional forms of representation, it is not one which radically subverts the notion of high art, as such. Picasso and Braque's Cubism, for example, reappropriates and relegitimises traditional genres such as the still-life, the nude, and the portrait, in terms of an aggressive subjectivity. Indeed, even in Cubist collage – where alien physical material is incorporated into the work – such material is thoroughly mediated. Any oppositional sense of its physical reality is lost within the totality of the overall artistic composition. Again, in the case of Surrealism's dislocations of form, these do not subvert art as such, but rather draw on the precedent of Romantic and Symbolist Fantasy, in order to evoke repressed depths of subjectivity. The function of Cubist space, in other words, is not to posit an antithesis to high art, but rather to refocus it in terms of a liberating affirmation of the subject. It is this affirmative dimension which provides the second, and most important bond between twentieth-century modernists. It even encompasses those American Abstract Expressionists who radically break with Cubist space after 1945. Barnett Newman, for example, declared that 'Instead of making *cathedrals* out of Christ, man, or "life", we are making it out of ourselves, out of our own feelings' (Newman in Chipp, 1968, p. 553). Compare this with the following set of statements:

When we invented Cubism, we had no intention of inventing Cubism. We simply wanted to express what was in us (Picasso in Chipp, 1968, p. 210).

Without much intention, knowledge, or thought, I had followed an irresistable desire to represent profound spirituality, religion and tenderness (Emil Nolde in Chipp, 1968, p. 146).

We ... create a sort of emotive ambience, seeking by intuition the sympathies and the links which exist between the exterior (concrete) scene and the interior (abstract) emotion (Umberto Bocciono in Chipp, 1968, p. 297).

The truly modern artist is aware of abstraction in an emotion of beauty (Piet Mondrian in Chipp, 1968, p. 321).

what interests me is the intensity of a personality transposed directly into the work; the man and his vitality; ... what manner he knows how to gather sensation, emotion, into a lacework of words and sentiments (Tristan Tzara in Chipp, 1968, p. 387).

On these terms, then, Newman's declaration that he and his contemporaries are making 'cathedrals' of 'our own feelings' is a statement that captures a profound theme running throughout modernist art – namely that the artwork receives its ultimate authentification as a vehicle for expression of *feeling*. What *sort* of feeling is expressed here varies (as the foregoing statements show) from artist to artist. In some, it is bound up with aesthetic experience and religious sentiments; in others, it is linked to the artist's affective response to technological change and Utopian political ideals. But what all these have in common is the view that what legitimises modern art and gives it its worth, is some kind of *elevating* expressive effect embodied in its creation and reception. I shall hereafter call this view the 'legitimising discourse' of art.

There are now two crucial points to be made. First (*contra* Danto) far from modernist art movements being engaged in a kind of war between mutually exclusive definitions of art, there exists a surprising degree of continuity between them at the level of both phenomenal appearance and theoretical justification. Second, the legitimising discourse of modernist art also gives it continuity with more traditional idioms. For since the Renaissance at least, the *raison d'être* of art in Western culture has been insistently tied to its elevating effects. As J.-J. David puts it somewhere, 'the purpose of the arts is to serve morality and elevate the soul'.

What demarcates modernist art from such sentiments as these is the different readings of morality and elevation which it involves, and the different pictorial means with which it operates. But the fundamental point is the same – art has its justification as a vehicle of – in the broadest terms – ethical and aesthetic improvement and elevation. If, therefore, we are to talk of a 'logic' of modernity in the visual arts at all, it can only be in the loose sense of a *radical transformation of the existing legitimising discourse of art*. This, however, should not be seen as a logic of 'necessary' progression; neither must it be viewed as a matter wholly internal to art itself. For, in modernist art, the different senses of elevation operative in the works of different artists and the means by which they are achieved are frequently enmeshed in complex responses to broader societal changes. Danto, then, is led astray in historical terms by his failure to look at the continuity of modernist art in its sociological context.

There is, however, one point in the growth of modernism which does seem more amenable to Danto's narrative. This is to be located in certain aspects of Pop Art – such as Warhol's *Brillo*

*Boxes* – and in the development of minimal and conceptual art in the 1960s and 1970s. The former tendency seems to insist on collapsing the distinction between art and life, whilst the latter tendencies (respectively) seem to declare – in the most strident terms – that the minimum conditions for something being an artwork, are mere objecthood, or embodying an 'idea' about what counts as art. Now even if (with Danto) we view these as quasi-philosophical statements about the definition of art, they point in a rather different direction from that which Danto's interpretation would lead us to expect. For if, as I have argued, the central feature of modernism is a radical transformation of the legitimising discourse, then, the fact that certain movements after 1960 seem to *break* with this carries with it the implication that we have here the beginnings of a break with modernity *itself*. What Danto's narrative of quasi-philosophical questioning *really* signifies, in other words, is not the underlying 'logic' of modernity, but the transitional point at which modernity begins to pass into postmodernity. In the next section of this chapter therefore, I will develop this interpretation by showing how the critique of the legitimising discourse can be construed as a definitive feature of postmodernism in the visual arts.


**III**


The key artist in understanding the transition from modern to postmodern is Malcolm Morley. In the late 1950s and early 1960s, Morley was working in an abstract expressionist idiom much indebted to Barnett Newman. However, around 1965 he began producing works such as *S.S. Amsterdam at Rotterdam*. Now at first sight, in utilising imagery derived from the mass-media – in this case a commonplace postcard – it might seem that Morley is linking himself to those aspects of Pop Art which overtly celebrate the virtues of mass-culture. This, however, would be a very superficial reading. For Morley's 'Super Realism' lacks any sense of the hedonism, humour, or gently irony which generally characterises Pop Art's relation to its sources. The internal resources of an image such as *S.S. Amsterdam* rather, declare it as more serious and critical through the very insistency with which it manifests its own origin in an image derived from mechanical reproduction.

246

*Figure 9.1*  Malcolm Morley, *S.S. Amsterdam at Rotterdam*

*Saatchi Collection, London*

(Even the margin of the postcard is, in fact, worked into Morley's image). This impression is consolidated by knowledge of how the work is created. In this (and kindred works of the late 1960s) Morley has small scale photographic-based material blown up into poster size. He then inverts the image, divides it up into a series of grid squares, and transcribes it – one square at a time (with the rest covered up) – in acrylic paint on to a canvas. Thus the process of making the work is reduced to the level of a quasi-mechanical reproduction. We have a framed picture offered in the 'big' format characteristic of 'high-art', but whose status as high art is subverted by the image's banal content. Other levels of negation are also operative. For here, a mechanically reproduced image (the postcard) is the original, whereas the high-art format painting is only a *copy* of this original. Indeed, whilst the common prejudices of the general public equate 'good' painting with verisimilitude ('it could almost be a photograph') here the 'good' painting is achieved by quasi-mechanical reproduction, rather than the virtuoso fluency of the skilled hand. Morley's Super Realism, in other words, is a critical practice which highlights, questions and thwarts our expectations of art as a 'high' cultural activity. It addresses not so much the minimalist and conceptualist preoccupation with the minimum conditions for something to be counted as art, but rather the legitimising discourse whereby art is justified as a vehicle of elevation and improvement. To some degree, this is anticipated in the blatant parodies of Duchamp, but in Morley's case the critical dimension is, as it were, painted into the image. We have not so much a kind of external 'anti-art', as art which internalises and displays the problematics of its own socio-cultural status. Now, in the work of a number of other Super Realist artists in the late 1960s and early 1970s – such as the paintings of Audrey Flack and Chuck Close or the sculptures of Duane Hanson, a broadly similar critical dimension is operative. However, the great bulk of work in this idiom has a much more superficial orientation. For, as the Super Realist tendency spread, it began to address itself to more traditional concerns and became simply a *style*. In the work of John Salt or Richard Estes, for example, we find close-up images of such things as cars or flashy shop frontages, which, whilst being derived from photographs, present themselves as ostensibly *virtuoso* performances. Super Realism becomes the means for intricate, aesthetically dazzling compositions on the grand scale. The work of

Morley and the other innovators, in other words, is reappropriated within the legitimising discourse. Indeed, Super Realism of this sort has overwhelming market appeal through its combining both the traditional and modernist exemplifications of this discourse. On the one hand, its flashy verisimilitude appeals to the traditional prejudices that art should uplift through its complexity and virtuosity; on the other hand, because such works look *so* much like photographs, they still seem odd – vaguely outrageous even – thus feeding on the demand for fashionable novelty and unexpectedness that is created by modernism.

One might trace a similar pattern in relation to the development and consumption of the tendency that began to displace Super Realism in the late 1970s – namely, 'Neo-Expressionism'. Again, the case of Malcolm Morley proves decisive here. Around 1970, he began to ruffle the surfaces of his photographic-derived works, by working them in more broken brush strokes. Of especial interest here is *School of Athens* (1972). This work is a copy of a photographic reproduction of Raphael's original. Raphael's work – in both content and handling – affirms art's status as a dignified and uplifting activity akin to the pursuit of those timeless essential truths which are the vocation of the great philosophers depicted in the painting. It is the quintessential icon of the very notion of high-art itself. Morley's treatment of Raphael's work, however, makes the artistic enterprise look earthy and contingent. This is achieved not only through the disruptions effected by the loose handling, but through the fact that Morley leaves a transcriptional *mistake* intact in the 'finished' work (namely a horizontal line of grid squares, that is manifestly asynchronous with the rest of the composition). Indeed, it becomes acutely difficult to locate Morley's *School of Athens* within the customary discourse of art history itself. Is it a copy; is it expressionist; is it a parody; is it surrealist; is it classicist? Perhaps all – yet none of these. Such dislocational effects are even more manifest in Morley's more recent works. In *Day of the Locust* (1977) for example, Morley not only completely mixes up such categories as expressionist and surrealist, but blatantly parodies that notion of 'stylistic development' which is so central to art history. Morley injects motifs drawn from his earlier work, but malforms them and screws them up. One must also note a further crucial dimension to this and kindred works. Morley does not simply overload us with images of breakdown and catastrophe,

*Figure 9.2* Malcolm Morley, *School of Athens*
*Saatchi Collection, London*

but rather tangles these up in a way that makes difficult to disentangle strands of depicted reality from strands of fiction. He does not offer an illusion of real space, but neither does he open up a surreal space of pure fantasy. We are left, rather, in a state of insecurity that seems to bear witness to painting's *inadequacy* in relation to articulating the complexity and/or horrors of contemporary existence. This felt inadequacy, in other words, arises from a pictorial *compromisation* of the legitimising discourse. A critical dimension of this sort is to be found in other innovative 'Neo-Expressionist' artists of the 1970s and 1980s, notably Anselm Kiefer, Georg Baselitz, and Philip Guston. Kiefer, for example, moves from large claustrophobic interiors that hint at unseen powers and violence, to devastated landscapes linked with symbols or inscriptions that allude more directly to catastrophe, and, in particular, the disasters of German history. In these works, the very overload of scale, catastrophic excess, and an insistence on the physical means of the medium itself, expressly thematises painting's inadequacy in relation to life. Now, whilst Morley, Kiefer, and others make Neo-Expressionism into a critical practice, their work created a stylistic precedent and climate which enabled less incisive, more market orientated Neo-Expressionism*s* to flourish. In relation to the work of Julian Schnabel, Sandro Chia, and Francisco Clemente, for example, the term 'Neo-Expressionism' is a catch-all phrase that picks out a discourse of painterly excess, and unbridled eclecticism. The overload of paint and imagery connects with its audiences fundamentally at the level of private and arbitrary association. If a dimension of public or collective significance is lacking in these works, it is taken as a signifier of the artist's profundity or depth of being. The viewer is invited to compensate for his or her own lack of experience by vicarious identification with the complex signs borne by the canvas. By engaging with the work, in other words, the viewer is elevated and improved.

I am arguing, then, that there are two fundamentally different aspects to postmodernism in the visual arts. First, in the late 1960s and 1970s there developed a kind of art which is sceptical about the legitimising discourse of art as a vehicle of elevation and improvement. Now, whereas radical modern movements such as Cubism and Surrealism redeploy traditional genres such as still-life and fantasy as a means of elevating subjectivity, artists such as

*Figure 9.3*  Anselm Kiefer, *Die Meistersinger*
*Saatchi Collection, London*

Morley and Kiefer radically question the affirmative discourse of high art, as such. They do so either by incorporating (in an *apparently* unmediated fashion) that which is most *directly* antithetical to high art – namely, mechanically reproduced imagery; or by thematising (within the particular work) the inadequacy of artistic categories, and, indeed, art's inability to express the complexities and catastrophes of concrete historical experience. We have, in other words, a new form of art whose very pictorial means embody a scepticism as to the possibility of high art. By internalising this scepticism and making it thematic within art practice, *Critical* Super Realism and *Critical* Neo-Expressionism give art a *deconstructive* dimension. Such work embodies the same kinds of strategy which inform contemporary poststructuralist approaches to discourse in general. They can, therefore, be defined as the definitive postmodern tendency. However, this deconstructive approach also created a market demand which was rapidly met by *Secondary* (uncritical) Super Realisms and Neo-Expressionisms. These works served to directly reinvigorate the legitimising discourse of art by tapping the traditional expectation of virtuoso performances and 'profundity' and the modernist appetite for the odd and the outrageous. Now in the latter half of the 1980s the Critical aspect of postmodern art has reached a crisis point. It is to a consideration of this phenomenon and some broader questions, that I now turn in the final section of this chapter.


**IV**


Much art practice of the late 1980s involves a kind of ironic deconstruction that recognises and internalises its own inevitable assimilation by the market. In the Neo-Geo abstractions of Phillip Taffe, for example, we find parodies and subversions of modernist colour-field painting and 'op' art. Barnett Newman's high Modernist *Who's Afraid of Red, Yellow, and Blue?* finds its riposte in Taffe's send-up *'We Are Not Afraid'*. Likewise Peter Halley's Neo-Geo electric cell and conduit paintings parody the high-falutin claims of Rothko-style colour-field painting by stating it and containing it in terms of banal imagery drawn from the technological base of postmodern culture. Again, the 'sculpture' of Jeff Koons and David Mach questions conventional notions of taste and represent-

*Figure 9.4* Julian Schnabel, *Starting to Sing: Untitled (2)* (1981) Oil and rustoleum on canvas 166″ × 228″ (415 × 570 cm)

*Saatchi Collection, London*

ation, through creating assemblages of quirky and comical ingenuity. Mach's *101 Dalmatians*, for example, turns Disney's hounds loose on the domestic environment. The disturbing sense of gravitational precariousness created by Barnett Newman's *Broken Obelisk* or Richard Serra's *Delineator* is here achieved through a Dalmatian balancing a washing-machine on its nose. Now, in all these Neo-Geo paintings and sculptures, a dimension of deconstruction is present, in so far as art's pretensions to elevation or improvement are called into question or shifted to the level of the humorous. But the very good humour of this strategy and the ludicrousness of its means bespeaks an overtly self-ironical and self-negating level of insight. We can deconstruct, but the legitimising discourse and the market will still have us – so let's have fun with the whole situation while we can. This comic fatalism is of some broader significance, in so far as it marks the point where critical postmodernism recognises its own limits. Any art objects set forth with internal critical intent will be assimilated by the legitimising discourse and market forces, and redistributed in the form of a *style*. This fate is promised as soon as the attempt to criticise the legitimising discourse of art is made internal to art itself. For here, the deconstructive tendency succeeds in fulfilling the legitimising discourse *despite* itself. To see why this is so, one must invoke the experience of the sublime, in terms of its two main expositors – Kant and Burke. In the Kantian version, when we encounter some phenomenon which overwhelms, or threatens to overwhelm our imagination or emotions, this can sometimes issue in a kind of rational counterthrust. In such a case, we recognise and comprehend that which overwhelms or threatens to over-whelm us. Indeed, the very fact that a phenomenon which so manifestly defeats our sensible capacities can nevertheless be articulated and thence, in a sense, contained by reason, serves to vividly affirm the extraordinary scope and resilience of rational selfhood. I would suggest that an affirmative response on some-thing like these lines is embodied in our engagement with certain aspects of Critical postmodernist art. Consider, for example, the overwhelming disaster motifs, and dislocational effects of Critical Neo-Expressionism. These signify art's essential inadequacy in relation to expressing the complexity and immensity of the real world and its problems. However, the very fact that such a profound insight can be articulated within the idioms of art serves, paradoxically, to *vivify* the extraordinary scope of art itself as a mode of rational artifice. The disaster of failure to signify is, as it were, contained and redeemed by the achieved signification of this failure within the visual means of art. The artist offers an affirmative and elevating experience of a kind of artistic sublimity. Now there is another – somewhat cruder – experience of the sublime which can also be related to Critical postmodernism (and, indeed, to any avant-garde art). One might call it the *protosublime*. Burke is its most effective expositor. According to him, prolonged states of inactivity and monotony are deleterious to our organic constitution. In order to counter this, we need to experience mild shocks – which will stimulate our sensibilities, but without involving any real sense of pain or danger. Experiences of this sort are provided by such things as vast or destructive objects encountered from a position of safety, or by human artefacts which outrage or thrill us in some way. Now, Burke's argument can be transposed into contemporary terms, on the basis of our response to patterns of work and social existence in a society characterised by the division of labour. In such a society, the reified and monotonous pattern of life demands a compensating substitute for real experience. The shocks and thrills provided by media news items, or such things as violent adventure films and the like, fulfil this function. It is this vein of compensatory affective response, I would suggest, which is tapped by Critical postmodernism. In the case of Critical Super Realism and Neo-Geo, for example, we have works which engage us fundamentally in terms of affective jolts – through thwarting or parodying expectations based on our intercourse with high art of the traditional or modernist kinds. They have a shock or surprise value which rejuvenates and heightens our very sense of being alive. The means may be banal or ludicrous, but in the midst of social monotony and accelerating standardisation, the 'whatever-will-they-do-next' aspect of artistic innovation is a life-enhancing force. Its affective jolt, indeed, may even thematise the notion that the individual creator *can* resist the forces of reification to some degree – however trivial.

I am arguing, then, both that the Critical dimension of postmodern art has ended up in a kind of comical recognition of its own limits; and that this kind of result was implicit in the very attempt to deconstruct art from within. Such a practice tends towards elevating experiences of the sublime in either the Kantian or Burkean modes. This interpretation raises two questions. First, is there any way in which Critical postmodernism in the visual arts can avoid assimilation by the legitimising discourse and market forces; and second, if it cannot, does this not mean that Danto is at least right in his claim that postmodernism is post historical? Let me address the former question. First, as I have already argued, internalised deconstruction is assimilated by the legitimising discourse in terms of the sublime. But what about those cases where the critique is conducted from a more external viewpoint? A good example here is the work of the feminist artist Mary Kelly. In her *Post-Partum Document*, Kelly seeks to break out of the patriarchal power-structures which have regulated what is admissible as art and what is not. The work consists of a series of largely documentary displays charting biographical facts about, and theoretical inter-pretations of, her relationship with her son – from earliest infancy to earliest childhood. Now the problem with this work (and, indeed, the problem faced by 'conceptual art' in general) is that the level of sensuous essentially visual meaning is almost entirely eliminated. It might, of course, be argued that the removal of this dimension is an extremely positive feature, in so far as it is art's sensuousness which appeals to the market and which provides the essential spectacle for the male gaze. However, on these terms, Kelly's work merely throws out the baby with the bathwater. For to remove the appeal to distinctively visual meaning is to render the notion of visual art itself superfluous. Collapsing the boundary between art and documentation in this way simply eliminates art. Interestingly, however, Kelly – as is the case with most conceptual artists – is not willing to allow her *Post-Partum* work to be judged *as* a series of theoretical statements, for its units are mounted so as to be hung in accordance with the presentational formats on conventional art. Thus the work takes on its deconstructive edge through the play-off between its primarily non-artistic content, and its conventional art format of presentation. Again, however, whilst this thwarts our normal expectations as to what should be counted as art, the fact that it is mounted *as* an-object-for-contemplation serves to contain the shock response. We feel that this is just the avant-garde thrilling us with the outrageous and extending our horizons once more. Our sensibility is, once more, elevated and improved. That the legitimising discourse should exert so profound a pull in relation to even the most (superficially) antithetical works, is hardly surprising. For whilst the concept 'art' is a social construct of Western culture, it is not *merely* a construct. The reason why it *needs* to be constructed is to pick out the fact that certain kinds of artefact bring about certain positive effects *through the mere contemplation of them*. It is the fact that certain artefacts *can* be valued in this way that necessitates the concept 'art'. The legitimising discourse, in other words, legitimises not just this art and that, but the very concept of 'art' as such.

I shall now finally return to Danto's implicit equation between postmodern art and posthistoricality. It will be remembered that, for Danto, the reason why this equation is justified is that modernist art – in the form of Warhol's *Brillo Boxes*, brings about a congruence between art and the statement of its essence. Thereafter, there cannot be anything artistically new – only a re-hash of old forms. Now, whilst I rehearsed the philosophical objections to this claim in Part I, it is worth looking at again in the light of my alternative historical account of modernity and post-modernity. First, I have tried to show that there is some continuity between the late modernism of Warhol, minimal art, and concep-tual art, and the Critical varieties of postmodern Super Realism and Neo-Expressionism. All these tendencies are energised by the philosophical implications of art. The difference between them consists in the fact that whereas the late modernists question the logical scope of art and take it to and beyond its limits, the Critical postmodernists question the social reality of art (i.e., the status of the legitimising discourse) from within. This latter fact is itself a concrete illustration of how postmodern art – working within and loosening up the limits of already established idioms (i.e., 'Real-ism' and 'Expressionism') – is authentically critical and historically innovative, rather than the mere product of market demands. Now, of course, I also argued that whilst Critical postmodernism shakes up and questions the legitimising discourse, it does not escape it; but this fact in no way restricts its historical possibilities. For, as I further suggested, the legitimising discourse is the very basis of our having a concept of art at all – indeed, it is the very basis of our interest in art's historical development. To escape the legitimising discourse, in other words, would involve giving up art. One might expect, therefore, that future postmodern art will become less obsessed with criticising the legitimising discourse, and will instead orientate itself towards new ways of exemplifying it. To some degree, this process is already under way. Therese Oulton's paintings, for example, draw on tradition in a way that redirects rather than criticises it. She articulates primeval experiences of place and presence through a collectively accessible vocabulary of form, texture, and colour. Ross Blechner's sinister memorial paintings referring to Aids victims likewise state private experience in a way that is collectively moving and enlightening. Here, in other words, we have the beginnings of a postmodern art that is profoundly creative, and which involves an elevating reappropriation of the *lifeworld*, rather than criticism or eclecticism alone.

In conclusion, then, one must concede only one major point to Danto – namely that all future art will have to work within the logical limits that were set out by late modernism, and this will involve operating with genres and categories already defined. Even this, however, would only rule out the possibility of future authentic artistic innovation on the assumption that such innovation is sufficiently definable in *negative* terms, i.e., as *simply* creating something the like of which has not been created before. But, of course, this assumption is false. Historical innovation in art has always been determined in the context of *creative* breaks with, *or* refinements of, what has already been given. We do not want new artefacts that are simply unprecedented – but rather ones whose unprecedentedness casts new light on the traditions of art or on our broader relation to the lifeworld. Artistic innovation, in other words, is a complex relation between art and its past, rather than the kind of absolute philosophical break which Danto's reading makes of it. The moral is clear. Art lives ... and will continue to do so whilstsoever artists see their world and, in particular, their discipline's history, from different viewpoints.

## Note

For a much fuller discussion of the general relation between art and Kant's theory of the sublime, see Crowther, 1989, Chapter 7.

**Bibliography**

DANTO, A. (1987), *The State of the Art*, New York, Prentice-Hall.
CHIPP, H. (1968), *Theories of Modern Art*, Los Angeles, University of
California Press.
CROWTHER, P. (1989), *The Kantian Sublime: From Morality to Art*,
Oxford, Oxford University Press.

# Chapter 10

# Architectural Postmodernism: The Retreat of an Avant-Garde?

Howard Caygill

---

a waalworth of a skyerscrape of most eyeful hoyth entowerly, erigenating from next to nothing and celescating the himals and all, hierarchitectitiptitoploftical, with a burning bush abob off its baubletop and with larrons o'toolers clittering up and tombles a'buckets clottering down. (Joyce, *Finnegans Wake*)

The 1987 *Internationale Bauausstellung (IBA)* held in Berlin offered itself as a laboratory of architectural postmodernism. The administrative division of the exhibition into *Neubau* (New Building) and *Altbau* (Old Building) corresponds to the two main critical factions in architectural theory to emerge from the collapse of architectural modernism. *Neubau* was represented by prestige buildings on prime sites in what may be described as 'postmodern international style', while *Altbau* encompassed the communal renovation of housing stock described as 'community architecture' in the UK and 'social architecture' in the USA. In this chapter, I will examine how these two broadly speaking 'postmodern' tendencies in architectural theory and practice stand with regard to each other and to the modernism which they claim to supersede.

The colour-supplement vision of architectural postmodernism as an eclectic historicism designed to refresh the tired shopper mistakes a symptom for a cause. At stake in this architecture are not simply the stylistic tics of technicolour pilasters, allusions to Borromini, or the inevitable atrium, but the relation of an avant-garde profession to its public. Postmodern architecture would re-cast the relation of avant-garde profession and retro public be-queathed it by the modern movement. The latter legitimated its architectural interventions according to an avant-garde ideology opposed to public opinion and officially-sponsored academic taste. The key elements of its avante-gardism were an extremely abstract understanding of space and a utopian conception of human needs. Modern interventions were legitimated by the conviction that it was possible to effect spatial solutions to political problems. The threat of 'Revolution', seen by Corbusier and his peers to follow from the irrational spatial distribution of social relations, could be alleviated by the rational, centralised reorganisation of space.

The distributive emphasis of the spatial solution to a political problem reduces politics to administration. The programme of architectural modernism seemed suited to bureaucratic implemen-tation. But while the abstract premises accorded with the adminis-trative values of the bureaucratic commissioning clients, they were divorced from those of the building's users. They experienced the bureaucratic administration of space as a violent imposition, and met it with forms of resistance ranging from resentment and apathy to vandalism and riot.

The ideology of architectural postmodernism arose against this background of popular dissatisfaction with modern building and planning measures. It was articulated in the language of philo-sophical postmodernism. One of the most powerful features of this philosophy is its claim that modern philosophy's concept of the autonomous and free subject is unsustainable without the violation of its opposite. In order to accomplish the subsumption of nature under the categories of the theoretical subject, it was necessary to posit nature as passive extension, the undifferentiated 'other' of the subject. Similarly, in order for the acting subject to represent the social universal, it was necessary to abstract from individual idiosyncrasies and differences in order to reduce them to complexes

of universal human needs and rights. Postmodern philosophy sees
in the freedom of the modern subject the subjection of its other; it
finds the other's passivity in its activity and hears in its voice the
other's silence.[1]

Such philosophical antinomies structure the ideology of avant-
gardism which dominated modern aesthetic and political practice.
The avant-garde is inherently reactionary since it defines its activism
against the passivity of its other. Aesthetic avant-gardists define
themselves against a body of philistines; a political avant-garde
legitimates its vanguard role by postulating the 'passive' or 'trade
union consciousness' of its constituency. In both cases, the revolutionary hyper-activity of the avant-garde legitimates itself through
the representation of its other as conservative and passive.[2]

Philosophical, political, and aesthetic postmodernisms invert
the dichotomy of an active avant-garde and its passive other.
Philosophical postmodernism discriminates between differences
found in the object, while political postmodernism prefers local
interventions, using improvised forms of organisation and 'temporary contracts' (Lyotard), over the global solutions proposed by
the vanguard party. Aesthetic postmodernism or 'trans-avant-
gardism' renounces its avant-garde status in favour of an accom-
modation to the figurative conventions of popular culture.

Architectural postmodernism mobilises anti-avant-garde ideology in its redefinition of the practice of architecture after modernism. It rejects the philosophical foundations of the modern movement, its self-definition as an avant-garde, along with its complicity
with bureaucratic techniques of implementation. The theorists of
Postmodern and community architecture accordingly describe
their work as a re-alignment of popular taste and the professional
ethos of architecture. Charles Jencks, speaking for the new postmodern international style, describes it as architecture which
'speaks to the elite and the man in the street ... Both groups,
often opposed and often using different codes of perception, have to
be satisfied' (1978, p. 8). In the ideology of community architecture,
architects are no longer the legislators of space, but 'enablers' who
use 'their skills to enable people to achieve better conditions for
themselves ... giving such people direct experience of controlling
their own futures' (Charles McKean, cited by Wates and Knevitt
1987, p. 149). The question arises of whether this refusal of the
avant-garde posture of modernism is sufficient to legitimate the

*Figure 10.1* Marco Polo Offices, London *Barbra Egervary*

theory and practice of an architectural postmodernism? In order to reach a judgement on this issue it is necessary to examine more closely the character of the modern avant-gardism which the post-moderns find so unacceptable.

## Avant-Gardism and Architecture

There *are* no architects today, we are all of us merely preparing the way for him who will once again deserve the name of architect, for that means: *lord of art*, who will build gardens out of deserts and pile up wonders to the sky (Gropius, 1919).

It is important to maintain a sense of proportion with regard to the achievements and failings of architectural modernism. Not every modern development suffered the fate of the award-winning Pruitt Egoe housing scheme (1952–55) in St. Louis, whose partial demolition in 1972 has been seen to mark the death of modern architecture.[3] Popular dissatisfactions with modern architecture rarely extends to the products of the architectural studios designated by such proper names as 'Corbusier' and 'Mies van der Rohe' which defined the modern style. The objects of its hostility are usually the outcome of the small but accumulative decisions of anonymous architects serving bureaucratic clients, whether private or public. Yet the very possibility of such bureaucratic interventions and the form they assumed ironically presupposed the existence of the avant-garde ideology constructed in the early decades of the century. It is in the extravagant and often grotesque fantasies of the modern manifestos that the ideological conditions for the bureaucratic implementation of a modern 'style' were established.

The means by which the architectural decisions of the avant-garde studios were transformed into a catalogue of architectural tropes have not been properly studied. This is unfortunate since, as said, popular resistance is directed less against modernism than against the unreflective application of the modern style. Part of the responsibility for the absence of thorough study of the institutional transmission of architectural information lies in the way an avant-garde systematically conceals its self-constitution. The cult of individual genius is one of the most effective techniques of avant-garde dissimulation, not only diverting attention from the institutions which create and reproduce architecture, but also abstracting from the intensely co-operative nature of architectural work. Even at the design level, the architectural studio is organised according to a highly differentiated division of labour. And once on site it is obvious that every hierarchitect needs an army of larrons o'toolers to celescate the himals. Yet the product of the co-operative design and construction process is fetishised as a 'Stirling' or a 'Rogers' or even – the ultimate irony for a 'community architect' – an 'Erskine' building.

It is paradoxical that while modern architecture seems blind to the social determinants of its practice, it justifies itself with a rhetorical appeal to social theory. To take a well known example: at the end of his seminal text *Towards an Architecture* (1923), Le Corbusier states the political ambitions of the architectural avant-garde with characteristic unsentimentality: 'It is the question of building which is at the root of the social unrest of today; architecture or revolution' (p. 251). Corbusier answers that 'Revolution can be avoided' (p. 269) through architecture's rational disposition of space and distribution of housing resources. This assumes, of course, that the causes of revolution lie in the irrational disposition and distribution of space and housing, an assumption which demands closer examination.

The identification of social with spatial order involves the transformation of social relations into spatial entities. But such reification abstracts social relations from the historical tangle of forms in which they are found, and through which they have developed. With this transformation, architecture placed itself in a long tradition of social thought which spatialised social relations, a tradition which began with Plato's *Laws*.[4] However, this same tradition had been drawn upon during the nineteenth century to justify the administrative ideologies of Comte, Saint-Simon and Bentham, along with the socialist versions of Owen and Fourier. These social theorists saw the maintenance of social order as the responsibility of an administrative stratum who intervened on the premiss that spatial order was the key to social order.

The spatialisation of social relations was an essential moment in the architectural profession's self-definition as an avant-garde. Architects defined themselves against the public: the public was confused, in the words of the Charter of Athens 'Opinion has gone astray'. The public's irrational spatial decisions led to disastrous consequences, and had to be rationally re-configured by the architect. But the legitimation of this claim required that architecture detach itself from its public, that it show itself to possess a knowledge in advance of, superior to, the public's.

An early stage in this separation – which it is the ambition of postmodern architectures to repair – is evident in the critique of ornament as the sign of a degenerate popular taste. Adolf Loos announced in his sentimental pamphlet 'Ornament and Crime' (1908): 'I have made the following discovery and I pass it on to the world: *the evolution of culture is synonymous with the removal of ornament from utilitarian objects*' (Conrads, p. 11). But he wasn't really announcing his discovery to the world since, 'I am preaching to the aristocrat, I mean the person who stands at the pinnacle of mankind and yet has the deepest understanding for the distress and want of those below' (p. 24). By the time of the immensely influential CIAM (Congrès Internationaux d'Architecture Modern) Charter of Athens (1933), the deepest understanding has become 'the perfect knowledge of man' possessed only by the architect. The architect has become the 'lord of art' – one whose mastery of space will ensure social order.

But the perfect knowledge was bought at the price of gross philosophical and political simplification, one which was to be paid by a later generation of architects. It abstracted from the historical and institutional complexities of social life such general categories as 'life', 'opinion' and 'basic needs'. These were considered as quanta which needed only to be rationally directed in order to achieve their optimal distribution. Perfect knowledge involved the separation of the architectural avant-garde as the bearers of the concept, from the blind intuition of 'life' and 'opinion'. And the possession of this knowledge legitimated their legislation of the spatial decisions for the rest of society. Furthermore, the case of the architect's knowledge conformed with the administrative ideology characteristic of modern bureaucracies.[5] This affinity perverted the libertarian intent of modern architecture: the lords of art, instead of piling wonders up to the sky – celescating the himals – found themselves designing Iron Cages.

The 'avant-garde ethic' of modern architecture was propagated through institutions such as the Bauhaus and CIAM. These institutions represented a break not only with popular culture, but also with the politically-defined architectural tradition of the Academies. The latter represented the history which had to be superceded. In

CIAM's La Sarraz Declaration (1928), the state is urged to 'tear the teaching of architecture out of the grip of the academies', for these are 'by definition and by function, the guardians of the past. They have established dogmas of architecture based on the practical and aesthetic methods of historical periods. Academies vitiate the architect's vocation at its very origin. Their point of view is erroneous and its consequences are erroneous' (Conrads, p. 112) The academies represent the past, while the new 'rational and standardised' architecture represents the future. This claim to avant-garde status required justification, since the accusation of 'error' presupposed a criterion of judgement. In the La Sarraz Declaration, this criterion is vaguely the 'economic and sociological plane', but by the Charter of Athens it has become explicit as the spatial ordering of social relations.

The Charter of Athens, probably the most influential document of architectural modernism, displays all of its philosophical and political limitations. The entire urban planning programme which it proposes rests on the reification of temporal social processes into spatial functions. Town planning deals with four functions: housing, work, recreation and traffic which the Charter analytically separates from the tangled reality of the city, reducing them to things which may be distributed on a Cartesian grid.

The temporal historical dimension of the city, a dimension in which the relation of these functions reveals a different, more complex order, is ignored in favour of an exclusively spatial disposition. It is in this spirit that tenet 78 of the Charter claims that:

> Town planning . . . will transform the face of cities, will break with the crushing constraint of practices that have lost their raison d'etre and will open an inexhaustible field of action to creators. Each key function will have its own autonomy based on the circumstances arising out of climate, topography and customs; they will be considered as entities to which will be assigned territories and locations . . . (Conrads, p. 139).

The language of this proposal is revealing. It is the *face* of the city, its visible or representative aspect, which is to be transformed: urban experience is rendered as spectacle. Furthermore, the key functions are considered 'entities' which are 'assigned' location. This reification of the function, and its assignment in quantified isotropic and homogeneous space, reduces the qualitative dimension of urban experience – its place between past/present/future – to the mere 'circumstances' of climate, topography and custom.

One outcome of the reification of the processes of housing, work, recreation and traffic was the possibility of planning their

*Figure 10.2*   Richard Rogers, Lloyds Building, London   *Barbra Egevary*

spatial disposition *in advance*. Tenet 84 of the Charter justifies avant-garde prescience regarding the city in the following terms: 'The city will assume the character of an enterprise studied in advance and subjected to the rigour of an overall plan. Wise foresight will have sketched its future, described its nature, anticipated the scope of its development and limited their excess in advance' (Conrads, p. 141). By rendering the inextricable processes of the city as things, it not only becomes possible to dispose them in space, but also to anticipate or 'plan' their optimal, future disposition. The masters of space inhabit the future perfect tense: they *will have* sketched the future of the city – they are avant-garde. The intricate temporality of urban experience, its roots in the past and its hopes for the future, is reduced into three discrete elements. The past which permeates every moment of urban experience is consigned to the Academies, the present is the confusion of the city's inhabitants, while the city's future is the responsibility of its prescient masters. The separation of past, present and future is used by the avant-garde both to distinguish themselves from Academic and popular opinion, and to justify their interventions. The repression of past and present results in the near deification of the avant-garde as the bearers of destiny. The identity of the profession of the future is revealed in an ecstatic passage which unconsciously evokes Cassius's speech on Brutus:

> Architecture presides over the destiny of the city . . . Architecture is responsible for the well being and beauty of the city. It is architecture which sees to its creation and improvement, and it is architecture's task to choose and distribute the various elements whose felicitous proportions will constitute a harmonious and lasting work. Architecture holds the key to everything (p. 144).

These claims are entirely justified if the definition of 'everything' is conceded to be 'everything considered as entities in space'. However, this universality is but the dominion of abstract space, one which can only be sustained at the expense of the violent repression of all other aspects of experience.

The exorbitance of the Charter of Athens demonstrates how the avant-garde distanced itself from the spatial and temporal irregularities of urban experience, only to return and legislate for it with inappropriate laws. The bureaucratic imposition of spatial solutions to non-spatial problems provoked resistance, one aspect of which was a cruel return of the repressed. For the very pretensions of their modern avant-gardism placed architects in an exposed position. The inevitable failure of the spatial solution to social problems was seen as an exclusively architectural failure, one for which the profession had to take responsibility. Architecture, then, became the stage for the symptomatic rehearsal of social conflicts whose origins ran deeper.

In a sense, the construction of modern architecture as an avant-garde profession with spatial solutions to political problems was all too successful – even in its failure. For the failure of modern architecture appears as the contingent failure of architectural talent, rather than being inevitable. The hope persists that the reform of architecture, or even architects, might deliver the modern promise that 'Revolution can be avoided'. The importance which architecture accorded itself in modern societies through its presentation as an avant-garde persists even after its 'failure'. The persistance of avant-gardism is evident in postmodern architectures. For while Postmodern and Community Architecture profess to reject the avant-gardism of modern architecture, they implicitly accept many of its axioms, albeit in an inverted form.

## Postmodernism

'is not Main Street almost all right?' (Venturi)

Venturi's *Complexity and Contradiction in Architecture* (1966) along with *Learning from Las Vegas* (1972), articulate a profound dissatisfaction with architectural avant-gardism. They anticipate postmodern re-coding of architectural design to accommodate popular taste, exceeding later statements in the clarity of their view. However, what emerges from Venturi's texts and the postmodern ideology they found, is less a resolution of popular and professional taste than the celebration of their incompatibility at the level of style. Nowhere in postmodernism does architecture renounce its pretention to mastery. The 'other' of popular culture is not recognised in its complexity and contradiction, but is instead constituted as the avant-garde's fantasy of popular culture.

In *Complexity and Contradiction*, Venturi consummately inverts many of the stylistic postulates of modern avant-gardism. On the first page, Mies' hallowed dictum 'less is more' is inverted and parodied. First of all, a complex and contradictory architecture embodies 'the difficult unity of inclusion rather than the easy unity of exclusion. More is not less' (p. 16). But there's worse sacrilege on the following page – 'Less is a bore', no less. But, strangely enough, this complex and contradictory architecture is justified through a reading of the history of architecture. Venturi's provocative deconstruction of the architectural tradition still acknowledges it as the sole arbiter of architectural taste. He is concerned with complexity and contradiction 'in' architecture, and not 'of' it. Architecture itself, in other words, is really not so bad after all.

*Learning from Las Vegas*, on the other hand, seems to represent an institutional inversion of avant-gardism in architecture. It begins to address the complexities and contradictions *of* architecture, but falls back, and finally remains within architecture. In the 'Studio Notes' prepared for students, the authors claim to be 'evolving new tools, analytical tools for understanding new space and form, and graphic tools for representing them. Don't bug us for lack of social concern; we are trying to train ourselves to offer socially relevant skills' (p. 73). Venturi et al., were to be continually bugged by their professional colleagues for their alleged lack of social conscience; but the accusations of irresponsibility and frivolity only succeeded in diverting attention away from the real challenge of their text. For *Learning from Las Vegas* is, at first glance, no less a refusal of architectural avant-gardism, a slap in the face of an honourable profession.

The title of the book captures the ambition to overturn avant-gardism: the architects learn *from* Las Vegas instead of prescribing to it. The discovery of new analytic and graphic tools are anticipated from the scrutiny of a 'popular' anarchitectural built environment. Instead of following the avant-garde in legislating space, the Venturi studio would open themselves to understanding the manner in which popular culture has established its own spatial relations. In the process of re-education, the architectural profession itself is found to be somewhat retro – the avant-garde have fallen behind everyone else: 'The representative techniques learned from architecture and planning impede our understanding of Las Vegas. They are static where it is dynamic, contained where it is open, two-dimensional where it is three dimensional' (p. 75). This is serious. It's the avant-garde who are meant to be dynamic and the popular culture static; the avant-garde are meant to be open, the rest contained; they're meant to think two-dimensionally, we're the ones with the extra dimension. The conclusion is inescapable: Las Vegas is avant-garde, it is architecture that has 'gone astray'!

Architecture is quickly rescued from the indignity of being square, for it becomes apparent that Las Vegas is only the architect's fantasy of popular culture. For Venturi et al., Las Vegas functions as a compensatory fantasy for the failure of architecture's avant-garde identity. This is the reason why their inversion of avant-gardism is so insistent; it does not threaten the dichotomy between the dynamic and the static and other correlates emerging from the opposition of avant-garde and its other. The field within which the oppositions are constituted remains unexplained, perhaps because it lies outside architecture. Consequently, the relation of master and slave persists, since changing the signs changes nothing but the signs. In the end, Las Vegas, the site of popular fantasy, becomes the architectural fantasy of the popular.

The antithesis of popular and professional culture is resolved in a new way. Popular culture supplies a style which may be deployed by architects: 'Meeting the architectural ´implications and the critical social issues of our era will require that we drop our involuted architectural expressivism and our mistaken claim to be building outside a formal language and find formal languages suited to our time' (p. 161). Instead of a *spatial* solution to 'critical social issues', Venturi et al., propose a stylistic one. They imperiously dismiss spatial avant-gardism with one hand while retrieving a stylistic avant-gardism with the other. The gesture of renouncing avant-gardism is retracted by a sleight-of-hand which, and this is characteristically modern, diverts attention away from 'critical social issues' to stylistic architectural ones. This retraction became axiomatic for subsequent Postmodern theory, which fantasises the popular in order to recuperate it for architecture. But most subsequent architectural Postmodernism holds back from Venturi's initial gesture of overturning avant-gardism, his risking the end of architecture, and retains only his stylistic recuperation. It toys with the dichotomy of professional and popular styles, but ultimately insists that proper distinctions be observed: that the popular be kept in its place (preferably the middle of the Nevada desert).

In Charles Jencks' influential definition of the meaning of post-modern architecture, the popular and the professional tastes are identified as diverse semiotic codes. In this semiotic all codes are equally valid although, as we shall see, some are more equal than others. In *The Language of Postmodern Architecture*, Jencks defines a postmodern building as one 'which speaks on at least two levels at once: to other architects and a concerned minority who care about specifically architectural meanings, and to the public at large, or the local inhabitants, who care about other issues concerned with comfort, traditional building and a way of life' (p. 6). There is little to distinguish this definition from the self-definition of modern avant-gardism. A typical avant-garde dicho-tomy is evident in the value hierarchy implied in the comparison of a creative 'concerned minority' (reminiscent of Loos's concerned aristocrat) who are noble and disinterested enough to care about 'architectural meanings' with the 'public at large' concerned with their creature comforts. The dichotomy reappears throughout Jenck's text in terms of the 'élite' and the 'man in the street', 'childhood and adulthood', 'mind and body', and, in a later pamph-let, *What is Postmodernism?*, in terms of Basil Bernstein's 'elabo-rated and restricted codes'.

Postmodern architecture is 'radically schizophrenic', addressing both 'popular and élite codes', but perhaps not in the way Jencks thinks. The populism of his claim that the profession is mentally ill is severely qualified by the difference of degree implied in the dichotomies within which postmodern architecture is theorised. As against Venturi's inverted avant-gardism, Jencks unequivocally re-states the pretentions of architectural modernism, but in the name of postmodernism. The distinction between a traditional popular language and a progressive avant-garde one reappears in his analysis of architectural 'schizophrenia':

It is *radically schizophrenic* by necessity, partly rooted in tradition, in the past – indeed in everyone's childhood experience of crawling around on flat floors and perceiving such normal archi-tectural elements as vertical doors. And it is partly rooted in a fast-changing society with new functional tasks, new materials, new technologies and ideologies. On the one hand architecture is as slow-changing as spoken language . . . and, on the other, as fast changing and esoteric as modern art and science (p. 24).

Popular culture is represented as childlike, slow moving and traditional, while the avant-garde is technological, fast-changing and esoteric. These are precisely the avant-garde pretensions which the Venturi studio tried to overturn. Jencks just won't learn from Vegas.

When analysing a postmodern building, Jencks forgets the popular contribution to architectural schizophrenia. For just as Venturi was ultimately only interested in the complexity and contradiction in, but not of, architecture, so schizophrenia for Jencks is just a matter of architectural style. He describes the schizophrenia of Portoghesi's Casa Baldi (1959–61) as internal to architectural discourse; the contribution of the popular language to the architectural disturbance is repressed:

> Here is the schizophrenic cross between the two codes that is characteristic of Postmodernism: the enveloping, sweeping curves of the Baroque, the overlap of space, the various foci of space interfering with each other *and* the Brutalist treatment, the expression of a concrete block, rugged joinery and the guitar-shapes of modernism (p. 82).

Here the popular contribution to Portoghesi's (stylistic) schizophrenia is unclear, perhaps it is the 'rugged joinery' ('rugged' *sounds* a bit popular)? The refusal to let the popular speak except in the voice of architecture suggests a misdiagnosis: this architectural discourse is not schizoid, it is psychotic.

In spite of occasional references to popular participation in design and the utterance of community architecture's shibboleth 'Byker wall', Jencks arrives at a denial of any mediation between popular and avant-garde codes. In an astounding insistence on the irreconcilability of popular and professional semiotics he concludes that:

> Since there is an unbridgeable gap between the elite and popular codes, the professional and traditional values, the modern and vernacular language, and since there is no way to abolish this gap without a drastic curtailment in possibilities, a totalitarian manoeuvre, it seems desirable that architects recognise the schizophrenia and code their buildings on two levels ... the double coding will be eclectic and subject to the heterogeneity that makes up any large city (p. 130).

The recognition proposed by Jencks remains a stylistic one. The dichotomy of avant-garde and the popular culture should be incorporated into architectural style. But this is more of an evasion than a recognition of difference; and the unification of difference at the level of spectacle is the definitive 'totalitarian manoeuvre'.

Jencks' reference to the heterogeneity of the city points to perhaps the most important aspect of Postmodern architectural ideology. This is the rejection of the zoning recommendations of the Charter of Athens. Once again, Venturi's texts are far more radical than their Postmodern heirs, although characteristically not radical enough. In both books, Venturi shows that urban experience is not spatial, nor is urban space isotropic and homogeneous. In *Complexity and Contradiction*, he elegantly demonstrates that urban experience is far more differentiated than was ever imagined in crude differentiation of function proposed by the Charter of Athens. The difference of inner and outer founds an experience of the city which is qualitative, not quantitative: the passage from the inside of a building to the street is catastrophic and not continuous. The CIAM traffic grid fails to recognise the qualitative differences between the regional and the local route: the one carrying traffic within a locale, the other within a region; if the difference is not respected, immense damage to the urban fabric may result. Venturi's basic point is that there are several differentiations to be taken into account of in urban planning, and not just the differences of function and location maintained in the Charter of Athens.

Although Venturi's contribution to the theory of urbanism transcends the spatial emphasis of modern planning theory, it fails to transcend the level of style. The differences he proposes in place of spatial zoning are always dichotomous: 'Our recent architecture has suppressed dualities'. However, Venturi's dichotomies – his 'both–and', 'inside and outside', 'back and front', 'ornament and structure' etc. – themselves suppress their process of constitution. The dichotomies are stylistic counters which are shuffled in the design game; the social and political histories which are inscribed in the dichotomies are erased on the architect's drawing board. Once again, architecture abstracts itself from society, restoring to itself a position of mastery.

Postmodern architectural theory recognises that the simple relation of avant-garde and popular culture is no longer valid.

However, while the dichotomies which characterise modern architecture have been transformed, they have not been fundamentally
questioned. The self-legitimation of the architectural avant-garde,
through its mastery of space, has been replaced by its mastery of
style. Instead of the modern movement's fantastical representation of its other as passive material awaiting form, the other is
reconstituted as active – but still lacking form. Popular culture
remains represented as an object of architectural manipulation, it
is not a partner in a dialogue. What is more, popular culture is still
reified; it is seen as a thing and not the complex and contradictory
product of a particular history.

The fundamental distinction of avant-garde and popular culture
persists behind the stylistic differences and schizophrenias of
postmodernism. And in this distinction the avant-garde maintain
their privileged position. They produce a fantastical representation
of the order which they recuperate stylistically. The 'popular code'
is a compensatory fantasy – Main Street, after all, was almost dead
when Venturi wrote *Complexity and Contradiction*. The advent of
the out of town shopping mall transformed it into a museum piece;
and, certainly, in the museum – site of myth and the canonical
postmodern building type – everything *is* almost all right.

## Community Architecture

> Just as, before putting up a large building, the architect surveys and
> sounds the site to see if it can bear the weight, so a wise legis-
> lator does not begin by laying down laws good in themselves,
> but examines whether they are appropriate to the community
> for which they are meant (Rousseau, *The Social Contract*).

If Postmodernism is an ideology in search of a practice, community
architecture is a practice inflated into ideology. Modern architecture was always accompanied by architects who rejected its
stylistic and organisational canons, but their interventions were
essentially individual, special solutions to particular problems.
When this approach is made an ideology it takes on a different
significance. This has been the case with the claims of community
or social architecture which, especially, in the UK, has been cast as
the answer to the collapse of the legitimacy of modern architec-

ture. Here, its patrons span the political spectrum, from the anarchist Colin Ward to the HRH Prince Charles, both of whom applaud its anti-bureaucratic and anti-institutional stances, and who in doing so misrepresent, even pervert its character and potential.

The anti-modern ideology of community architecture antedates the accession of Rod Hackney to the presidency of RIBA in 1986. It was articulated as an ideology by the Dutch architect John Habraken as early as 1961 in his book *Supports: an alternative to mass housing*. Habraken's text is structured around the antithesis of nature and artifice. Against the mechanical abstractions of CIAM he proposes an organic architecture whose design not only incorporates the processes of change and decay, but also the adaptations of the structure made by its eventual users. Organic architecture rethinks the relation of architectural form and content. The architect's job is to devise structures or 'supports' within which the inhabitants may improvise their own environments or 'infill'.

Habraken's organicism does not admit of a contradiction between the personal and the community; there is a natural harmony between the decisions of the individual and the requirements of the community. Form, or the 'support' represents the public realm, and content or 'infill' the private; the dichotomy is assumed to be reconcilable. He theoretically justifies the natural harmony between form and content in terms of a metaphysics of 'possession'. Possession is distinguished from property, as being a spontaneous activity through which human beings form their environment: 'the natural relationship between man and his dwelling', he claims, 'is universal' (p. 97). However, this notion of possession abstracts from real differences in property ownership within a society. The community cannot be united by a common possession, nor can that notion be generalised quite so easily.

One of the consequences of the blatantly ideological definition of possession is the notion of architecture as a 'communal' process. The architect intervenes in an 'all embracing process' (p. 90) characterised by the workings of quasi-natural forces and the 'pressure of events'. While such a reduction of human to natural history is the diametric opposite to the machine ethic and aesthetic of modernism, it results in the same abstraction from the complexities and contradictions of history. The architect as engineer is replaced by the architect as gardener; both remaining firmly in

charge of their plots. Habraken pushed the horticultural metaphor of organic architecture to near dementia in 1985, when he
informed us that:

> To have a good garden we sometimes must make an infrastructure:
> dig the soil, make paths and provide water. Sometimes we must
> re-organise the distribution of plants. Sometimes we must weed
> and trim ... The new practitioner is the one who accepts the
> fluid movements of the everyday environment and rejoices in
> them (cited in Wates and Knevitt, p. 146).

What might it mean, in the context of a housing crisis, to 're-
organise the distribution of plants' or to 'weed and trim'? These
apparently benign metaphors become chilling when we remember
that Habraken is talking about 'weeding and trimming' people's
housing. Is there any real difference between modern architecture's 'rationalisation' of space and Habraken tidying up the
garden?

Habraken's opposition of an organic to a mechanical metaphor
allows him, like Venturi, to make several apparently critical
points against the modern movement without endangering the
sovereignty of architecture. His architectural 'other' is the natural,
harmonious community, growing organically and requiring the
interventions of a gardener to keep its 'fluid movements' from
overflowing the paths. But if the community was harmonious and
without differences in this way, why then would it need architect
gardeners to keep it in order? It needs them, we are told, because
the natural expression of the community has been perverted by its
representative institutions. The notion of the organic community
itself is preserved, as is the innocence of the architect, for she/he is
outside of representation, with an immediate relation to the community.

The sentimental idyll of community architecture turns sour on
site. The natural community of the ideology becomes an extremely
complex and contradictory phenomenon in reality. This is underlined with refreshing realism by Ralph Erskine and his site architect Vernon Gracie when discussing their experience in redev-
eloping Byker. The regeneration of public housing in a working-
class area in Newcastle is often used as a justification of community
architecture. However, the circumstances were quite unique and
cannot bear the ideological weight which the project has been

given. First of all, the inhabitants did not wish to conserve the existing building stock of their neighbourhood: 'Contrary to our expectations, they did not share our or other outsiders' interest in the existing houses and streets – they wanted their Byker, but a new Byker, and expressed this vocally' (Erskine, p. 188). In order to build a new Byker it was necessary to educate the inhabitants in how to articulate their desires, and the architects in how to recognise them. The architect had to be both educator and educated: it was not enough simply to be an engineer or a gardener. The avant-garde dichotomy of architect and public had to be re-nounced; the architect had to educate: 'In doing our normal architect's job, we could also help people to understand the thought processes involved and help them realize that they could insist on changes in the plans if they could understand how and why decisions are made and analyze and justify their needs' (p. 191). But the architect also had to be open to the lessons given by the public: 'we have at times and with demonstrable success listened to the wisdom of residents rather than the wisdom of experts'. In order to achieve this, the site architect had to act as a focus for the community, occupying the now legendary funeral parlour, selling flowers.

*Figure 10.3*   Ralph Erskine, 'Byker Wall', Newcastle     *Caroline Caygill*

The role of educator and educated is too sensitive and fragile to be elevated into a prescriptive ideology. Indeed, Gracie explicitly warns against a global generalisation of the experience at Byker:

> While things go right, the degree of involvement and commitment of a professional team to consultation and the giving of information will be considerable. But if things should go horribly wrong, it is difficult to see a professional team taking a hammering for year upon year without the goodwill vanishing and the more traditional approach to redevelopment reemerging (p. 197).

This caution is echoed by many of the reports of community architecture projects which were successfully completed.

This caution has been abandoned in the elevation of the practice of community architecture into an ideology. It has come to represent an alternative exit from the modern, one to set against postmodernist international style. Theorists find in it a new architecture, one whose 'emphasis on process, in the involvement of users and the democratic control of the environment confounds the Postmodernists on their home ground and points to new and fruitful directions for architecture' (De Carlo, p. viii). C. Richard Hatch arrives at the Marcusean conclusion that social architecture 'will lead us to that world whose aesthetic is not the quality of isolated objects, but of life itself' (p. 10). This kind of claim might hold for individual projects, but then it would do for countless individual modern projects. However, as an ideology, community architecture experiences the same fate as modern architecture, when it became the 'modern movement'. Indeed, as ideologists there is little to distinguish community architecture from modern avant-gardism.

Community architecture arises from the same tearing asunder of avant-garde and popular culture that is recognised in differing ways in architectural modern and postmodern international style. In their manifesto for community architecture, Wates and Knevitt characterise the division in the following way:

> People cannot solve their own problems because they lack the knowledge and skills and because the whole system is geared to intervention only by experts. Experts cannot solve the problems because they have been divorced from the people they are meant

to serve and are not given relevant training. A web of red tape stifles creativity or innovation by both citizens and experts, leading to an environment which is increasingly mediocre, unresponsive and unrelated to people's needs (p. 68).

The move this passage represents is characteristic of the British community architecture movement. First of all, the division between popular culture and the architectural profession is acknowledged, and then it is blamed on representative institutions, more technically – 'red-tape'. It is in direct ideological descent from Habraken's architectural organicism, and shares many of its undesirable sociological assumptions.

The phrase 'red-tape' – central to the ideology of community architecture – comes to designate anything that obstructs the immediate relationship between the architect and the client. It refers to the representative institutions which impede the harmonious expression of the community, leading, so the story goes, to social despair and bad buildings. Prince Charles used the phrase in the celebrated RIBA speech of 1986: 'To restore hope we must have a vision and a source of inspiration. We must sink our differences and cut great swathes through the cat's cradle of red-tape which chokes this country from end to end' (ibid., p. 15). But when the community is extended to the nation in this way, and when local interventions such as Erskine's are given universal significance, architecture resumes its avant-garde posture. The architect's other is a simplified organic community without any internal differences, without a history. The social problems of this community arise from the distortions of its harmonious development by red-tape. And as the modern movement believed, these problems may be resolved through architecture: 'The lesson seeming to be that if you rehabilitate houses you don't need to rehabilitate people' (p. 73).

The affirmation of community architecture by the Crown, the Judiciary in the shape of Lord Scarman, and the Conservative Party in the wake of the inner-city riots of the early 1980s, is reminiscent of the earlier co-option of modern architects by the post-war welfare state. Architecture, once again, has solutions to social problems which remain at the level of representation, and so do not threaten the bases of real social inequality. But architects now have an alibi for their inevitable failure in 'red-tape' and

*Figure 10.4*  Byker, Newcastle                              *Caroline Caygill*

'institutional and bureaucratic restrictions'. Architectural interventions are now legitimated by the 'community', but since this is
an inchoate term, defined against representative institutions and
only existing in the architectural fantasy, it comes to mean everything and nothing.

There are more structural similarities between the ideologies of
community architecture and modernism. Along with the prefer-
ence for an architectural solution is the familiar fantastical representation of the architects' other. The retarded public of the
modern movement has become the sentimental 'community'.
There is an almost Rousseauesque quality to community architecture's evocation of the goodness of the community which they wish
to 'serve'. As with Habraken's garden, there is little recognition
that the community may be divided internally, and that the sources
of the division may lie elsewhere than in planning and architecture. In a society which allocates its housing resources through the
market, there are fundamental differences within the 'community'
which issue from unequal access to resources. The unified community is an exception, and may only occur in regard to specific

issues which over-ride such fundamental differences. This is, of course, recognised by most practitioners of community architecture, if not by their ideologues.

The hollowness of community architecture's populism is repeatedly exposed by Prince Charles. He does not hesitate to universalise the local community – which under certain circumstances may achieve a concerted intervention in the built environment – to the National Community. The reward of community architecture, he maintains 'will be nothing less than a Great Britain once again' (p. 40). But the fantasy of the National Community is unequivocally ideological. There is no immediacy of national sentiment to which anyone might justifiably appeal in their judgements, say, of the Mansion House and National Gallery Extention schemes.

The sentimental ideology of community architecture obscures the lessons of its practice for architecture. These include the elaboration of new working methods and the inscription of accountability into the design process. The 'new analytical tools for understanding new space and form' are better learnt in Newcastle than in Las Vegas. However, the lessons of a new architectural form are forgotten in the ideological appropriation of community architecture. This re-states its lessons in terms of avant-garde oppositions. The community is reduced to a natural essence in which there is assumed to be an automatic harmony between individual and community, one which is distorted by representative institutions. But this community is itself a representation. The differences in the community are not respected; only those between the community and its representative institutions are acknowledged as significant. Instead of a responsible architecture which would understand and teach differences in full awareness of the violence of its intervention, architecture casts itself as the neutral, innocent voice of a community whose discord it has silenced.

Architecture retains its avant-garde role since both the engineers of CIAM and the gardeners of community architecture claim prescience. The ideology of community architecture offers an architectural solution to a social problem. As 'inperts', community architects have snatched the keys to a social order from the modern experts. Yet they can retain their position only by representing themselves as the voice of their own fantasy of the community. In this regard, they remain the heirs to Corbusier's claim 'Architecture or Revolution. Revolution can be avoided'.

**Torn Halves of an Integral Freedom?**

> Its account with its previous shapes is thereby closed ... Yet
> they still fall apart within its consciousness as a *movement* of
> distinct moments, a movement which has not yet brought them
> together into their substantial unity (Hegel, *Phenomenology of
> Spirit*).

The two main currents of postmodernism in architecture present
partial antitheses to modern architecture, but do not attain to a
new synthesis or 'substantial unity'. Neither postmodernist international style nor community architecture have overcome the
avant-garde ideology of modernism; their resistances to it remain
at the level of symptom. Both mutually antagonistic postmodern
factions remain deeply implicated in each other and in the modern
avant-garde posture which they desire to negate.

This mutual implication is readily apparent in the peculiar dichotomy in which postmodern and community architecture find themselves. The one is an architecture of artifice and irony, the other of
nature and sincerity. The exaggerated opposition of the ideologies
suggest that they are perversely dependent on each other. The
irony of the one is parasitic upon the sincerity of the other, and the
reverse. Architectural postmodernism, in the broad sense, finds
itself internally divided between innocence and experience.

The exaggerated dichotomy in which architectural postmodernism finds itself expresses the partiality of the postmodern rejec-
tions of the role of avant-garde. In many respects, they maintain
characteristically modern postures. Both privilege the architectural intervention, both rely on a simplified fantasy of the popular
and both seek to reconcile the profession and the public on the
basis of this fantasy. Instead of the modern movement's representation of the popular as passive and awaiting form, it is now seen as
active, yet still it awaits form. Behind the fantasy of the 'popular'
or 'community' lies the desire to simplify the public the better to
order it.

The factions of postmodernism re-inscribe the modern opposition
of the avant-garde and the popular. But the very fact that they are
now internally opposed brings this opposition to consciousness.
The elements of the opposition have now 'fallen apart', and the
exaggerated form in which they are manifest offers a chance to

move beyond them. But what would be the nature of such a movement, a movement which would deserve the name 'postmodern'? It would not be the attempt to rescue avant-gardism at the level of spectacle, nor would it offer external mediations between the poles of the popular/professional dichotomy. It would, rather, question the field within which this dichotomy is placed. It would take Adorno's challenge to think avant-garde and popular cultures as 'torn halves of an integral freedom, to which however they do not add up' (Adorno, 1977, p. 123).

The integral freedom to which Adorno referred and to which architecture, modern and postmodern, aspires cannot be achieved by moving the demarcation line between the torn halves. What he said of music in elucidating his proposition is also important for architecture:

> The unity of the two spheres of music is thus that of an unresolved contradiction. They do not hang together in such a way that the lower could serve as a sort of popular introduction to the higher, or the higher could renew its collective strength by borrowing from the lower. The whole cannot be put together by adding the separated halves, but in both there appear, however distantly, the changes of the whole, which only move in contradiction (1978, p. 275).

Current postmodern theory and practice succumb to the desire to reconcile the two spheres by resolving their contradiction. Both critical factions achieve this reconciliation through the erasure of differences between the profession and the public, and within the public itself.

This 'forced reconciliation' at the level of representation is manifest in the practice of postmodernism. Returning to the division of IBA into Altbau and Neubau, it is apparent that most of the projects do not fully achieve the desired 'critical reconstruction of the city' which formed the brief of the exhibition.[6] This reconstruction sought to reconcile the city plan with the elevation of buildings, and the elevation with interior plan. However, much of the Neubau emphasised the relation of façade and the city plan over the interior: it remained at the level of style and spectacle. It has been widely remarked that at the level of interior plan, many Neubau projects were unadventurously 'modern' or even 'submodern'.[7] Inversely, many of the Altbau projects, while adventurous at the level of plan, pointing to new, flexible dispositions of domestic space, were extremely conservative with regard to elevation and their relation to the city as a whole.

The Director of Neubau, Josef Paul Kleihues, distinguished the postmodernism of IBA from the postmodern international style. In place of stylistic irony he called for re-inscription of architecture within a 'world' characterised by the 'letting-differ of poeisis

*Figure 10.5*   Baller/Baller, Fraenkelufer Housing, Berlin *Howard Caygill*

and reason (logos), metaphor and function, existential risk and institutional form' (1987, p. 9). However, the distinction of the poiesis of Altbau and the logos of Neubau persists throughout the exhibition. However, on the rare occasions on which the borders of the two were crossed, as in Baller/Baller's Fraenkelufer project, intimations of a synthesis may be perceived. Here poeisis and logos, the two relations of interior and façade, façade and street, street and city, combine into a fragile whole which, as formed fragments of a complex and contradictory history, is more than the sum of its parts. The building points beyond the opposition of poeisis and logos, an opposition which, as another dichotomy, re-inscribes the avant-garde ideology into architectural theory and practice.

The building, in other words, exceeds the ideology through which it is interpreted. A proper postmodern architectural theory has, in its turn, to transcend the dichotomies within which it finds itself. A first step is to understand the whole within which its dichotomies move historically and sociologically. Architecture and its theory must recognise its predicament as an avant-garde detached from its public. This recognition is an essential first step toward a reflexive architectural theory for which architecture and the categories through which it constitutes and understands itself is an object. Without such reflection, postmodern architectural theory will continue to repeat the dichotomies bequeathed it by the modern avant-garde.

## Notes and References

As always, my thanks to Gillian Rose and Greg Bright for their criticism.

1. For a statement of philosophical postmodernism, see Jean-François Lyotard's *The Postmodern Condition: A Report on Knowledge.* For critiques, see Gillian Rose, *Dialectic of Nihilism*, Jürgen Habermas, *The Philsophical Discourse of Modernity* and Howard Caygill, 'Post-Modernism and Judgement', *Economy and Society* vol. 17, 1988.

2. Peter Buerger's seminal *Theory of the Avant-Garde*, does not fully develop the paradoxes of an avant-garde's self-definition. This follows largely from his underestimation of Adorno's theory of the avant-garde, which he misreads as a one-sided defence of avant-garde art against Lukacs' socialist realist critique of it.

3. In a surreal combination of precision and vagueness, Jencks claims

'Modern Architecture died in St Louis Missouri on July 15, 1972 at
3.32 p.m. (or thereabouts) when the infamous Pruitt-Igoe scheme, or
rather several of its slab blocks, were given the final *coup de grace* by
dynamite' (1978, p. 9).

4. As in *Laws* VI: 'If men must have a wall of sorts, they should
construct their own dwellings from the outset in such a fashion that the
whole town forms one unbroken wall, every dwelling house being
rendered readily defensible by the uniformity and regularity with which all
face the streets'. *The Collected Dialogues of Plato*, Princeton, 1978,
p. 1355.

5. For the relation of spatial order and bureaucracy, see Georg Lukács,
*History and Class Consciousness*; Michel Foucault, *Discipline and Punish*;
and Walter Benjamin, *Charles Baudelaire*.

6. 'Critical Reconstruction of the City' is theorised with reference both
to Heidegger and to Critical Theory, see Kleihues 1987a and b.

7. Inken Baller commented, 'The housing plans [in Neubau] are for the
most part worse than those of the Hansa-Quarter during the last
Bauausstellung in 1957'. Interview in Tip Magazine, Berlin, 20/87, pp. 18–
20.

# Bibliography

ADORNO, THEODOR (1977), 'Letters to Walter Benjamin', *Aesthetics
and Politics*, London, NLB.
ADORNO, THEODOR (1978), 'On the Fetish Character in Music and
the Regression of Listening', (eds) Arato and Gebhardt, *The Essential
Frankfurt School Reader*, Oxford, Blackwell.
BENJAMIN, WALTER (1983), *Charles Baudelaire: A Lyric Poet in the
Era of High Capitalism*, tr. Harry Zohn, London, NLB.
BUERGER, PETER (1984), *Theory of the Avant-Garde*, Minneapolis,
Minnesota U.P.
DE CARLO, GIANCARLO (1984), 'Beyond Postmodernism', in Hatch,
op. cit.
CONRADS, ULRICH (1970), *Programmes and manifestoes on 20th-
century architecture*, tr. Michael Bullock, London, Lund Humphries.
LE CORBUSIER (1923), *Towards a New Architecture*, tr. Frederick
Etchells, London, Architectural Press.
ERSKINE, RALPH (1984), 'Designing Between Client and User', in
Hatch op. cit.
FOUCAULT, MICHEL (1977), *Discipline and Punish: The Birth of the
Prison*, tr. Alan Sheridan, Harmondsworth, Penguin.
GRACIE, VERNON (1984), 'Pitfalls in Participation: A Cautionary Tale
(of Success)', in Hatch op. cit.
HABERMAS, JÜRGEN (1988), *The Philosophical Discourse of
Modernity*, Oxford, Polity Press.
HABRAKEN, N. J. (1972), *Supports: an Alternative to Mass Housing*, tr.
B. Volkenburg, London, Architectural Press.

HATCH, RICHARD (ed.) (1984), *The Scope of Social Architecture*, Wokingham, Berkshire, Van Nost. Reinhold.

JENCKS, CHARLES (1978), *The Language of Post-Modern Architecture*, London, Academy Editions.

JENCKS, CHARLES (1980), *Late Modern Architecture and Other Essays*, London, Academy Editions.

JENCKS, CHARLES (1982), *Current Architecture*, London, Academy Editions.

KLEIHUES, JOSEF PAUL (1987a), 'Kritische Rekonstruktion der Stadt' in *750 Jahre Architektur und Stadtebau in Berlin*, Berlin.

KLEIHUES, JOSEF PAUL (1987b), 'Die Gebiete des Stadtneubaubereichs, Bauten und Projekte', *IBA Projektubersicht*, Berlin.

LUKÁCS, GEORG (1971), *History and Class Consciousness*, tr. Rodney Livingstone, London, Merlin Press.

ROSE, GILLIAN (1984), *Dialectic of Nihilism*, Oxford, Blackwell.

VENTURI, ROBERT (1966), *Complexity and Contradiction in Architecture*, London, Architectural Press.

VENTURI, ROBERT et al. (1972), *Learning from Las Vegas: The Forgotten Symbolism of Architectural Form*, London, MIT Press.

WATES, NICK and KNEVITT, CHARLES (1987), *Community Architecture: How People are Creating their own Environment*, Harmondsworth, Penguin.

# Notes on Contributors

**Roy Boyne** is Principal Lecturer at Newcastle upon Tyne Polytechnic. He has published widely on contemporary European social thought and is currently working on a book about late twentieth-century French cultural theory. The author of *Foucault and Derrida: the Other Side of Reason*, he is a member of the editorial advisory board of *Theory, Culture and Society*.

**Alex Callinicos** teaches politics at the University of York. His most recent books include *The Great Strike* (with Mike Simons), *Making History, South Africa between Reform and Revolution*, and *Against Postmodernism*. He also regularly contributes to *Socialist Worker* and *International Socialism*.

**Howard Caygill** is Lecturer in Sociology at the University of East Anglia. He is the author of *Art of Judgement*.

**Stephen Crook** is Lecturer in Sociology at the University of Tasmania. He is the author of *Modernist Radicalism and its Aftermath*.

**Paul Crowther** is Lecturer in Art History at the University of St Andrews. He is the author of *The Kantian Sublime: From Morality to Art* and *Critical Aesthetics and Postmodernism*.

**Jean-Jacques Lecercle** is Professor of English Language and Literature at the University of Nanterre. He is the author of *Philosophy Through the Looking Glass* and *Frankenstein: mythe et philosophie*.

**Sabina Lovibond** is Fellow and Tutor in Philosophy at Worcester College, Oxford. She is the author of *Realism and Imagination in*

*Ethics.* Her philosophical interests include meta-ethics, the theory of value and subjectivity, as well as feminist theory.

**Christopher Norris** is Professor of English at the University of Wales in Cardiff. His books include *William Empson and the Philosophy of Literary Criticism, Deconstruction, The Deconstructive Turn, The Contest of Faculties, Jacques Derrida, Paul de Man, Deconstruction and the Interests of Theory* and *What is Deconstruction* – (with Andrew Benjamin). He has also edited volumes on Shostakovich, George Orwell, the politics of music and post-structuralist criticism, as well as contributing numerous essays to British and American journals.

**Ali Rattansi** is Lecturer in Social Sciences, City University, London. He is the author of *Marx and the Division of Labour*, editor of *Ideology, Method and Marx* and co-editor of *Radicalism in Education.* He is currently working on issues around racism, cultural difference and social theory. He is a member of the editorial board of *Economy and Society.*

**Elizabeth Wilson** teaches Social Studies at the Polytechnic of North London. She is the author of a number of books, including *Adorned in Dreams: Fashion and Modernity, Only Halfway to Paradise, Hidden Agendas* and *Hallucinations: Life in the Postmodern City.*

**Janet Wolff** is the author of several books on the sociology of the arts, including *The Social Production of Art* and *The Culture of Capital: Art, Politics and the Nineteenth-Century Middle Class*, edited with John Seed. A book of her essays on women and culture, entitled *Feminine Sentences*, is forthcoming. Until recently, she was Reader in the Sociology of Culture at the University of Leeds. She is currently Visiting Scholar in Sociology at the University of California, Berkeley.

# Index